AT THE TOP OF THEIR GAME

BOOKS BY ROBERT H. BOYLE

Sport, Mirror of American Life
The Hudson River, a Natural and Unnatural History
The Water Hustlers (with John Graves and T. H. Watkins)
The Fly-Tyer's Almanac (edited with Dave Whitlock)
The Second Fly-Tyer's Almanac (edited with Dave Whitlock)
Malignant Neglect (with the Environmental Defense Fund)
Bass (photographs by Elgin Ciampi)
Stoneflies for the Angler (with Eric Leiser)

At the Top
of Their Game

ROBERT H. BOYLE

NICK LYONS BOOKS
WINCHESTER PRESS

Published and distributed by
WINCHESTER PRESS
New Century Publishers
220 Old New Brunswick Road
Piscataway, New Jersey 08854

Produced by
NICK LYONS BOOKS
212 Fifth Avenue
New York, New York 10010

PRINTED IN THE UNITED STATES OF AMERICA
10 9 8 7 6 5 4 3 2 1

Designed by Shari De Miskey

All the articles in this book originally appeared in *Sports Illustrated.* "Step in and Enjoy the Turmoil"
(June 13, 1977), "The Deuce with Love and Advantage" (August 28, 1972), "Trick or Truite"
(November 8, 1971), "Frank Merriwell's Triumph" (December 24, 1962), "The Man Who Lived
Two Lives in One" (April 29, 1968), "Kind and Canny Canines" (January 15, 1968), "Nobody
Touches Me with Impunity" (March 15, 1971), "Really the Greatest" (March 7, 1966), "A Champ
for All Time!" (April 19, 1965), "He Beats the Drums for Champs and Bums" (July 8, 1963), "An
Absence of Wood Nymphs" (September 14, 1959), "With a Quack, Quack Here" (September 27,
1971), "The Obsessions of a Late Bloomer" (August 18, 1969), "The Strange Fish and Stranger
Times of Dr. Herbert R. Axelrod" (May 3, 1965), "Absolutely Stuck on Stamps" (August 23,
1971), "He's Got a Very Fishy Look" (September 3, 1979), "Spare the Rod(s) and Spoil the Cast"
(April 7, 1980), "Shhh! It's the Black Ghost" (December 8, 1980). Reprinted courtesy of *Sports
Illustrated.*
© 1959, 1962, 1963, 1965, 1966, 1968, 1969, 1971, 1972, 1977, 1979, 1980
by Time Inc.

Library of Congress Cataloguing in Publication Data

Boyle, Robert H.
  At the top of their game.

  "A Nick Lyons book."
  1. Sports—Biography—Addresses, essays, lectures.
I. Title.
GV697.A1B596   1982   796'.092'2   [B] 82-20292
ISBN 0-8329-0274-8
ISBN: 0-8329-0283-7 (paperback)

To Sophie Delar-Githens

Contents

I wish to thank *Sports Illustrated* not only for permission to reprint these pieces but for indulging me initially in writing them for the magazine. I give my thanks to Sidney L. James, the late André LaGuerre, Roy Terrell and Gilbert Rogin, all understanding managing editors, plus Jeremiah Tax, Robert Creamer, Merv Hyman, Arthur Brawley, and Bob Brown. My thanks also to John Cushman and Nick Lyons, and to the late Jane Sanger Boyle and to Kathryn Belous-Boyle who have partaken of my life and put up with my odd hours and odder friends with the greatest love and understanding.

Foreword

ALL THE characters portrayed in this book—and they *are* characters, be they alive and thriving (as the majority of them are), deceased or fictional—have a number of attributes in common. They are driven. They have gusto. They are often amusing and, on occasion, outrageous. They would stand out in a crowd, even a mob. They act. They are not acted upon. They march to the beat of a distant drummer who doesn't even know he's pounding away. They have their wits about them. Above all, the characters here are utterly obsessed with a sport or hobby, be it playing handball, casting a fly, breeding dogs, promoting fights, collecting stamps, tropical fish, decoys, or butterflies, or shooting a slingshot. They relish what they are doing, outlandish or preposterous as it may seem, and they excel at what they do. They are *at the top of their game.*

Now, you might ask, as some readers of *Sports Illustrated* have—and all these articles, or "pieces" as we call them in the trade, first appeared in *SI*—"What does collecting stamps or shooting a slingshot have to do with sports?" Everything to me, the magazine, and *Webster's*, which defines sport as "any activity or experience that gives enjoyment or recreation; pastime, diversion." You don't have to play quarterback for the Pittsburgh Steelers to get written up in *SI*. When I was choosing the pieces for this book, I reread at least sixty I've done over the past twenty-five years, and those concerned with professional or college sports just didn't hold up. They lacked either depth or edge, they were dated, or they didn't fit the theme of the book.

Let me confess to a personal bias. I *like* all the characters selected for the book, even though some can obviously be difficult. They add spice to life. Another confession: I am personally interested in many of the activities that obsess the characters here, and while interviewing them I learned what I could to better my own game. I now fly-cast more proficiently because the master, Lefty Kreh, showed me how; I have greater insight into the morphology of insects because of the late Vladimir Nabokov; and I tie a dandy stonefly thanks to Charles E. Brooks.

Since I usually know something, sometimes a great deal, about the field that enthralls my subject, I can readily climb inside his mind to pick the faraway notes that would elude a newcomer to his particular area of expertise. Moreover, the fact that I know something about a subject's field has on several occasions allowed me to get my foot in the door when otherwise the door would have remained firmly double-bolted. Dr. Herbert R. Axelrod said he wouldn't have seen me unless I had been a nut, too. At the time, I was keeping a three-and-a-half-pound largemouth bass in an enormous aquarium in my living room.

There are a few men in the book who practice a sport that holds no interest for me, such as soaring, but when Dick Wolters, whom I had sought out because he trained field-trial Labradors, told me that the enormous crate in his backyard contained a sailplane, I knew there was a story in Wolters. The same occurred when Chanler Chapman allowed that he had just bought 600 pounds of gravel as ammo for his slingshot. I was eleven or twelve when I last had an interest in sling-shots, but Chapman was then seventy-six and the word "story" just kept lighting up in my mind after I looked at his gravel pile. In fact, whenever I meet anyone who piques my interest, I immediately think, "Story?" There has to be a sporting peg, of course, but I'll do this with anyone: a plumber who comes to the house, a hot-dog vendor, an Episcopal nun, a bookmaker. My wife complains, "Stop interviewing people." Until the other day I hadn't taken a long-distance train in fifteen years but on the way out to Toledo and back by Amtrak I interviewed Chang K. Chang, my Taiwanese sleeping car attendant. Chang—I'm using his last name rather than his first because I am not trying to be familiar—wasn't a story but he did tell me how to prepare the small shrimp, *Palaemonetes pugio*, which abounds in local waters and which is ordinarily used as fish bait, into a great dish for the table. Don't clean the shrimp, Chang advised. Just net them out of the water and drop them in a jar with salt. The salt will kill everything. Put in three ounces of salt for every pound of shrimp and, if you wish, add a shot of vodka. Let the shrimp sit a week, then eat heartily.

Once I finally decide that someone is a story, I'll check with the editors at the magazine. I've seen my share of raised eyebrows and heard guffaws, but I take even the slightest shrug of dismay as assent, and off I go to read everything I can about him or her. I make notes of everything I can find, talk discreetly to a few of the subject's friends or enemies, and then I write out the chronology of the subject's life in one of those "Reporter" notebooks that fit snugly into the back pocket. A typical entry: "Van Alen imported European robins. Why???" Van Alen told me why. While going through the Van Alen clips, I also ran across the 1948 headline, CANDY VANDERLIP TIPTOEING TO ALTAR WITH JIMMY VAN ALEN A LA HUSH HUSH. I used it. It gives the flavor of Van Alen's world.

Background notes in hand, I then start to interview the subject, preferably in his native habitat or haunts. You can learn a lot about a person just seeing the kind of books, pictures, or knick-knacks he has. When I did the piece on Joe Hyde, I worked with him in the kitchen while he catered a party in New Jersey, I watched him cook at home in Sneden's Landing, and we fished together at Martha's Vineyard. Turnabout is fair play, and Hyde even came to my house to cook. At the time I was planning to sell the house, but Hyde spotted some mushrooms by the front steps. "Morels!" he shouted. "You can't move." I stayed another seven years.

I have used a tape recorder several times but in my experience they are unreliable devices. I once spent several days tracking down a former pro quarterback who didn't want to say anything to anyone about his problems with drugs and the police. I finally found and persuaded him to talk. He talked for a couple of hours into a tape recorder that I had brought along. I called *SI* in New York and said, "Listen to this. It's a scoop!" All we heard was a low-pitched whine. Thanks to good fortune, I was able to interview the quarterback again, and this time I took notes with a ball-point pen in my Reporter's notebook.

Interviewing is fun; the hard part is writing the story. Sometimes a story will write itself, and occasionally it won't. But while doing the interviewing and research, certain points, incidents, anecdotes, quotes, whatever, stick in my mind, and I'll say to myself, "That's the end of the piece," or "That's the lead," or "The stuff about his grandfather goes in the middle." I have these key points or coordinates in my mind, and I'll write them out when I sit down at the typewriter. Sometimes I'll write the end or middle of a piece before I write the lead. I write out my selected chunks and start filling in the blank spots between them. After I do the first draft, I'll polish it. Writing is mostly rewriting, editing, sandpapering. After I complete a second draft, I'll do a third, then more if necessary.

I want a piece to do several things. I want it to capture the essence of the subject's personality and approach to life. I know a published article is a complete success when friends of the subject say, "You really captured old Joe," and at the same time his enemies say, "Thank God you nailed the son of a bitch." I want the story to interest the reader who may not be interested in the subject at hand, and to do this, I want the lead to be compelling. Then I want the story to move briskly, and that can mean cutting material that might impede the flow of the narrative. I want the story to have the right proportions. Here I adhere to the admonition of James Parton, a now-ignored nineteenth-century American biographer, who wrote, "The art is, to be short where the interest is small, and long where the interest is great."

Except for a few small changes in phrasing, these pieces appear as they originally did in *SI*, when the subjects were, so to speak, caught on the wing. To me, all the characters are still vibrantly alive, no matter when the individual pieces were first published, but I have appended an italicized tailpiece to almost all the stories to update the subject's latest interests, obsessions or lunacies.

—ROBERT H. BOYLE

AT THE TOP OF THEIR GAME

STEP IN AND ENJOY
THE TURMOIL

CHANLER CHAPMAN

June 13, 1977

I T WAS a splendid day in Paris in the 1920s when
William Astor Chanler, former African explorer, big-game hunter,
Turkish cavalry colonel and patron of the turf, limped into Maxim's for
lunch with a friend. The colonel had lost a leg, not on the field of battle
but as the result, it was whispered, of a brawl in a bordello with Jack
Johnson, the prizefighter. A familiar figure in Maxim's, Colonel Chanler informed the headwaiter that he wished to be served promptly
because one of his horses was running at Longchamps that afternoon.
The colonel and his friend sat down, and when, after taking their order,
the waiter did not reappear swiftly, the colonel began tussling with
something beneath the table. With both hands he yanked off his
artificial leg, bearing sock, shoe and garter, and hurled it across the
restaurant, striking the waiter in the back. Colonel Chanler shouted, in
French, "Now, may I have your attention?"

Back home in the United States, the colonel's oldest brother, John

1

Armstrong Chanler, known as Uncle Archie to members of the family, had a simpler way of obtaining service: when dining out, Uncle Archie would carry a pair of binoculars around his neck to keep close watch on his waiter's comings and goings. His manners at table were memorable. He would consume a fish as though he were playing a harmonica, and a fellow member of one of his clubs was intrigued to watch Uncle Archie douse a dozen batter cakes with melted butter and maple syrup and then roll them up and tuck them behind his ears like a Polynesian adorned with hibiscus blossoms. Wherever he went, Uncle Archie was likely to get attention. He sported a silver-headed cane engraved with the words LEAVE ME ALONE. He had spent three and a half years involuntarily confined in the Bloomingdale lunatic asylum in White Plains, New York, because, among other peculiarities, he liked to dress as Napoleon and often went to bed wearing a saber. In a farewell note he left the night he escaped from the Bloomingdale asylum in 1900, Uncle Archie wrote to the medical superintendent, "You have always said that I believe that I am the reincarnation of Napoleon Bonaparte. As a learned and sincere man, you therefore will not be surprised that I take French leave."

Given the drabness of the present age, it is heartening to note that the spirit of the eccentric sporting Chanlers lives on in Barrytown, New York, one hundred miles up the Hudson River from New York City. Here, in the decaying but still gracious estate country on the east bank of the river, a handful of Chanler descendants carry on in their own fashion. There is Richard (Ricky) Aldrich, grandnephew of Uncle Archie and grandson of Margaret Livingston Chanler Aldrich, who fought for the establishment of the United States Army Nursing Corps. Ricky, thirty-six, manages Rokeby, the family seat and farm, where he collects and rebuilds antique iceboats (such as the *Jack Frost*, a huge craft that won championships in the late nineteenth century), and ponders the intricacies of Serbian, Croatian and Polish grammar. Ricky studied in Poland for a spell, but left in 1966 after he was caught selling plastic Italian raincoats on the black market. The most noticeable fact about Ricky is that he seldom bathes. As one boating friend says, "Ricky would give you the shirt off his back, but who'd want it?"

Then there is Chanler A. Chapman, regarded by his kin as the legitimate inheritor of the family title of "most eccentric man in America." As Ricky's brother, J. Winthrop (Winty) Aldrich, says, "Only members of the Chanler family are fit to sit in judgment on that title." Winty, who is Chanler Chapman's first cousin once removed, says, "Television has done *Upstairs, Downstairs, The Forsyte Saga* and *The Adams Chronicles*, but they should do the Chanlers. The whole story is so improbable. And true."

Everyone who has met Chanler Chapman regards him as brilliantly daft. While teaching at Bard College, Saul Bellow, the Nobel laureate, rented a house on Chapman's estate, Sylvania ("the home of happy pigs"), and found in him the inspiration for his novel *Henderson the Rain King*. In the novel, written as an autobiography, Henderson shoots bottles with a slingshot, raises pigs and carries on extravagantly in general. "It's Bellow's best book," Chapman says, "but he is the dullest writer I have ever read."

At seventy-six and possessed of piercing brown eyes, a bristling mustache and wiry hair, Chapman nearly always wears blue bib overalls and carries a slingshot. He is fond of slingshots, because "they don't make any noise," and he shoots at what tickles his fancy. Not long ago he fired a ball bearing at a Jeep owned by his cousin, Bronson W. (Bim) Chanler, former captain of the Harvard crew, inflicting what Chapman calls "a nice dimple" in the left front fender. Ball bearings are expensive ammunition, however, so, for four dollars, Chapman recently bought 600 pounds of gravel. He calculates this supply of ammo should last at least five years.

Before his infatuation with slingshots, Chapman was big on guns. He hunted deer, small game and upland birds and ducks, mostly on his estate. Indeed, at one time he had 115 guns, and his shooting habits were such that friends who came to hunt once never cared, or dared, to return. Chapman had only to hear the quack of a duck and he would let loose with a blast in the general direction of the sound. On a couple of occasions it turned out that he had fired toward hunters crouched in reeds, using a duck call. "Almost got a few people," he says matter-of-factly.

Chapman is the publisher of the *Barrytown Explorer*, a monthly newspaper that sells at the uncustomary rate of twenty-five cents a copy at the newsstand and four dollars a year by subscription. The paper's slogan, emblazoned above the logo, is WHEN YOU CAN'T SMILE, QUIT. "You can abolish rectitude," Chapman once expatiated opaquely, "you can abolish the laws of gravity, but don't do away with good old American bullshit."

The *Explorer* prints whatever happens to cross Chapman's lively mind. "Opinions come out of me like Brussels sprouts," he says. There are poems by Chapman (who always gives the place and date of writing, for example, Kitchen, September 13, 7:15 A.M.), and a regular spiel column, also by Chapman, in which he offers his unique observations of the world ("A sunset may be seen at any time if you drink two quarts of ale slowly on an empty stomach" or "What's good for the goose is a lively gander" or "Helen Hokinson has turned atomic" or "Close the blinds at night and lower the chances of being shot to death in bed. That goes for the district attorney who wants to be a judge"). Chapman always signs the spiel column, "Yrs. to serve, C.A.C., pub."

The *Explorer* publishes pieces about nature, written by Mrs. Stuyvesant Chanler under the nom de plume of "Country Cousin," and about horse racing. "Racing entertains me," says Chapman. "It's an absolute fool's game. It is the incense of the ethos. It's glorious!" For years, Chapman has been a close friend of Abram S. Hewitt, who recently completed an eighty-seven-part series on sire lines in *The Blood Horse*. Any contributions by Hewitt, even personal letters, are welcomed by Chapman. Last year Hewitt sent a letter from Lexington, Kentucky, and Chapman printed it in part in his paper: "Your kind note finally caught up with me here, where I am enthroned for the moment, having taken charge of N. Bunker Hunt's matings (not personal!) for 1976. He is a Texan who does things in true Texas style— the sky's the limit. His training bills in France alone amount to about three-thousand five-hundred dollars a day!

"The horse copers in this area have kept the W. C. Fields tradition alive, of swindling one and all—especially 'outsiders'—with an air of fraudulent dignity. Once you know what is going on, the spectacle has its entertaining aspects—like sending a crew of men out in the night to move the three-eighths pole one hundred and fifty feet, so that the New York millionaire . . . would be sure to see a high-priced two-year-old work three-eighths of a mile in world-record time! . . ."

Chapman likes the W. C. Fields touch, and on occasion he will print Fields' picture in the *Explorer* for no reason other than this fondness. People in the news sometimes get worked over by Chapman in Fieldsian fashion. Of Leon Botstein, the new president of Bard College, Chapman wrote, "His diction seems to be improving. Obviously he has never been trained to speak, so that every word can be understood when it is uttered. There is no elocution." The Reverend Sun Myung Moon, the Korean messiah who bought the old Kip estate across the road from Chapman, gets evenhanded headlines: DARK SIDE OF THE MOON and THE MOON RISE OBSERVED. Chapman is not prejudiced against any race, creed or color, but he does harbor a grudge against the state of Ohio. "It is occupied by blind, moneyed baboons," he says.

Chapman has been married three times. His first wife, from whom he was divorced, was Olivia James, a grandniece of Henry and William James. Robert, a son by that marriage, lives in a house in Florence, Italy, which his father thinks is called "the place of the devil." (Robert reportedly used to live in a cave, where he made kites.) Another son by this marriage, John Jay Chapman II, lives in Barrytown. After attending Harvard, he went to Puerto Rico, where he became a mailman. He married a black woman, and they have several children. When Chanler Chapman's old school, St. Paul's, went coed, he was enthusiastic about his grandaughter's chances of getting a scholarship. "She's a she," he said, ticking off the reasons. "She's a Chapman. She's a Chanler. And she's black."

Five years ago, John Jay Chapman II persuaded post office authorities to transfer him from Puerto Rico back to Barrytown, where he now delivers the mail. Asked if his son truly likes delivering mail, Chapman exclaimed, "He can hardly wait for Christmas!" Not long ago, Chapman and Winty Aldrich, who lives with Ricky at Rokeby, the ancient family seat next door to Sylvania, were musing about the twists and turns in the family fortunes. Winty observed, "Isn't it remarkable, Chanler, that Edmund Wilson called your father the greatest letter writer in America, and now your son may be the greatest letter carrier!" Chapman, who is, upon occasion, put off by his cousin, let the remark pass without comment. ("Winty is the essense of nothing," says Chapman. "He has the personality of an unsuccessful undertaker and he uses semicolons when he writes. He knits with his toes.")

Chapman's father was John Jay Chapman, essayist, literary critic and translator. A man of strong convictions, John Jay Chapman atoned for having wrongly thrashed a fellow student at Harvard—it happened to be Percival Lowell, the then future astronomer—by burning off his left hand. At the same time, Chapman used to go to bed at night wondering, according to Van Wyck Brooks, "What was wrong with Boston?"

Chanler Chapman's mother, Elizabeth Chapman, was one of the orphaned great-grandchildren of John Jacob Astor, each of whom came into an inheritance of some one million dollars. They were called the "Astor Orphans" by Lately Thomas in *A Pride of Lions*, a biography of the nineteenth-century Chanlers. Winty Aldrich says, "There was never anything wrong with the Chanler blood until crossed with the yellow of the Astor gold."

By blood, the Chanler descendants are mostly Astor, with an admixture of Livingston and Stuyvesant. Knickerbocker patricians, they are related, by blood or marriage, to Hamilton Fish Sr., Franklin Delano Roosevelt, Jimmy Van Alen, Francis Marion the Swamp Fox, Julia Ward Howe and General John Armstrong. It was the last who built Rokeby in 1815 after he blotted his copybook as Secretary of War by letting the British burn the Capitol and the White House.

It has been said of Chanler Chapman that the genes of the Chapman side of the family provided the polish, while the Chanler genes imparted the raw psychic energy. Chapman's middle name is Armstrong; he was named in honor of Uncle Archie, his mother's oldest brother. "Archie was a pure bedbug," Chapman says. That may be understating the case. After escaping from the Bloomingdale asylum, where he had been committed by his brothers (with the help of Stanford White, the architect and a close family friend), Uncle Archie fled first to Philadelphia, where he was examined by William James, and thence to Virginia. He changed his last name to Chaloner and started a long legal battle to have himself declared sane in New York.

At his Virginia estate, Merry Mills, Archie indulged his love of horsemanship and hatred of automobiles. He discovered an obscure state law requiring the driver of a motor vehicle to "keep a careful look ahead for the approach of horseback riders, [and] if requested to do so by said rider, [such driver] shall lead the horse past his machine." Mounted on horseback, clad in an inverness cape and armed with a revolver, Uncle Archie would patrol the road in front of Merry Mills demanding that motorists comply with the law. "A green umbrella was riveted to the cantle of his saddle, a klaxon to the pommel," J. Bryan III, one of his admirers, wrote in *The Virginia Magazine of History and Biography*. "After nightfall, he hung port and starboard lights from the stirrups and what was literally a riding light from the girth. The klaxon was his warning, the revolver his ultimatum."

In the midst of the legal battle for his sanity, Uncle Archie shot and killed a wife beater who had invaded his house. To commemorate the encounter, he sank a silver plate in the floor with the cryptic inscription

HE BEAT THE DEVIL. He was absolved of the killing, which occurred in 1909, shortly after Harry L. Thaw shot Stanford White, but the *New York Post* noted, "The latest prominent assassin has taken the precaution to have himself judged insane beforehand." Archie sued for libel, and the case dragged on to 1919, when he won both the suit and his fight for sanity in New York.

By now Uncle Archie had come to love automobiles and made peace with his brothers and sisters. He came visiting in a Pierce-Arrow he had had custom-made. Parts of the rear and front seats were removed to make room for a bed and a field kitchen, and the car was painted with blue and white stripes copied from a favorite shirt. Chanler Chapman would meet Uncle Archie in Manhattan, and they would drive back and forth between the Hotel Lafayette and Grant's Tomb. "He told me he was the reincarnation of Pompey," Chapman says, "but that he was going to have more luck than Pompey and take over the world. His eyes would gleam and glitter. He would also rub an emerald ring and say to the chauffeur when we came to a light, 'Watch, it's going to turn red! See!' " In Barrytown, Uncle Archie dined, as family members pretended not to notice, on ice cream and grass clippings.

At St. Paul's, Chanler Chapman was nicknamed Charlie Chaplin, after his own exploits. From the start Chapman had what the masters at St. Paul's called "the wrong attitude." Some years afterward he wrote a book with that title about his days at St. Paul's. (In *Teacher in America*, Jacques Barzun praises *The Wrong Attitude* for Chapman's "penetrating remarks.") Once young Chapman jumped into an icy pond to win a fifty-dollar bet, and he collected a purse of one hundred dollars for promoting a clandestine prizefight in which he was knocked out. On another occasion, boys each paid fifty cents to watch Chapman fill his mouth with kerosene and strike a match close to it. Flames shot across the room. On the side, he dealt illegally in firearms, selling the same Smith & Wesson .32 over and over again. It jammed every third or fourth round and, invariably, Chapman would buy it back from the disgruntled owner at a reduced price. A center in club football, he practiced swinging a knee smartly into the ribs of an opponent, but when he cracked the rib of a boy he liked, he felt such remorse that he gave the boy a silver stickpin shaped like a broken rib with a diamond mounted over the break.

Chapman was too young to serve in World War I. He desperately wanted to serve after his half-brother, Victor, was shot down and killed while flying for the Lafayette Escadrille. Fortunately, he was distracted by his Uncle Bob, Robert Winthrop Chanler, the youngest, biggest and, in many ways, the most raffish of the Chanlers. "Uncle Bob dreaded the thought that Chanler would be filled with the pieties," says Winty Aldrich.

After studying art in Paris for nine years, Uncle Bob settled on a farm near Sylvania and ran for sheriff of Dutchess County. He won the election after acquiring acclaim by hiring a baseball team, which included Eddie Collins of the Philadelphia Athletics and Heinie Zimmerman of the Cubs, to play against all comers. While sheriff, Uncle Bob wore a cowboy suit and retained Richard Harding Davis as his first deputy. Having divorced his first wife, Uncle Bob returned to Paris, where he vowed to marry the most beautiful woman in the world. He fell in love with Lina Cavalieri, an opera singer, who, if not the most beautiful woman in the world, was certainly one of the most calculating. After only a week of marriage to Uncle Bob, she left him to live with her lover. That was bad enough, but then it was learned that Uncle Bob had signed over his entire fortune to her. Uncle Archie, down in Virginia busily fighting for his sanity, remarked to reporters, in words that became famous, "Who's loony now?"

Uncle Bob divorced Lina, who settled for a lesser sum than his entire fortune, and back in New York he began living it up again, with his nephew, Chanler, sometimes in tow. During this period he was doing paintings of bizarre animals and plants, which became the vogue, and he bought three brownstones in Manhattan, made one establishment of them, and called it the "House of Fantasy." The place was filled with macaws and other tropical birds, and parties held there (orgies, some said) lasted for days. Ethel Barrymore is reputed to have remarked of the House of Fantasy, "I went in at seven o'clock one evening a young girl and emerged the next day an old woman."

Chapman found two of his other Chanler uncles tedious. One, Winthrop Astor Chanler, was extremely fond of riding to hounds. Indeed, when Uncle Winthrop died, his last words were, "Let's have a little canter." Then there was Lewis Stuyvesant Chanler who, like all the Chanlers, was a staunch Democrat. In 1906 he ran for the lieutenant governorship of New York—at the time the candidate for that office ran separately—and in 1908 he was the Democrats' choice to run for governor against Charles Evans Hughs. Hughs won, but the memory of the campaign waged by Uncle Lewis, which began with an acceptance speech on the front steps of Rokeby, still stirs the family. Not long ago, Hamilton Fish Sr. visited Rokeby, where he strongly urged Winthrop Aldrich to run for office. When Winty demurred, Uncle Ham, sole survivor of Walter Camp's 1910 All-American football team, six-feet four-inches tall and ramrod straight at eighty-eight years of age, said, "Look at your Uncle Lewis!" Winty replied, "But Uncle Ham, Stanley Steingut [State Assembly speaker] and Meade Esposito [Brooklyn Democratic leader] wouldn't know anything about Uncle Lewis. Nobody remembers Uncle Lewis." Eyes blazing, Uncle Ham exclaimed, "Everyone remembers Uncle Lewis!"

Chanler Chapman went to Harvard in 1921. "He ran a gambling den there," recalls Peter White, a cousin, who is a grandson of Stanford White. "He had a bootlegger, and all the gilded aristocracy from St. Paul's, St. Mark's and Groton as his customers. Chanler and his partners took in $300 to $400 a week. They didn't drink until their customers left at three in the morning, but then they drank themselves blind."

While in Cambridge, Chapman joined the Tavern Club, founded by nineteenth-century Boston literati. "Two years ago Chanler celebrated his fiftieth anniversary as a member of the club," Winty Aldrich says. "It is a tradition to present a gold medal to a man who has been a member for fifty years. Being proper Bostonians, the members do not have a new medal struck, but give the honoree one that had been presented to some deceased member. Chanler was very excited—I had heard he was to get the gold medal that belonged to Oliver Wendell Holmes—but for one reason or another he couldn't attend the ceremony. The members were relieved. They thought Chanler might bite the medal in half, or hock it."

After Harvard, Chapman went to Paris where he acquired his lasting affection for horse racing. He went broke at the track, and his Uncle Willie, Colonel William Astor Chanler (also known as African Willie, because he had explored parts of the Dark Continent where Stanley said he would not venture with a thousand rifles), gave him a job at an ochre mine he owned in the south of France. Six weeks in the mine were enough. Seeking fresh adventure, Chapman joined an acquaintance who was sailing a forty-seven-foot ketch, the *Shanghai*, from Copenhagen to New York. But Chapman found the trip a bore—"The ocean is the dullest thing in the world. The waves just go chop, chop, chop"—

except for the stop in Greenland, where he swindled the Eskimos by trading them worn-out blankets for furs. Off Nova Scotia he lost the furs and almost everything else when the *Shanghai* foundered on rocks, forcing all to swim to shore.

Back in the United States, Chapman undertook a career as a journalist. He worked for the *Union* in Springfield, Massachusetts for two years and then joined *The New York Times*. "Anyone who spends an extra week in Springfield has a weak mind," he says. The *Times* assigned Chapman to the police beat on the upper East Side but Chapman decided that crime, like the ocean, "bores the hell out of me." He spent a year playing cards with the other reporters and then quit to work for a book publisher.

In 1932 Chapman took over Sylvania and became a full-time farmer. He devoted a great deal of effort to organizing dairymen so they might obtain better milk prices, but division in the ranks made the task impossible. Then, during World War II, Chapman, with the seeming compliance of President Roosevelt, worked up a plan to seize from Vichy France the islands of St. Pierre and Miquelon located off Newfoundland. However, Roosevelt, who had apparently been having a lark at his neighbor's expense, called off the plan at the last moment. Chapman next volunteered as an ambulance driver for the American Field Service and served in Africa and Burma. Nautically, his luck seemed to pick up where it had left off with the sinking of the *Shanghai*— a freighter taking him to Egypt was torpedoed 600 miles southeast of Trinidad. "It was very entertaining," he recalls. "The vessel was carrying 1,900 tons of high explosives." Fortunately, the ship, which had been struck in its boilers, went down in seven minutes and did not explode. Chapman had the foresight to stick $200 in traveler's checks and a bottle of Abdol vitamin pills inside his life jacket before scrambling into a lifeboat. After a week's sail, he and the other survivors made it to Georgetown, British Guiana.

After the war, Chapman and his wife were divorced and he married Helen Riesenfeld, who started the *Barrytown Explorer* with him. She died in 1970, and three years later Chapman married Dr. Ida Holzberg, a widow and psychiatrist. "It's convenient for Chanler to have his own psychiatrist in the house," says Winty Aldrich. Like the second Mrs. Chapman, Dr. Holzberg is Jewish. While chaffing her recently Chapman said, "Jesus Christ, maybe I should have gone Chinese the third time around." Mrs. Chapman, or Dr. Holzberg, as she prefers to be called, is listed on the masthead of the *Explorer*, but her duties are undefined. "She wants to get off the masthead because she gets angry at me every other day," Chapman says. Dr. Holzberg is petite, and Chapman affectionately refers to her as "Footnote" or "Kid," as in "O.K., Footnote" or, "Kid, I like you, but you've got a long way to go." As Chapman figures it, his wives are getting shorter all the time, but he likes that because they have a lot of bounce-back, Dr. Holzberg especially, "because she's got a lower center of gravity."

Over the years, Chapman has conducted his own radio interview show, but at present he is off the air. His last sponsor was a dairy, for whom he used to deliver remarkable commercials, such as, "Their man is on the job at five in the morning. You might even see him back at a house for the second time at nine, but let's skip over that." Some of Chapman's taped interviews are memorable, like the one in which he kept referring to the mayor of San Juan, Puerto Rico, where Chapman happened to be on vacation, as the mayor of Montreal. "San Juan, Señor," the mayor would say plaintively every time Chapman referred to Montreal.

Perhaps Chapman's greatest accomplishment with a tape recorder came at a great family gathering at Rokeby in 1965. About 150 Chanlers, Astors, Armstrongs and other kin assembled to celebrate the sesquicentennial of the house. Among those present at the main table were William Chamberlain Chanler, who is known as Brown Willie, and Ashley Chanler, the son of African Willie. Ashley is generally accounted a bounder by the rest of the family, and on this occasion he was wearing a Knickerbocker Club tie, which disturbed Brown Willie, a retired partner in the proper Wall Street firm of Winthrop, Stimson, Putnam, and Roberts. Believing that Ashley had been dropped from the Knickerbocker Club (as indeed he had been previously, for nonpayment of dues), Brown Willie voiced his annoyance and a loud debate ensued. "No one knew what was going on," says Winty Aldrich. "It wasn't until later that we found out it was all over a necktie. But Chanler was seated near them, and the moment the argument started he turned on his tape recorder, held up the microphone and began egging them on. When Ashley said that he had been reinstated in the Knickerbocker Club, Chanler shoved the microphone at Brown Willie and said, 'You lose that round, counselor.' "

Nowadays Chapman is primarily confining his attentions to the *Explorer* and his slingshot, with an occasional reversion to his guns. "Stop the presses!" he exclaimed the other day to a caller. "We're replating for wood alcohol! An unlimited supply of energy. No fermentation at the North and South Poles, so the penguins and Eskimos are out of luck. First flight to Venus by booze." He also was elated about reprinting a piece by Abraham Hewitt on War Relic, "really a second-rate horse, still being promoted as quite a stud."

The shooting in early spring, Chapman said, had been superb. The frozen Hudson was breaking up, and he liked to go down to the river with a .22 to shoot at pieces of ice. The most challenging shot was at twigs floating by. "Crack a little twig when it's just barely moving!" he exclaimed. "It's better than any shooting gallery. You feel like a newborn baby." Friends who happen along at this time of the year may be greeted as was William Humphrey, the novelist. Chapman insisted he shoot his initials into the snow next to the front porch. "Chanler can be trying," Humphrey says. "A few years ago I broke my right foot playing baseball barefooted with a gang of ten-year-olds. It was not put in a cast. Chanler came to dinner. He had stowed away six or eight martinis when he got out of his chair, crawled across the drawing room floor, took my bare foot in his big hands and broke it all over again. I beat him in the face with my crutch until he let go." Despite this, Humphrey considers Chapman a great friend.

Chapman is hopeful that this year will be a good year for seventeen-year locusts. Good, that is, from his point of view, not theirs. "They don't come every seventeen years, you know," he says. "They come every five or six. I use twenty-two longs with birdshot in them and, boy, those locusts can absorb a lot of dust. They're only three-quarters of an inch long, but they're built out of armor plate. You have to hit them just right. I like to take a little stool that unfolds and pop them when they're swarming. Shooting on the wing. That's the only way. I wouldn't shoot them while they're sitting down."

Chapman says now he's just looking for things that give him plea-sure. Has he a word of advice for others who would seek a happy life? Yes. "Things are going up and coming down," he says. "Earthquakes are expected. Step in and enjoy the turmoil."

* * *

Shortly after this article appeared, Winty Aldrich wrote me to say, "Bob Chanler's surviving daughter, Julie Laurin, died at home in Paris. They say she went out with a belly laugh, a copy of Sports Illustrated *clasped to her ample bosom.*

"The most bizarre consequence of the article occurred next door," Winty continued. *"Chanler acquired a couple of hundred copies of the article, which fill the back of his VW, and he wrote a letter to the Red Hook Central School Board arguing the article's transcendent significance in illuminating American civilization (or whatever) and demanding that it be made required reading for every graduating class at the High School. The letter was to be signed 'Ida Holzberg, M.D.' Whether it was sent, I know not, but Jay Chapman's wife and daughter told me this, with much rolling of eyes and shaking of heads."*

Not long ago, my wife and I attended a birthday party for Chapman at Sylvania, and the cast of characters came out of Eleanor and Franklin *and* Arsenic and Old Lace. Chapman's son, Jay, the mailman, was there in uniform, chatting with members of the river gentry as his buttons gleamed in the candlelight. Ricky Aldrich was attired in an ancient Brooks Brothers suit with spots all over it, and there were streaks of dirt on his hands and face. When he saw me he beamed—he bore me no grudge for the article—and when I introduced him to my Serbian-born wife, Ricky extended an earth-caked paw and said in fluent Serbian, *"Ya sam selyak"*—I am a peasant. Members of the Chanler clan are in general agreement that Ricky is the heir-apparent to Chanler Chapman's title of *"most eccentric man in America."*

Chapman died in 1982.

THE DEUCE
WITH LOVE
AND ADVANTAGE

JIMMY VAN ALEN

August 28, 1972

B Y HIS own definition, James Henry Van Alen, a millionaire sportsman of 69 who looks like a cherub, is "a busy little body." He has been called "the first gentleman of Old Guard society in America" and "Newport's last *grand homme*," and, given his money and position, Van Alen could have been just another social gadabout, but he is driven by an almost manic spirit of *noblesse oblige*. In his efforts to make the world a better place than he found it, Van Alen has espoused the cause of Santa Claus, put up the money to rescue the journals of James Boswell from Malahide Castle in Ireland, edited the *North American Review*, rejuvenated the Soldiers', Sailors' and Airmen's Club in New York, saved the landmark Newport Casino, collected the greater bustard and other rare Iberian birds for the American Museum of Natural History and promoted the reformation of scoring in tennis with such fervor that he was recently given a new sobriquet, "the Rolls-Royce radical."

Of all his interests, Van Alen is most intense about tennis. A tournament player in his younger days, he says, "I don't want you to think I'm a nut, but tennis established me *on my own.*" As far as Van Alen is concerned, millions upon millions of people should be playing tennis regularly, but in his opinion the sport will never achieve the great popularity it deserves as long as matches drag on and the scoring is obscured with terms such as "love" and "deuce," pseudoarchaic words imposed on tennis, Van Alen says, by the English in 1873.

In line with this, Van Alen, who turns out verse on any subject that engages him, has written a poem, "The Facts of Love," which goes in part:

> *The French think English crazy*
> *For the way they score at tennis—*
> *To claim that 'love' means nothing*
> *To a Frenchman makes no sennis.*
> *'Love all' the English umpire*
> *   cries,*
> *And means a double zero;*
> *What more's required to prove*
> *The English thinking's out of*
> *   gear-o?*
>
> *It's true that 'l'oeuf' means 'egg'*
> *   in French,*
> *And sounds like 'love' in English;*
> *But Frenchmen claim a moron*
> *   should*
> *Be able to distinguish;*
> *For love is love the world around*
> *And zero's always zero.*
> *And they who claim they mean the*
> *   same*
> *Must be a trifle queer-o.*

To reform tennis Van Alen has thought up the Van Alen Simplified Scoring System, known as VASSS. In VASSS, zero replaces the term love, and deuce and advantage are eliminated entirely. Briefly put, individual games are simply scored one, two, three instead of fifteen, thirty, forty, and the game goes to the first player who wins four points. Should players be tied six-six in games, they then play a nine-point sudden death with the set going to the player who first scores five points. By using VASSS, no match can last longer than about an hour and ten minutes or, as Van Alen puts it, "Just about as long as I care to watch people play tennis."

As the result of devising VASSS, Van Alen is convinced that his name will go down in history. "Pasteur pasturized milk. I will VASS-Sify tennis," he says. His Humber touring car has Rhode Island plates that proclaim VASSS, and for a brief while he even considered changing the name of his Newport cottage, Avalon, one of four residences he maintains in the United States and Europe, to VASSSalon, but thought better of it. When Van Alen can't use VASSS to (excuse the word) advantage, he goes around marking everything with his family initials, an intertwined VA. Thus the towels in Van Alen's bathroom look as though they had been stolen from the Veterans Administration, and the VA that he attached to the hood of his Rolls-Royce, in place of the figure of the lady, made his Rolls dealer apoplectic. The dealer complained that Van Alen was making the Rolls look like a Volkswagen. In his spare time, Van Alen designs jewelry with a VA motif for his wife Candy, who says, "I love to have Jimmy doodle in gold or diamonds or whatever."

Tennis is not the only sport that Van Alen would reform. Indeed, he has so many ideas about other sports that he is thinking of going into business as VASSS Inc., Spectator Sports Specialist. "I'm going to look at any game from the point of view of the spectator," he says. "People want blood! Out at Forest Hills people get blood with sudden death. If I go to a baseball game I want to see runs made, hits made, action! They've lowered the mound. That's not enough! I'd like to see ball games won twenty-eight to twenty-seven!" To accomplish this Van Alen would move the pitcher's rubber back five feet—"The pitcher in baseball was supposed to put the ball into play, not end it with a strikeout"—and have the ball slightly softened. Van Alen has little regard for home runs. He finds no excitement in the ball soaring over the fence, but doubles and triples are the very stuff of blood to him. To make sure that batters hit slews of doubles and triples with the softened ball, Van Alen would do away with the center fielder and the shortstop.

Yacht racing is another sport Van Alen deems in need of reform, particularly the America's Cup which, he says, is "deader than Admiral Nelson's left arm." Van Alen's low opinion of the cup races stirs up Newport, especially when he endorses Ring Lardner's idea of taking the yachts to the Niagara River and starting the race one hundred yards above the falls. As Van Alen sees it, no foreign yacht ever has a chance because of the United States edge in hull design and sailmaking. To make the cup truly a test of seamanship, he proposes that competing crews swap boats after each race.

For a supposed radical in sports, Van Alen has impeccable credentials. He was captain of the lawn tennis team at Cambridge, a well-known amateur player in the 1920s, thrice United States court tennis champion in the 1930s, and nowadays holds the presidencies of both the Newport Casino and the National Lawn Tennis Hall of Fame as well as membership in such plush clubs as Piping Rock, Racquet and Tennis, River, Knickerbocker and Spouting Rock in this country and Buck's and the Bath in England. Knowing everyone in the Establishment, he has the contacts and the time and energy to do "my yammering, squawking and shouting" about VASSS practically nonstop. If Van Alen can't corner a sympathetic audience in person to extol the merits of VASSS he relies on the telephone, and he calls with such frequency that the numbers and letters have disappeared from the dial faces of the phones in his Fifth Avenue apartment.

On occasion Van Alen will even take to his car and hunt for someone to talk to about VASSS. A couple of years ago he stopped at the home of a sportswriter on his day off. The writer was not there, but his wife was. "That's all right, I'll wait," Van Alen announced cheerfully, and he thereupon sat himself down at the piano for three hours, playing and singing songs of his own composition. All his life Van Alen has reveled in poetry and song. One of his earliest recollections is standing at attention with his father's letter opener for a sword and reciting "How Well I Remember the Days of '61." Van Alen has a great interest in the Civil War; his great grandfather and namesake, Brigadier General James Henry Van Alen, raised and equipped the Third New York Volunteer Cavalry and served on the staff of Fighting Joe Hooker. "Fighting Joe Hooker. His name more than described certain interests," Van Alen mused recently before plunging into his own poem "Pickett's Charge." His favorite poem by another author is Clement C. Moore's *A Visit from St. Nicholas*. As a boy Van Alen always thought that the poem ended too soon, and moreover, he worried that Father, who is standing by the open window as the poem closes, would catch cold, and to rectify this he has written additional verses in which Father climbs back into bed and pulls "the covers right up to my head. . . . My heart full and happy, my cap pulled on tight, I settled myself for the rest of the night."

Every Christmas Van Alen dresses up in a velvet Victorian suit to read *A Visit from St. Nicholas* to youngsters at Clement Moore's old home in Newport. As president of the House of Santa Claus Society, Van Alen has hopes of buying the Moore place and setting it aside as a Museum of Santa Clausiana replete with stalls for Donner and Blitzen and the rest of the reindeer. On Christmas Eve he would like to read *A Visit from St. Nicholas* in the White House. The idea is not farfetched. An ardent Republican, Van Alen composed and sang the song "Good Evening, Mr. President" at Eisenhower's first inaugural ball. It begins:

> *The country, Mr. President, is sure*
> *that you will keep*
> *Our people freedom-minded, and*
> *not governmental sheep.*
> *'Bang!' goes inflation; corruption's*
> *on the run.*
> *Before you've really started, the*
> *whole free world is shouting,*
> *Well done!*

Ever on the go, Van Alen is the last man to shirk a challenge. "If you don't risk in depth, you can never reach in height," he says. Even so, he occasionally comes a cropper. Back in the 1950s Van Alen decided that the European robin, a bird he fell in love with as a child after reading *The Death and Burial of Cock Robin* and *The Babes in the Wood*, should be in the United States. He imported three robins from Belgium and put them in a specially constructed "Robin Room" in the basement of his house in Washington, where he was then serving as an Eisenhower appointee on the Selective Service Commission. Van Alen built the Robin Room "so I could have little ones," but no little ones were forthcoming, since all three turned out to be males. A year later, Van Alen took the robins to Newport and released them. "It was autumn," he recalls. "I said, 'Goodbye, little robins.' 'Goodbye,' they said." As much as Van Alen loves robins, it is doubtful he will ever try the experiment again, since federal authorities have warned him that introduction of exotic birds is prohibited by law.

Born in Newport, Van Alen is of old New York stock with Astor and Vanderbilt blood in his veins. Raised in both the United States and England, he spent a good part of his childhood alone, tended by servants. At Rushton Hall, his grandfather's 4,000-acre estate in Northhamptonshire, a groom in top hat, cutaway and butcher boots was assigned to take Master James, wearing white breeches and a white cockade in his hat, pony riding every day. Since Van Alen's mother was fearful that the pony might run away with her son, the groom was instructed to go alongside with a lead. "I would say, 'Trot, George, trot!' " says Van Alen. "He would say, 'Yes, Master James.' I had no idea that the man was being degraded." Inasmuch as Master James spoke with an American accent in Britain and a British accent here, he found himself challenged to fights until his father's valet, John Dono, taught him to defend himself. As a result, whenever Master James met a new youngster, he would shoot out a clenched fist beneath the boy's nose and shout fiercely, "Smell this!" Van Alen's combative nature occasionally surges to the fore even now. Several years ago, while serving as a linesman in a match at Newport, Van Alen jumped to his feet after Pancho Gonzalez angrily hit a ball over the Casino roof while playing VASSS tennis. Van Alen went straight up to Gonzalez and told him in no uncertain words that such behavior would not be tolerated. Gonzalez backed off, muttering.

Looking back on his childhood, Van Alen finds his upbringing of immense value. "Having been brought up in the servants' hall, I know the servant's mind," he says. "I know all the waiters and the people who play in bands. Whenever I arrive at a party and Meyer Davis' band sees me, they stop and play 'My Shining Hour.' My theme song, a wonderful song. The words are right, and the melody has that warmth."

After attending preparatory school in England, Van Alen was supposed to go to Eton, his father's public school, but the start of World War I caught Van Alen in the United States and he was sent off to St. George's in Newport and then to the Lake Placid School. Summers were spent at Newport, where he took up lawn tennis under the tutelage of Craig Biddle, the father of a friend. When Van Alen proved adept, Biddle suggested that he enter the juniors at Forest Hills. However, Van Alen's father refused to let him go. "What!" he exclaimed. "Send James down to a place like *that* to play scalawags!"

In 1920 Van Alen went to England where he enrolled at Christ College, Cambridge. Not knowing any of the other students, he discovered, to his pleasure and surprise, that tennis opened the way for him. "This game was my passport," Van Alen says. "Tennis made a life for me. James Van Alen—my name was on the boards. I became captain of the Cambridge lawn tennis team. I became a personality." The student magazine, the *Granta*, described Van Alen as "a considerable personage who shines in any society . . . if America has any more James Henry's, let's have 'em."

With his stylish placement game Van Alen captained an Oxford-Cambridge team that beat Harvard and Yale at Eastbourne. This was at the height of what Van Alen calls "my great period, my lawn tennis period." He went to Wimbledon and the south of France, where he once was to play doubles with King Gustav of Sweden, "but then," he says, "I fell off a battleship, a British battleship, where there are no problems with getting brandy." In between tennis seasons Van Alen indulged in shooting and stalking, both still passions. (Van Alen's wife Candy, who is fond of traveling, says, "I know I can get him to go if there's something to shoot.")

Returning to the United States he and his younger brother Sam almost beat Bill Tilden and Frank Hunter at Newport, losing the third set seven to five. "No dinner parties were on time that night," Van Alen says. When he realized he was not going to be the greatest tennis player in the world, he gave up competing in the sport, and when he married his first wife, Eleanor Langley, he even stopped going to Newport because she hated it. His wife's family was very horsey, and with his usual zest Van Alen rode to hounds and played polo. But horses could never take the place of racket sports. Under the guidance of World Champion Pierre Etchebaster, the court tennis professional at the Racquet and Tennis Club, he took up the intricacies of that sport. He won the United States championships in 1933, 1938 and 1940. "Jimmy had beautiful classic strokes," says Allison Danzig, who covered court tennis for the *New York Times*. "I wouldn't say he was the best amateur who ever lived in this country, but he was a very smart player who got the most out of his abilities." In 1954 Van Alen persuaded clubs in Philadelphia, New York and Boston to let Princeton, Yale and Harvard students practice the game so they could compete against an Oxford-Cambridge combine for a trophy—a cup Van Alen found in a secondhand shop in London. The matches are now held every two years with Van Alen usually on hand to present the trophy.

When not off sporting somewhere, Van Alen, his wife and their two sons lived most of the time on Long Island, where he busied himself with the *North American Review* and a chain of weekly newspapers. Sensing that war was coming, he joined the Navy in 1939 and was commissioned a lieutenant in the reserve. Called to duty in 1941, he was first put in charge of the Navy's New York publicity office, where he was responsible for getting William H. White of the *Reader's Digest* to write the bestseller *They Were Expendable.* Later Van Alen served in England, where he came up with the idea of preloading ships for the Normandy invasion. After Normandy he ran a novel rest and rehabilitation camp at which he personally led the men on a mile run at six every morning. Throughout the war Van Alen carried on with his customary flair. When an enterprising fellow officer found himself suddenly billed £50,000 for the construction of a sailors' club in London, Van Alen used his Old Boy friendships with the British to see to it that the bill was charged off against lend-lease.

Returning home, Van Alen found his marriage had gone sour, and he and his wife were divorced. In 1948 he married again, this time with a front-page headline in the *New York World-Telegram* which read: CANDY VANDERLIP TIPTOEING TO ALTER WITH JIMMY VAN ALEN A LA HUSH HUSH. Unlike the first Mrs. Van Alen, Candy liked Newport and got along famously with her husband's mother, Mrs. Louis Brugière, who ran Wakehurst, the last "proper" house in Newport, staffed by twenty-three servants who piled up freshly cut flowers grown on the grounds in the ballroom lit by 146 candles.

Early on in his second life in Newport, Van Alen was offered the presidency of the lavish Newport Casino, a private club founded by James Gordon Bennett in 1880 and designed by Stanford White in Victorian Chinese style. The Casino had seen better days before World War I, when it annually held the United States National Lawn Tennis Championships which were later removed to Forest Hills. At great personal expense Van Alen set about refurbishing the Casino, and in 1954 he was able to get the USLTA to authorize the establishment of the Tennis Hall of Fame there.

Under Van Alen's direction, the Newport invitational tournament took on added gloss. His mother would attend, seated either in a peacock wicker chair or in the back of her chauffeured Rolls parked within a few feet of the grass courts. It took several years for the germinal seeds of VASSS to sprout within Van Alen's brain. He first had a clue that all was not well when he realized that a number of people who had been buying boxes for years hadn't the foggiest idea of what was going on in a match because they did not understand the scoring and were too timid to ask. Then matches had a way of dragging out interminably. In 1957 the idea for changing the scoring came to Van Alen when there was a marathon singles final between Ham Richardson and Straight Clark. A dull match to begin with, it lasted three and one-half hours, and as a result, no one ever got to see the exciting doubles final between Lew Hoad-Ken Rosewall and Mervyn Rose-Rex Hartwig, who were forced to play on a side court.

VASSS offers various alternatives. Instead of playing games to make a set, one system allows players to compete in a thirty-one-point set, something like table tennis, and as far as Van Alen is concerned, it makes handicapping simple and practicable and permits round-robin medal play that is ideal for club weekend tournaments. Above all, VASSS controls the number of points in a set and thus limits the length of a match, enabling players, spectators and TV programmers to plan an accurate time schedule. Van Alen is convinced that once big-time tennis fully adopts VASSS, the sport will become more popular than ever because matches will be able to start and finish at the time announced. Above all, Van Alen believes VASSS will allow fellow senior citizens to play a match to a conclusion without suffering undue fatigue.

Van Alen also feels strongly about the big serve. He is against it on the grounds that it makes matches dull with its weak return and smashing volley. To minimize the importance of the power serve, Van Alen advocates drawing a server's line three feet behind the baseline or eliminating the second serve. This idea has not gone down as well as his concept of sudden-death play in a set. Even there, he finds that the pros have altered sudden death from nine to twelve points. "The other players have gone along with Rod Laver and twelve-point sudden death," says Van Alen. "A twelve-point sudden death favors Laver in the percentages, but all the other players have jumped up and down like a lot of little monkeys shouting, 'Woo, woo!' "

While Van Alen waits impatiently for the rest of the tennis world to fall in line with VASSS, he has embarked on an even more ambitious program—saving all the United States, including tennis players. A newly dedicated member of the Committee to Unite for America, he has been instrumental in getting out buttons and bumper stickers that proclaim, "For America." Van Alen wants to organize the "sound-thinking majority to rebuild patriotism and armaments" because, in his opinion, "The chips are down, our backs are to the wall, the fight is for survival. Time is short. Dr. Edward Teller told a meeting of the committee that the Russians will be able to overwhelm us in just two years unless we build up our strength and, moreover, we are threatened by dissidents with unkempt locks and shoddy habits who foment strikes and campus disorders. We've got to get back to the good old days."

Several months ago Van Alen tried to do his best by his old service, the Navy, in his For America campaign. He went to Washington to call upon John Chafee, a fellow Rhode Islander, then Secretary of the Navy. As Chafee, a captain and a commander listened, Van Alen detailed his program to get sailors into fighting trim. As part of the program, he recommended the installation of chinning bars aboard ships at sea so sailors could strengthen their grips. "Nobody cares about good strong hands," Van Alen told them. The captain and the commander pointed out, with deferential hems and haws, that Van Alen's program would cost considerable money and time to get it underway, and it really wouldn't be helpful for the sailors. "But this will be for the officers, too," Van Alen replied. And no sooner had he said that than he realized he had lost his audience, such as it was.

No matter whether he is trying to save the United States, or tennis, Van Alen refreshes his morale with purely personal projects. At present he is trying to find a publisher to bring out his odes to Scotland, *Songs of Heather, Fur and Feather*, illustrated, at his commission, by Lionel Edwards, the late British sporting artist. "It has," Van Alen says, "some memorable poems, such as 'Little Hans, the Partridge Hound.'" Uncharacteristically, Van Alen refuses to recite it. "Whenever I read this, I burst into tears," Van Alen says. But then, smiling cheerfully, he leans close and asks, "But what's a tear or two?"

* * *

Jimmy Van Alen says "I'm gummed up with three or four things. I'm trying to create a House of Christmas for the children of America, I'm still reading A Visit from St. Nicholas *at Newport and Palm Beach, and VASSS is coming along."*

TRICK OR TRUITE

JOE HYDE

November 8, 1971

ELEGANCE AND simplicity are the why and the wherefore of Chef Joe Hyde, sportsman, savant of fish and game and author of the new cookbook *Love, Time & Butter*. At Gay Head on Martha's Vineyard, where fishing for striped bass can be a pretentious production calling for belted waders, plug bags and floating flashlights, Hyde once appeared on the beach carrying a rod and wearing a dark blue suit, brightly polished black shoes and a derby hat. As the other anglers watched in silence, Hyde waded into the surf up to his armpits, caught two twenty-pound stripers, tipped his bowler to onlookers and departed, dripping wet.

On the Vineyard, in New York City, Kansas City, Jupiter Island and Santa Barbara, all locales where he has cooked or taught cooking, Chef Joe Hyde is, in the words of novelist Robert Crichton, "sort of semilegendary." Should a client's dinner party flag, Hyde, looking like a white-hatted Brendan Behan, has been known to bound from the

25

kitchen to supply the missing ingredient, his own good cheer. At one dull gathering in New Jersey, he enlivened the proceedings by Indian wrestling with the guests. Some years ago at a garden party for Patrice Lumumba's delegation to the United Nations, he showed the befuddled Congolese how to eat corn on the cob. Having done so, he threw the finished ear behind him with a flourish. A week later, at least so the story goes, the Congolese attended a formal dinner in the state dining room at the United Nations. Corn on the cob was served and the Congolese startled everyone by tossing the cobs over their shoulders. But Hyde has his shy moments, too. When Elizabeth Taylor sought him out to congratulate him on a dinner, he hid under the kitchen table, where he pretended to fuss with pots and pans. "I didn't want to get involved," he says.

Gastronomically, Joe Hyde belongs to the classic French school, with the emphasis, as an admiring food critic of *The New Yorker* once put it, on "preserving the essential greatness of the ingredients, rather than exalting them to complicated and unrecognizable heights." Hyde preaches the gospel of simplicity in food with such fervor that he sometimes refers to himself as "the backlash to the Galloping Gourmet and other TV chefs. While the bird is drying out more and more, they just confuse and snow the audience. Teaching cooking should be about detailed simple processes."

Hyde does about sixty dinner parties a year, and one of his simple spreads—enhanced with a touch of game fish here, a game bird or so there—can cost the host up to twenty dollars a guest. Hyde and his family live in Sneden's Landing, New York, but they also have a house on the beach at the Vineyard, which Hyde visits often for seafood. "I love nothing better," he says, "than to have a client ask, 'Is this fish fresh?' And I say, 'Yes sir, I caught it myself last night on Martha's Vineyard. Would you like some more?' " Among Hyde's favorite seafoods are minnows, known as spearing, dipped in beer and then in a mixture of bread crumbs and flour and fried in deep fat; bay scallops, either smoked or sautéed meunière (the floured scallops are in the hot pan only one minute; if they stay longer they toughen); boiled periwinkles served cold with a vinaigrette dip of chopped onions, salt, pepper, oil and vinegar; fresh mussels and poached fish, preferably a striped bass or salmon of from five to twelve pounds. "The way to cook fish is to poach it whole," Hyde says, explaining that this is the best method to keep it juicy. "People have simply gotten used to fish being dry, because it is so often served that way."

Dryness is only one of the horrors that Hyde sees in American cooking of fish and game. He is aghast at the idea of storing venison or rabbit in a freezer. Instead he marinates them in crocks filled with red wine. Similarly, he feels game birds should be hung for a sufficient period of time. Adhering to French custom, he hangs a woodcock until it has one or two maggots in it. "Not fifty or one hundred," he says. "Just one or two." He also contends that all birds, except turkeys with exceptionally large breasts, should be roasted breast down and not up. "The hottest part of the oven is the top," Hyde explains, "and the back should stick up in the hot air because it has little meat on it." As fond as he is of game, Hyde regrets that he cannot get it often enough. Recently he roasted some starlings for a friend. "They weren't bad," he says, "but I suspect blue jays are better."

Hyde, who is now forty-three, was born surrounded by the "Beautiful People." His maternal grandmother, Mary Tonetti, a sculptress, started the artistic colony at Sneden's Landing on the Hudson River. Hyde's neighbors have included Orson Welles, John Steinbeck, Katharine Cornell, Jerome Robbins, Mike Wallace, Aaron Copland, Noel Coward, Vivien Leigh, Laurence Olivier and Burgess Meredith. As a youngster, Hyde taught Olivier how to sail; his boat was named *Fiddle-dee-dee*, a favorite expression of Scarlett O'Hara in *Gone with the Wind*.

Hyde's father, Robert McKee Hyde, was a well-to-do eccentric. He occupied his time writing ("His *Winds of Gobi* is a perfectly beautiful book about China," says Hyde. "He had never been there."), practicing nudism, collecting spiders and hunting mushrooms, an avocation inherited by his son. Joe went to prep school at Millbrook and then to college at Trinity in Hartford. Upon graduating from Trinity in 1950, Hyde decided on a conventional enough career, the hotel business, because he enjoyed meeting people. He went to work at the Hotel Raleigh in Washington, D.C., and there he started in the kitchen. He perceived immediately, he says, that cooking was his destiny. He spent three weeks with the roast cook, two weeks in the pastry shop, three weeks in cold meat and a week in the storeroom, where his first task was to clean all the cans on the shelves. He had no sooner absorbed the location of the canned goods than he was drafted into the Army. There, amazingly, he wound up serving as a cook for a heavy-mortar company in Korea. Hyde took along a Betty Crocker cookbook. "When the menu said steak, I always made stew," he recalls. "I made a casserole with the hamburger meat. I browned the meat, poured off the fat, added garlic, bay leaf, onion and tomato puree and simmered the sauce for two hours. Then I put layers of cooked elbow macaroni, sauce and sliced American cheese into the deep pans until they were full. The whole affair was baked for an hour; one pan went to each platoon. The boys liked it. They called it 'Holy Mattress.' "

On return to civilian life, Hyde worked as a room clerk at the Statler Hilton in New york for six months before going to France. There, through UNESCO, he got a job as an apprentice in Chez Nandron, a two-star restaurant in Lyons, a city considered by some to be the culinary capital of France. His first day was almost a disaster. The usual apprentice is a 13-year-old, and here was Hyde, the only American apprentice in the country, twenty-five years old, burly—almost six feet tall with a beard that needed shaving every twelve hours. When he appeared in the kitchen dressed in white, the dozen cooks stopped working to stare in amazement. With an atrocious accent, Hyde introduced himself. *"Bond jour!"* he exclaimed. *"Je m'appelle Joe!"* Several of the cooks almost swooned. "I was the grossest thing that had ever happened to French cooking," Hyde says. "They'd never seen anyone like me before. And the name Joe. They flipped out over it. It sounds like a peasant's name. Even today French chefs who have known me for years recoil at the mention of it. They always call me Joe-ceph!"

Given his appalling debut, Hyde was assigned the lowest job in the scullery, plucking larks beneath a splashing drainboard. Eventually, because of his age, the first cooks allowed Hyde to eat with them, and he acquired a taste for fried tripe, pig heads and coq au vin made with just the peeled chicken gizzards.

Hyde next became an assistant *poissonier*, or fish cook, at the Pyramide in Vienne. At the time it was regarded by many as the best restaurant in the world. While there, Hyde, a follower of the turf, won $1,000 in the *tiercé*, a form of French off-track betting. According to local custom, a winner is supposed to spend it all on one spree. Hyde invited nearly two dozen friends including the man who had sold him the ticket, to dine at the famed Pont de Collonges. "It was a fantastic, endless meal," he recalls. "I ate two pheasants. We had a meringue and ice cream dessert that was four feet tall. Each tier was covered with spun sugar and illuminated with a little light inside. We drank the finest of champagne—it didn't have anything written on it except dust."

After two years in France, Hyde returned to the United States to become chef at the Jupiter Island Club in Hobe Sound, Florida. One of his triumphs there was a chicken poached inside a pig's bladder, which he prepared for Sir Osbert Sitwell and Marshall Field. Hyde had brought back with him a supply of pig bladders from France, but when he later tried to import more, United States Customs seized them, and ever since he has had to make do with ones obtained from local slaughterhouses. Once, while he was cooking at Chalet Frascati in Santa Monica, California, he procured some bladders, washed them, blew them up through a stick of macaroni and set them out to dry on a clothesline. One of them got away and sailed over the fence like an expiring balloon. Hyde's wife, Gail, ran next door, shouting to the neighbors, "Excuse me, but one of my husband's bladders just landed in your yard."

Hyde spent a summer as head chef at the Misquamicut Club in Watch Hill, Rhode Island, but then quit to work, once again, as an assistant because "I felt I had to learn a great deal more." Cole Porter wrote a letter of introduction to Le Pavillon—how chic—but Hyde says, "It was the wrong way to come in. I should have entered through the cellar." He was shunted off to the Waldorf in 1956 as assistant sauce cook and afterward spent a year at the Brussels. A little while later he decided to teach cooking at UCLA. When his mother's home in Sneden's Landing fell vacant, he returned East to teach in the family mansion known as the Old Library because it had served as one in the nineteenth century. Built in 1685, the house was also celebrated as a meeting place of George Washington and Lafayette. Although Washington never slept there, he had eaten there, and Hyde's classes were held in the enormous kitchen with its original fireplace.

In a roundup of cooking schools, *The New York Times* went beyond the city line to include Hyde's school because his classes had "too much merit." Similarly another Manhattan food expert wrote, "It is not my custom to concern myself with matters beyond the limits of my own borough, but I have an excuse in this case—that I would go a lot farther afield than Rockland County to find a teacher with Mr. Hyde's combined gifts for cooking and teaching."

In 1966 Hyde gave up teaching to devote himself full-time to catering. He shifted his kitchen from the Old Library to a sort of miniature palace nearby that had been built by his uncle, Eric Gugler, an architect and designer of the executive offices in the West Wing of the

White House. There, amid historic frescoes, triumphant arches and heroic busts, Hyde turns out smoked bluefish, stuffed eggs, poached salmon, orange mousse and other dishes that can be prepared in advance for a dinner party. Hyde is thus well prepared when he arrives at a client's house with his staff of six, headed by Selma Andersen, a brisk Swedish woman who superintends the table setting while Hyde himself prepares the canapés, heats the oven for the saddles of lamb, sautés endives air-expressed from Belgium and chops shallots. Hyde never goes anywhere without shallots. Just in case he might find them unavailable, he keeps a supply in the glove compartment of his truck. "And I always have kosher salt with me," he says. "I just love the feel of it."

Hyde has cooked and catered in all sorts of places. At a party at a manufacturing plant, he used a forklift truck to serve the appetizers. When the Broadway musical *Camelot* opened, he catered the party for lyricist Alan Jay Lerner. He has also catered parties for the Josh Logans, including one party in honor of Princess Margaret and Anthony Armstrong-Jones. Armstrong-Jones was so pleased that he shook the hand of one of Hyde's assistants under the mistaken impression that he was Hyde. "Another first for Chef Joe Hyde," says Hyde, who sometimes refers to himself in the third person when things go awry.

Occasionally Hyde falls out with a client. Robert Montgomery objected to the bill, and Carter Burden, the social New York City councilman, wrote Hyde several letters complaining he could not find the persimmon ice cream that was left behind.

Every so often Hyde caters a dinner for the New York Mycological Society. The mushroom enthusiasts often show up with unusual fungi, and they joyously sing their anthem:

> *"Deep, deep in the murky shadows,*
> *There where the slime mold creeps,*
> *With joy the stout mycologist*
> *His pallid harvest reaps."*

A year and a half ago Hyde and Everett Poole, who runs a fish market in Menemsha, on Martha's Vineyard, began turning out a line of frozen fish and shellfish dishes, prepared by "Famous Chef Joe Hyde." They sell soups, chowders, bouillabaisse, Menemsha thermidor (lobster and fish) and stuffed clams direct to customers or through fancy food stores in cities all across the country. (While Hyde objects to many frozen foods, he believes these dishes, prepared his way—with juices to conserve fresh taste—are worthy of a first-class chef.) One Vineyard resident went to three dinner parties in a week, and all the hostesses passed off Hyde's dishes as their own. They should know better, the Vineyard being true Hyde territory. It is there that Hyde does some truly debatable things. For example, he will take one of his antique bass boats and head south five miles for the deserted island called No Man's Land. When Hyde gets to No Man's, he either trolls off the beach or goes ashore for a stroll. There is only one difficulty. No Man's Land is used as a bombing and target range by the armed forces. Hyde rather likes trolling offshore, especially when the planes are strafing. With the fastidious taste of a haiku poet, he is fond of describing the puffs of smoke that are emitted from the wings of an attacking plane.

But for all this *joie de vivre*, he has moments of depression. On occasion he wonders if he does not repeat himself too much with menus. A couple of years ago he got so depressed by this thought that he consulted a psychiatrist. The doctor was elated because Hyde had such an unusual cause for depression. "People are eating your art!" the psychiatrist exclaimed. To which Hyde adds, "That was still another first for Chef Joe Hyde."

Wild Duck à la Chef Joe Hyde

3 or 4 wild ducks for 6 persons (four ducks offer a second helping)	2 cloves garlic halved but unpeeled
	1 tbs. peppercorns
2 medium-size onions cut into eighths	8 juniper berries
	1 cup white wine
1 onion chopped fine	1 quart water salted to taste
1 stalk celery roughly cut	1 stick butter
1 carrot roughly cut	1 bunch watercress

Pluck ducks. Cut necks flush with bodies of birds. Split and clean gizzards. Fry gizzards and necks with liver in one-half stick of butter over medium-high heat in a large cast-iron skillet. When brown, add cut-up onions, celery and carrot, garlic, peppercorns and juniper berries. When all are tinged with brown, remove to saucepan, add white wine and let simmer for two hours. Strain off resulting juice and boil down to one-half cup liquid. Refrigerate. (You can do all this the day before the dinner.)

On day of dinner preheat oven to 500°. Salt and pepper ducks; smear with one-half stick of soft butter. Place in oven breast down on top shelf and roast for 25 minutes. This will cause some smoke. Don't worry. Remove ducks, sprinkle with chopped onion, and perhaps a handful of pine needles or several branches of rosemary. Return to 350° oven for 10 minutes.

Remove ducks. Make an incision between second joint and breast and rip off the legs. Make another cut at top of wishbone and on both sides of the backbones and strip breasts from carcasses. Place breasts skin down on platter and put to one side.

Place legs in a duck press or orange juice squeezer. If neither is available, simply squeeze the blood from meat with hand, and set aside.

Place the carcasses in a roasting pan. Pour one-half cup of the cooled juices over them. Put in oven and let simmer. Remove from heat and pass the juice through a sieve. Simmer again.

Place dinner plates and platter of breasts in the oven at 100° for three minutes. (Plates should be warm when served, not hot.) Garnish breasts with watercress. Just before serving, remove juices from heat, whisk in blood and pour over duck breasts.

Venison Steak au Poivre

6 1½-inch-thick venison steaks cut ⅔ stick butter
    from haunch 1½ tbs. finely chopped shallots
3 tbs. peppercorns

Put peppercorns on chopping block or cutting board. Using heel of heavy pot or round stone, crack corns. Do not grind. Distribute peppercorns on both sides of steaks and press in with palm of your hand. Heat 12-inch cast-iron skillet and put in 1 tbs. butter. Let butter brown and begin to smoke over high heat. Put in steaks. Brown three minutes to a side. Remove steaks, wipe out pan and put in remaining butter over medium high heat. When butter is brown, add shallots and remove from fire. Stir briskly and pour shallot-butter sauce over steaks. Serves six.

If steaks are frozen, do not thaw completely before cooking; too much juice will run. One of the important principles of game cooking is preservation of all juices. Do not presalt steaks. Salt draws juice from the meat. Let your guests salt their own venison at table.

* * *

Chef Joe Hyde now does catering from his yacht Constellation, *which is ordinarily berthed at City Island, New York in the warmer months, and in Florida during the winter.*

FRANK MERRIWELL'S TRIUMPH

December 24, 1962

O F ALL the bold Americans who have appeared on the sporting scene, none ever aroused the admiration or left so enduring an impression as one who never really existed: Frank Merriwell of Fardale Academy, Yale College and the world at large. The hero of the most widely read juvenile saga ever published, his very name is synonymous with the spectacular in sports. From 1896 to 1914 he performed unmatchable feats of derring-do in *Tip Top Weekly*. He was a whiz at boxing, baseball (his "double shoot," which curved in both directions, was always good in the clutch), football, hockey, lacrosse, crew, track, shooting, bicycle racing, billiards, golf—in fact, any sport he deigned to play. No matter what plots the villains hatched, Frank always emerged triumphant. The schemers—sneaky Roland Ditson, swaggering Herbert Hammerswell, the son of "a pompous, vain, conceited, narrow-minded, back-number politician," and the rest of their ilk—were routed.

Frank Merriwell, in the words of his creator, Gilbert Patten, stood for truth, faith, justice, the triumph of right, mother, home, friendship, loyalty, patriotism, the love of alma mater, duty, sacrifice, retribution and strength of soul as well as body. Frank was manly; he had "sand." He was tolerant. Although he neither smoked nor drank—"Frank had proven that it was not necessary for a man to drink at Yale in order to be esteemed a good fellow"—he gladly "blew off" his chums to fizz at Morey's while he quaffed ginger ale. He was honest. When some prankish classmates stole a turkey from a farmer's coop, Frank risked capture by staying behind to nail a five-dollar bill to the roost. "Have all the sport you like over it," he told his laughing friends, "but I feel easy in my mind."

Above all, Frank was modest. As a freshman in a boarding house on York Street, he tolerated Spartan furnishings, but as a sophomore in South Middle he did up his rooms with souvenirs of his adventures in South America, Africa, Europe, Asia and Australia. On the floor were grizzly-bear and tiger-skin rugs; on the walls, bows and arrows, pistols and "a heavy ax, the blade of which was rusty and stained with blood"; and, as a final touch, up near the ceiling, "safely out of reach," a strange knife, tipped with green, in a glass case with the sign, THE SNAKE KNIFE OF THE PAMPAS POISON! Frank's friends—Bart Hodge, Jack Diamond, Bruce Browning and the rest of the crowd—were wont to meet there once or twice a week for "jolly gatherings," but whenever anyone asked about the unusual decor, which "elicited no small amount of surprise," Frank would sigh, "What's the use of talking about what one has done? It's not that which counts here."

Such a hero could dazzle any generation. There is no counting the number of youngsters he inspired. Among Merriwell's admirers were Stanley Ketchel, Franklin P. Adams, Jess Willard, Floyd Gibbons, Jack Dempsey, Jerry Giesler, Fredric March, Christy Mathewson, Woodrow Wilson, Babe Ruth, Al Smith and Wendell Willkie. George Jean Nathan was so moved by Merriwell that he laid aside his acerbic pen to plead for a biography of Patten, and Westbrook Pegler once lamented that Patten had never received the Pulitzer Prize. "When I read Hemingway, Jack London and Skinny Caldwell of Tobacco Road, all fellows with scant respect for womanhood, nor reticence in matters which never should be mentioned in mixed company," Pegler wrote, "I pine for the fresh clear nobility which walked in gleaming armor even though dens of infamy flourished in all big cities and unwary daughters of our farmers vanished into Kansas City with straw suitcases."

Nowadays, *Dime Novel Round-up*, a monthly magazine devoted to old-time popular literature, gives over column after column to Merriwell minutiae, and its editor, Edward T. LeBlanc of Fall River, Massachusetts, is such an enthusiast that he is compiling a plot synopsis of each issue of *Tip Top*. So far, he has read his way through the first 375. Another contributor, J. P. Guinon of Little Rock, Arkansas, has analyzed the letters column that ran in *Tip Top* for almost twenty years. In New York, the Friends of Frank Merriwell, an informal society, meets over the luncheon table in the name of fair play. Started by Joseph Graham, an insurance executive who is fond of introducing himself to newcomers as "the president and beloved founder," the society has the motto, "No bullies or toadies allowed." One member, a reporter on *The New York Times*, was banished not long ago after a daily-double notation was found on the back of his membership card.

The closest any real-life Yale athlete has come to Merriwell was Albie Booth, who won eight varsity letters and captained the football and basketball teams. (He turned down the baseball captaincy "to give someone else a chance.") As a sophomore, Booth almost single-handedly defeated Army and Chris Cagle in a football game that Army was winning thirteen to zero. Booth went in and scored three touchdowns, the last on a sixty-five-yard punt return through the entire Cadet team. He kicked all the extra points as Yale won twenty-one to thirteen. In 1932 Booth made his sporting farewell by hitting a bases-loaded homer in the ninth to beat Harvard four to three. Sportswriters invariably called him Frank Merriwell.

For seventeen years, Patten, under the pen name of "Burt L. Standish," ground out 20,000 words a week on Merriwell. It was mentally taxing and physically arduous. He bruised his typing fingers so badly that he had to hire a secretary. He walked furiously as he dictated. When he walked slowly, the narrative came hard. The faster he walked, the better it flowed. One morning he attached a pedometer to his leg and clocked four and a quarter miles in three hours.

In practically every way, Patten was unlike his fictional hero. Patten was a spindly small-town boy with a sense of inferiority. His pacifist parents constantly warned him against the shamefulness of fisticuffs. When he created Merriwell, he simply turned himself inside out. "It was natural for me to wish to make Frank a fellow such as I would like to have been myself," he said.

Patten was born in Corinna, Maine on October 25, 1866, the son of a carpenter, "a good, solid, honest Maine man of no distinctive talents." His mother was "simple and merely a good housewife and a loving, almost adoring mother." From the start, he was a storyteller. "I was trying to write stories even before I knew how to spell some of the simplest words," he later recalled. "My thirst for reading was fed at first upon Sabbath-school literature and such worn and tattered books as I found in my home." He started smoking at fourteen, when he indulged in two-cent cheroots. He also got drunk on hard cider, but the experience, while "interesting, even exciting," helped make him into a Prohibitionist. When he was fifteen, he shocked his parents by running away. For six months he worked in a machine shop in Biddeford, Maine, and when he returned home, unrepentant, he announced he was going to be an author. He promptly wrote two stories, *A Bad Man* and *The Pride of Sandy Flat*, which he sent to Beadle & Adams, the leading dime-novel publishers. He received a total of six dollars for both stories. "That," he said, "settled my career."

For the next thirteen years Patten wrote westerns for Beadle & Adams. To get local color for such epics as *Hurricane Hal, The Cowboy Hotspur* and *Nobby Nat, The Tenderfoot Detective*, he once took a train as far west as Omaha, where he spent a day before returning east. For a brief spell he also ran a weekly newspaper and managed a semipro baseball team. In 1886 he married the first of his three wives, Alice Gardner, who corrected the grammar in his copy. In 1891 they moved to New York.

After several years of routine success, Patten quit Beadle when the firm deducted ten dollars from a one-hundred-dollar payment because he asked for the money ten days before publication of a story. To get by, he wrote boiler-plate pages for small country newspapers, 60,000-word juveniles for *Golden Hours* and, after much persistence, a series of boys' stories for *Good News*, a Street & Smith weekly. He also wrote a play, *Men of Millions*, which opened in New Haven. The leading lady, who played a social-climbing wife, so overacted that she was hissed from the stage and refused to return. The comedian got drunk. Patten decided it would be best to return to Maine. He was twenty-nine, the father of a three-year-old son and close to broke. His big chance came a couple of months later, in December of 1895.

Shortly before Christmas, Ormond Smith, senior partner in Street & Smith, wrote to say that the firm was interested in putting out a weekly series, "something in the line of the Jack Harkaway stories, Gay Dashleigh series which we are running in *Good News* and the Island School series . . . the idea being to issue a library containing a series of stories covering this class of incident, in all of which will appear one prominent character surrounded by suitable satellites. It would be an advantage to the series to have introduced the Dutchman, the Negro, the Irishman, and any other dialect you are familiar with.

"It is important that the main character in the series should have a catchy name, such as Dick Lightheart, Jack Harkaway, Gay Dashleigh, Don Kirk, as upon his name will depend the title for the library.

"The essential idea of this series is to interest young readers in the career of a young man at a boarding school, preferably a military or naval academy. The stories should differ from the Jack Harkaways in being American and thoroughly up to date. Our idea is to issue, say, twelve stories, each complete in itself, but like the links in a chain, all dealing with life at the academy. By this time the readers will have become sufficiently well acquainted with the hero, and the author will also no doubt have exhausted most of the pranks and escapades that might naturally occur.

"After the first twelve numbers, the hero is obliged to leave the academy, or takes it upon himself to leave. It is essential that he should come into a considerable amount of money at this period. When he leaves the academy he takes with him one of the professor's servants, a chum. In fact any of the characters you have introduced and made prominent in the story. A little love element would also not be amiss, though this is not particularly important.

"When the hero is once projected on his travels there is an infinite variety of incident to choose from. In the Island School series, published by one of our London connections, you will find scenes of foreign travel with color. This material you are at liberty to use freely.

"After we run through twenty or thirty numbers of this, we would bring the hero back and have him go to college—say, Yale University: thence we could take him on his travels again to the South Seas or anywhere. . . ."

Patten was enthusiastic. He knew next to nothing about military schools, so he read a number of brochures and books about them. Having made notes, he thereupon wrote the first story in four days. He christened his hero Frank Merriwell, explaining, "The given name of Frank was taken to express one of the hero's characteristics—open, on the level, aboveboard, frank. Merriwell was formed by a combination of two words: 'merry'—expressive of a jolly, high-spirited nature—and 'well'—suggesting abounding physical health."

Patten adopted the pseudonym Burt L. Standish because of his love for Longfellow's poem, "The Courtship of Miles Standish." Street & Smith accepted the story and offered Patten a contract to write Merriwell stories for three years, each story to be 20,000 words long, the salary a flat fifty dollars a week with no royalties. Patten signed for several reasons. "One," he said, "was that I was married and wanted a steady weekly income. Secondly, my father had been crippled by a fall and it had become necessary for me to support my parents. A third reason was that I believed I'd always be able to turn off my weekly Merriwell yarn in four days, which would leave me two extra working days a week in which to labor at the great American novel, which I still dreamed of writing."

The first story, *Frank Merriwell; or, First Days at Fardale*, Volume I, Number I, appeared on April 18, 1896, and it began:

"Get out!"
Thump! A shrill howl of pain.
"Stop it! That's my dog!"
"Oh, it is? Then you ought to be kicked, too! Take that for your impudence!"
Cuff! A blow from an open hand sent the boyish owner of the whimpering poodle staggering to the ground, while paper bags of popcorn flew from his basket and scattered their snowy contents around.
"That was a cowardly blow!"
The haughty, over-dressed lad who had knocked the little popcorn vendor down, after kicking the barefooted boy's dog, turned sharply as he heard the words, and found himself face to face with a youth of an age not far from his own.
As they stood thus, eying each other steadily, the two boys presented a strong contrast. The one who had lately been so free with foot and hand had a dark, handsome, cruel face. He was dressed in a plaid suit of a very pronounced pattern, had patent leather shoes on his feet and a crushed felt hat on his head, wore several rings on his fingers and had a heavy gold double chain strung across his vest, while the pin in his red necktie was set with a "sparkler" that might or might not be genuine.
The other lad was modestly dressed in a suit of brown, wore

well-polished shoes and a stylish straw hat, but made no display
of jewelry. His face was frank, open and winning, but the merry
light that usually dwelt in his brown eyes was now banished by a
look of scorn, and the set of his jaw told that he could be firm and
dauntless.

This, of course, is Frank Merriwell, fresh off the train at Fardale, and
the bully is Bart Hodge, destined to become, as most bullies were,
Frank's "admiring and unwavering friend." Frank challenges Hodge to
a fight for cuffing the little popcorn vendor, but Hodge refuses and
drives off to Snodd's boarding house, pausing only to lean out of the
barouche and whip the poodle as he goes by. At Snodd's, Hodge
further demonstrates his villainy by trying to kiss Belinda Snodd, the
plump daughter of the proprietor. "Belinda—what a sweet name—how
poetic!" exclaims Hodge. "You have the brown eyes of a fawn. The
sight of those tempting lips makes me burn with a desire to taste their
dewy freshness. Belinda, give me a kiss!"

Fat but frisky, she eludes him, and Hodge is further enraged at
dinner when Frank makes sport of him with ventriloquism. Frank, it
turns out, is a top-notch ventriloquist. When Hodge angrily leaves the
table, Frank gets the other boys on his side: "Being a born diplomat,
Frank decided that then was the accepted time to make himself solid at
Snodd's, which he proceeded to do by keeping up a string of funny
stories and witty sayings that convulsed the boys and made them
decide that he must be a jolly good fellow."

Hodge arranges to have Frank slugged over the head and sprinkled
with hard cider from Snodd's cellar. Despite Frank's protestations that
"I do not know the taste of liquor," Snodd takes him for a thief and
orders the popcorn vendor to drive Frank back to the railway station.
But the little vendor refuses; as Patten put it, "The urchin was loyal."
Snodd relents, and Frank and Hodge try to settle their differences with
a fight. "You and I both can't attend Fardale Academy!" shouts Hodge
during the melee. Though battered, Hodge refuses to give up. Frank
offers to make peace, but Hodge shows himself to be "a sulker and a
cad by his refusal to shake hands."

Enter Inza Burrage, who comes to picnic with Belinda and the boys.
She is a dark-haired, red-lipped, jolly girl, and Frank is smitten. "For a
moment Inza Burrage's dark eyes had looked straight into his brown
orbs." (Later in the series, Frank would also be attracted by blonde

Elsie Bellwood. It took him years to make up his mind which one he preferred.)

Alas, Hodge gets Inza as his tennis partner in a doubles game, and Frank looks bad as he is forced to cover the territory of his partner, plump Belinda. Just as Frank is striving extra hard, the popcorn vendor runs wildly toward them screaming, "Run! run! run! Mad dog! Mad dog!"

Hodge, the cad, flees. Inza trips, but Frank gently picks her up and moves her to the side as he prepares to battle an obviously hydrophobic canine with a jackknife.

> "What are you going to do?" panted Inza. "You are not going to fight the dog?"
> "Yes!"
> "He will kill you!" she screamed. "Remember that one scratch from his teeth means sure death!"
> "I know that!"
> "Then run—run!"
> "And leave you and these girls to be bitten by that beast! Not much! Better that he should bite one than a dozen."

As the dog pounces, Inza stops panting. "What a brave, noble fellow he is!" her white lips whispered. "How terrible that he should give his life for me! How grand!" Snodd arrives and shoots the dog as Merriwell grapples with it. Again shown up by Frank, Hodge retaliates by locking him in a cemetery vault so he'll miss the entrance examinations for Fardale. As Frank is trying to find a way out, he hears a rustling. Rats! ("Surely the situation was one to appall the stoutest heart.") Here the scene fades, opening next at Fardale on the day of the exams. To the astonishment of Hodge, Merriwell bursts into the room. Foiled again. Witness to the dark deed, the loyal urchin had let Frank out. Hodge agrees to mend his ways, and he and Frank enter Fardale together. There, along with Barney Mulloy ("Begobs! Oi filt that Oi had to do it. Two min were oudt, an' it samed loike th' last chance!") and Hans Dunnerwurst ("By shimminy! dot peen der pest gatch yr efer saw my whole life in!"), he becomes one of Frank's satellites.

Within a few months, the circulation of *Tip Top Weekly* was 75,000 copies. Eventually it reached 300,000. After further adventures at Fardale—Frank, of course, was the star of all the athletic teams—his uncle Asher Merriwell dies, and his will directs that Frank leave the academy "and begin a series of travels through the United States and other countries." Professor Horace Orman Tyler Scotch, nicknamed "Hot" Scotch, becomes his guardian and traveling companion. After a series of daring feats around the world, in issues twelve to thirty-nine, Frank announces he is going to try for Yale College. "Good," says Inza, "I know you will cut as much of a dash there as you did at Fardale."

And, of course, Frank does. He is no sooner in quarters on York Street with his spooneristic roommate, Harry Rattleton ("I seel filly—I mean, I feel silly"), than he gets into a hassle with Jack Diamond, a hotheaded Virginian who has been "drinking beer with the boys, and is in a mighty ugly mood." They fight, and Frank, who has a habit of laughing through a bout, wins. Diamond is so angry he keeps his roommate awake all night by grinding his teeth "at regular intervals." At Billy's, a freshman hangout, he dashes champagne into Frank's face and challenges him to a duel with rapiers. "Merriwell smiled and wiped the champagne from his face with a white silk handkerchief." Unbeknownst to his Yale chums, he is an expert fencer. "At Fardale he had been champion of the school, and he had taken some lessons in France while traveling." Frank disarms Diamond twice, gallantly permitting him the retrieve. A faculty raid causes the lads to flee, but "from that hour there seemed to be a sort of truce between Merriwell and Diamond. It was a long time before they showed signs of friendliness, but they fought together against the sophomores and Bruce Browning."

Giant Bruce Browning is "the king of the sophomores," and he deems the freshmen impertinent. He goes into training to take care of Merriwell, but Frank couldn't care less. "Whenever anyone told him about it, he merely smiled." When they meet in the ring, Browning can do little. "Frank Merriwell continued to laugh, and it had been said at Yale that he was most dangerous in an encounter when he laughed." Frank gets the better of it, but the bout is sportingly declared a draw and Browning admits Merriwell "to be a comer."

Frank is busy on other fronts. He is one of "the best freshmen halfbacks ever seen at Yale." He not only strokes but coaches the freshmen crew ("something never attempted before—something said to be impossible") that defeats the sophomores. On the mound for the freshmen nine, he is a dazzler. The only way a Harvard batsman can get on is through an error. When Blossom, the Yale third baseman, fumbles a grounder, Frank says gently, "Steady, Blos, old boy! You are all right. The best of us do those things occasionally. It is nothing at all." Then he retires the side.

Frank does so well that he is invited to try out for the varsity nine by Pierson, the manager. Even Frank is surprised by this, and his heart gives a great jump. "On the regular team! Why, he had not dreamed of getting there the very first season. Was Pierson giving him a jolly?"

Pierson was not. At Yale, the Yale of Merriwell anyway, democracy rules, and athletics are at the heart of this democratic spirit:

> Merriwell knew well enough that Phillips men were given preference in everything at Yale as a rule, for they had friends to pull them through, while the fellows who had been prepared by private tutors lacked such an advantage. But Frank had likewise discovered that in most cases a man was judged fairly at Yale, and he could become whatever he chose to make himself, in case he has the ability.
>
> Frank had heard the cry which had been raised at that time that the old spirit of democracy was dying out at Yale, and that great changes had taken place there. He had heard that Yale was getting to be more like another college, where the swell set are strongly in evidence and the seniors likely to be very exclusive, having but a small circle of speaking acquaintances. In the course of time Frank came to believe that the old spirit was still powerful at Yale. There were a limited number of young gentlemen who plainly considered themselves superior beings, and who positively refused to make acquaintances outside a certain limit; but those men held no position in athletics, were seldom of prominence in the societies, and were regarded as cads by the men most worth knowing. They were to be pitied, not envied.
>
> At Yale the old democratic spirit still prevailed. The young men were drawn from different social conditions, and in their homes they kept to their own set; but they seemed to leave this aside, and they mingled and submerged their natural differences under that one broad generalization, "the Yale man."
>
> And Merriwell was to find that this even extended to their social life, their dances, their secret societies, where all who showed themselves to have the proper dispositions and qualifications were admitted without distinction of previous condition or rank in their own homes.
>
> Each class associated with itself, it is true, the members making no close friendships with members of other classes, with the

possible exceptions of the juniors and seniors, where class feeling did not seem to run so high. A man might know men of other classes, but he never took them for chums.

The democratic spirit at Yale came mainly from athletics, as Frank soon discovered. Every class had half a dozen teams—tennis, baseball, football, the crew and so on. Everybody, even the "greasy" grinds, seemed interested in something, and so one or more of these organizations had some sort of a claim on everybody.

Besides this, there was the general work in the gymnasium, almost every member of every class appearing there at some time or other, taking exercise as a pastime or necessity.

The Varsity Athletic Organization drew men from every class, not excepting the professional and graduate schools, and, counting the trials and everything, brought together hundreds of men.

In athletics strength and skill win, regardless of money or family; so it happened that the poorest man in the university stood a show of becoming the lion and idol of the whole body of young men.

Unlike the Harkaway novels, which Patten was supposed to follow, there is no snobbishness in Merriwell. In *Jack Harkaway at Oxford*, for instance, Sir Sydney Dawson, one of the better-minded characters, shows he has a kind heart by musing, "I wonder what a poor man at Oxford is like. I should like to see him. Perhaps an hour or two with a poor man would do me good, always supposing he's a gentleman. I can't stand a cad." But to Patten, who styled himself an embryo socialist, such sentiments were unthinkable. In point of fact, the most villainous of Merriwell's enemies at Yale are well-to-do. There is Roland Ditson, who betrays the freshmen by informing the sophomores about their plan for the crew race. ("Ditson's parents were wealthy, and they furnished him with plenty of loose change, so that he could cut quite a dash.") To Frank, Ditson was a traitor, "a contemptible cur," and he gives him "a shake that caused the fellow's teeth to click together." "Tar and feather him!" shouts an outraged freshman, but Frank advises, "Let him go. He is covered with a coating of disgrace that will not come off as easily as tar and feathers." Ditson sneaks away, "the hisses of his classmates sounding in his ears."

In Merriwell's sophomore year there are tougher opponents: Dartmouth, Harvard and Princeton. The Dartmouth football players are "full of sand . . . being mostly sons of farmers and country gentlemen."

Against Princeton, Frank stops the Tigers on the one-yard line and then scores the winning touchdown with only seconds left. At New Haven he rows with such ferocity against Harvard that he swoons as the shell cuts across the finish. "Did we win?" he asks, coming to. "You bet! It's hard to beat Old Eli!" "I am satisfied!" gasps Merriwell, swooning again. A stranger hurriedly offers a flask, but Frank revives to turn it away. "I never touch liquor," he says firmly. "I do not want to start now."

To keep the series going, Patten arranged to have Merriwell leave Yale temporarily. It develops that Frank has lost his fortune because of bad investments by Professor Scotch, and he goes to work for a rail-road, settles a strike and writes a hit play, *John Smith of Montana*. Yale is sorely pressed by his absence. Harvard, Jack Diamond writes, is "arrogantly jubilant," while the nine is "putting up the yellowist kind of ball." When Yale plays the New Yorks at the Polo Grounds "in that city," the team is "white-washed, shut out, monkeyed with." Diamond laments for Old Eli, and the very mention of Merriwell causes Bruce Browning to grind his teeth and shake "his huge fist at the empty air." Frank is downcast. "Dear Old Yale!" he writes:

> I see in fancy the elm-shaded campus, the fence, the buildings, my old room and—dearer than everything else—my friends, the friends I love! I see them gathered about me at the fence; I listen to their talk, their jokes, their laughter and their songs. Oh, those dear old days! Oh, those dear old songs! In fancy I am beneath the elms; you are there, Browning is there, Jones is there, Rattleton is there, Hodge is there! We are singing *Stars of the Summer Night, Bingo, Here's to Good Old Yale* . . .
>
> I can't write about it, Jack—I can't! My heart is too full. Oh, I long to be back there again! I long to come back in time to have you with me. I long to line up with the eleven again. I long to pull an oar with the crew! I long to go into the box for the nine! And, by heavens! I want Bart Hodge behind the plate to catch when I pitch. He can handle my pitching as no other fellow ever handled it!

Frank does return to New Haven, with a new smash hit, *True Blue*, the finale of which shows him on stage in a racing shell. But since he has "been away from college, winning fame and fortune," he is obliged to spend the summer abroad catching up on his studies. In the British

Isles, further adventures await; he beats the Irish Gamecock in a sparring match, even though blinded, buys a horse that wins the Derby (he outrages some onlookers by shaking hands with Toots, the colored jockey) and plays golf at St. Andrews, where he ties the course record after a few lessons.

Back at Yale, he rejoins the eleven. But by the time of the Harvard game, he is a frightful mass of bruises. Although he tries to hide his injuries, he has obvious difficulty trying to stand up. "What's the good of saying anything?" he asks. He sits out a scoreless first half, then yields to the demands of the crowd. "Well, how are you going to stand it out on the field?" Jack Diamond inquires. "I'll have to stand it there," was the grim answer. With a minute to go, he pounces on a Harvard fumble.

Frank felt a fearful pain running through him. It seemed to stop his wind, but it did not stop him.

"I must do it," he thought.

He became blind, but he still managed to keep on his feet, and he ran on. Had Frank been at his best he would have crossed the Harvard line without again being touched; but he was not at his best, and Hollender came down on him. Ten yards from Harvard's line, Hollender tackled Merry.

Frank felt himself clutched, but he refused to be dragged down. He felt hands clinging to him, and, with all the fierceness he could summon, he strove to break away and go on. His lips were covered with a bloody foam, and there was a frightful glare in his eyes. He strained and strove to get a little farther, and he actually dragged Hollender along the ground till he broke the fellow's hold. Then he reeled across Harvard's line and fell.

It was a touchdown in the last seconds of the game. There was not even time to kick a goal, but Yale had won by a score of four to nothing!

He was carried from the field by his friends who took him to a hotel and put him to bed. A doctor came to see him and prescribed for him. They came round his bedside and told him what a noble fellow he was.

"Don't, boys!" he begged. "You make me tired! And I'm so happy! We won, fellows—we won the game!"

"You won it!" cried Jack Diamond fiercely. "They can't rob you of that glory! They've tried to rob you of enough!"

"No, no! We all did it. Think how the boys fought! It was

splendid! And that was the best eleven Harvard ever put on the field. Oh, what a glorious Thanksgiving!"

"Is there anything that Merriwell can't do?" asks a Yale student shortly afterwards. And the answer is no. At a shooting gallery Frank shows that he is a crack marksman, not only by pinging the target head-on but also by firing over his shoulder using a hand mirror to see the target. Challenged to billiards, he defeats the best of the day with "one of the handsomest massé shots ever seen." And there is no need to inquire what happens after a friend suggests that they take in a game of roller polo at a New Haven rink. Frank replies, "I'm with you. Used to fool a little with roller polo myself."

When Frank was in his senior year at Yale, Street & Smith suggested that another character, closely related to Frank, appear on the scene. Since this new character had to be old enough to enter Fardale, the firm suggested a brother instead of a son. The inventive Patten solved this with little difficulty. It seemed that before dying out West, Frank's father had remarried and sired another son. This is Dick Merriwell, whom Frank discovers in the Rockies. Dick is not only a half brother to Frank but also half-savage; he has risen to young manhood in the wilderness under the care of Joe Crowfoot, Indian guide. Dick resists Frank's efforts to send him East to the civilizing influence of Fardale and Yale, but after Indian Joe tries to shoot Frank, half blood proves thicker than water, and Dick becomes Frank's protégé. He matriculates at Fardale and eventually Yale, where he carries on in the family tradition.

Out of Yale, Frank founds the Bloomfield Home for Wayward Boys, marries Inza Burrage and takes time out from world adventures to father Frank Jr. As Dick leaves Yale, Frank Jr., to the dismay of all bullies and toadies, enrolls at Fardale. So the saga ends. Patten carried it only to the birth of Frank Jr., where other hacks took over, but it did not last much beyond that, and the old spell was gone.

To the purists, Frank is the only one of the Merriwells who counted, and the series undoubtedly began to decline after Dick entered the scene. Patten himself realized this. "The reason was that Dick was not the character that Frank was," he recalled years later for James M. Cain. "I couldn't make him a replica of Frank, you know; he had to be different. But it was Frank who really stood for every boy's dream. Dick was all right, but not many boys wanted to be like him. And then I suppose I got careless. Frank's ventriloquism was a big hit. But Dick's capacity to talk with wild animals never went over. It just didn't click. I guess I had written Merriwells too long."

In 1914, after 20 million words of Merriwell, Patten asked for relief. He complained that he felt "like a horse in an old country treadmill." Once, when he wanted to get away on a trip, he did 50,000 words, two and a half stories, in a week, but that was his "best record." Merriwell took all his time. In the morning he would plot two or three chapters, before his secretary arrived at nine. Then he would dictate until noon or one o'clock. "At the end of the stretch I was often worn out and compelled to lie down for ten minutes or so before I could eat lunch," he later wrote in a biographical memoir. "After lunch I had a nap of thirty or forty minutes. Then I got out into the open air for a while. Persons who saw me walking about or loafing in the afternoon occasionally said: 'Well, you have a snap. Don't you ever work?' "

Street & Smith assigned a fresh team to Merriwell, but the series lasted for only three more years, devoted, for the most part, to the exploits of Frank Jr. Patten attributed its demise to the rise of the movies. "Instead of buying a book with it, the boy who had a nickel spent it on a motion picture," he said.

After giving up Merriwell, Patten continued to write at a furious pace through most of the 1920s. He finished more than two dozen novels for boys (Lefty Locke is probably the most memorable of his later characters), and worked briefly in Hollywood. He found he could command only sixty dollars a script, so he returned to New York. The going was difficult. He tried his hand at a few Merriwell stories, but he had a hard time convincing editors that he could write other stories besides Merriwells. In desperation, he began grinding out stuff for Bernarr MacFadden's *Snappy Stories, Saucy Stories* and *True Story*. "It made me pretty sick," he said, "but the editors were convinced. It won me a market for adult adventure stuff." Patten drifted farther into the anonymous reaches of hackdom. In 1930 a feature writer for the *World* interviewed him and reported that Patten's favorite writers were Zola and Proust.

In 1934 Frank Merriwell became a radio program, but if Patten shared in the profits they must have been small. Several years later he was threatened with eviction from his apartment. In 1939 he was in the news again when he wrote a radio script for the Council Against Intolerance in America. The central figure was Dick, not Frank, and the role was played by Richard Merriwell Erickson, a pitcher for the then Boston Bees. According to the script, the pitcher for Fardale leaves the school to enroll at Eton, a rival school. On the day of the Fardale-Eton game, the pitcher beans Sam, a Jewish player for Fardale, and then hits Dick. There is a rumpus, but Dick stands up for the pitcher, saying he is sure the pitcher would not hit a batter on purpose. Later the pitcher admits to Dick, "I did do it on purpose," and Dick says, "Yes, I know you did." And thus the pitcher sees that Dick saved him, and he apologizes to all concerned.

In 1941 Patten wrote his final Merriwell story. It was called *Mr. Frank Merriwell*, and it was published as a hardcover novel. The scene is Elmsport, a town not far from New York. Frank is fifty years old and lives with Inza and their daughter Bart (named for Bart Hodge) in a house called "The Nest." Frank Jr. is a war correspondent "over there somewhere close to the blazing, blasting battlefront in stricken Holland." (He is later reported missing in action, but Frank *père* discovers him by chance as an amnesiac panhandler in Madison Square Park: "Suddenly, like the rending of a black cloud by a flash of lightning, recognition and remembrance came. He leaped to his feet, his eyes shining with a great joy. 'Father!' ") Merriwell is looked upon as a warmonger by old Harry Willwin, the villain and local millionaire. Frank, who is anti-Communist and anti-Fascist, wants America to prepare, and to that end he starts the Young Defenders of Liberty. He keeps track of the organization's growth on a huge map of the United States in his office: "Daily the map was becoming increasingly bespattered with pin-anchored tags."

The two high points in the novel come when Frank thrashes four ruffians with a cane and when Gladys, the town floozy, tells him, "If there were more men in the world like you there'd be less women like me." There is no reference to athletics, except for a brief note that Frank coaches the high school football and baseball teams on the side. The novel sold only 4,000 copies, and Patten blamed the publisher for poor distribution. Not long afterward, Patten moved to Vista, California, near San Diego, where he lived with his son, Harvan Barr Patten. On January 16, 1945 he died in his sleep. He was 78 years old.

"Did I love Merriwell?" Patten once answered an interviewer, James M. Caine. "Not at first. Those early stories were more of a joke to me than anything else. But when it got so that half a million kids were reading him every week—and I think there were that many when you stop to think how the stories were lent from hand to hand—I began to realize that I had about the biggest chance to influence the youth of this country that any man ever had. And when you get the messiah complex you are lost. Yes, I loved him. And I loved him most because no boy, if he followed in his tracks, ever did anything that he need be ashamed of."

* * *

The keeper of the Merriwell flame these days, Edward T. LeBlanc, the editor of Dime Novel Roundup, *has compiled not only a plot synopsis of all 850 issues of* Tip Top Weekly, *but also has published Number 851, "Frank Merriwell's All Star Opponents," a new short story by Robert McDowell. At present, LeBlanc and McDowell are collaborating on a Merriwell bibliography.*

THE MAN WHO LIVED
TWO LIVES IN ONE

ZANE GREY

April 29, 1968

T HERE NEVER has been anyone quite like Zane Grey. Famed as the author of *Riders of the Purple Sage* and fifty-seven other Westerns tinged with purple prose, Grey ranks as the greatest best-selling novelist of his time. For years the total sales of his books fell behind only the Holy Bible and McGuffey Readers. At his death in 1939 his novels had sold more than 15 million copies in the United States alone, and they are still selling at the rate of 750,000 to a million books a year. Magazines paid Grey as much as $85,000 for the serial rights to a single work, and Hollywood transferred epic after epic to the silver screen. Gary Cooper, Cary Grant, Warner Baxter, Warner Oland, Richard Arlen, Richard Dix, Randolph Scott, Wallace Beery, Roscoe Karns, Harry Carey, William Powell, Jack Holt, Jack LaRue, Billie Dove, Lili Damita, Fay Wray, Jean Arthur and Buster Crabbe are among the stars who got their start in Zane Grey movies.

On film or in print Grey's Westerns enthralled the public. The books were stilted, awkward and stuffed with painful dialogue ("If you think I'm wonderful and if I think you're wonderful—it's all really very wonderful, isn't it?"), but they throbbed with the narrative drive of a true storyteller and the fervor of a moralist who made certain that virtue triumphed over evil on the range. "Never lay down your pen, Zane Grey," John Wanamaker, the white-haired merchant prince, once advised, putting a friendly hand on the novelist's shoulder. "I have given away thousands of your books and have sold hundreds of thousands. You are distinctively and genuinely American. You have borrowed none of the decadence of foreign writers. . . . The good you are doing is incalculable."

Grey received acclaim and money (and some critical brickbats) for his writings, but in another field his distinction was almost beyond compare—he was one of the finest fishermen the world has ever known. In the words of Ed Zern, who edited the anthology *Zane Grey's Adventures in Fishing*, "It is reasonable to assume that no one will ever challenge his right to be known as the greatest fisherman American has ever produced." It has been said that the dream of many American males is to have $1 million and go fishing. "Well," writes Zern, "Zane Grey had $1 million, and he really went fishing."

Grey is the classic case of the compulsive angler. He was truly obsessed by fish. "Not many anglers, perhaps, care for the beauty of a fish," Grey wrote in *Tales of Fishes*, one of his eight books on angling, "but I do." He would rhapsodize on the beauty of a huge tuna that "blazed like the sword of Achilles" or marvel over the shimmering colors of a dolphin, only to feel a pang because the dolphin was dying and he was "the cause of the death of so beautiful a thing." The leaping of fish absolutely fascinated him, and even fish fins and fishtails had what he called, with a flourish, "a compelling power to thrill and excite me."

From black bass to blue marlin, Grey pursued fish the world over with unmatched avidity. He explored and established new fishing grounds and techniques in Florida, California, Nova Scotia, New Zealand and Australia. He took great delight in fishing where no one had ever fished before, and his sense of anticipation was so keen that even arranging tackle for a trip gave him exquisite pleasure. He was the first man to catch a fish weighing more than 1,000 pounds on rod and reel. In his day he held most world records: 582-pound broadbill swordfish; 171-pound Pacific sailfish; 758-pound bluefin tuna; 318-pound yellowfin tuna; 1,040-pound striped marlin; 1,036-pound tiger shark; 618-pound silver marlin; 111-pound yellowtail; and a 63-pound dolphin. The record for the yellowtail and the yellowfin tuna have not been beaten since the International Game Fish Association began keeping records in 1938. Grey was held in such high regard that the Pacific sailfish was named for him, *Istiophorus greyi*. Hardy's in England manufactured a Zane Grey reel, while in the United States there was a Zane Grey bass bug, a Zane Grey steelhead fly and a Zane Grey teaser.

Grey had his bad days fishing—he once passed 88 days without a strike—but he remained enthusiastic. "The enchantment never palls," he wrote. "Years on end I have been trying to tell why, but that has been futile. Fishing is like Jason's quest for the Golden Fleece. . . . Something evermore is about to happen." When something did, Grey wrote about it exuberantly. If he made an unusual catch he would wire *The New York Times*. There were some critics who thought him guilty of exaggeration. A friend, Robert H. Davis, the editor of *Munsey's Magazine*, wrote Grey, "If you went out with a mosquito net to catch a mess of minnows your story would read like Roman gladiators seining the Tigris for whales." Davis added, "You say, 'the hard diving fight of a tuna liberates the brute instinct in a man.' Well, Zane, it also liberates the qualities of a liar!" Grey cheerfully reported these comments himself in *Tales of Fishes*. Such criticisms did not bother him. But he was vexed and angered when his sportsmanship was called into question, as it was on a couple of occasions.

Zane Grey's passion for fishing, which, by his own admission, grew stronger through the years, started in his childhood. "Ever since I was a little tad I have loved to chase things in the water," he wrote. He was born in Zanesville, Ohio, on January 31, 1872. His Christian name was actually Pearl, and the family name was spelled Gray. After college he dropped Pearl in favor of his middle name of Zane, and he changed the spelling of Gray to Grey. He also shaved three years off his age, according to Norris F. Schneider, the foremost authority on Grey, and upon his death obituaries reported he had been born in 1875.

Grey came from pioneer stock. His great grandfather, Colonel Ebenezer Zane, settled what is now Wheeling, West Virginia in 1770 and moved into Ohio after the Revolution. Zanesville is named for him. Zane Grey's father, Dr. Lewis Gray, was a farmer and a preacher who eventually became a dentist with a practice in the Terrace section of Zanesville.

The oldest of five children, young Pearl was so mischievous that he was known as "the terror of the Terrace." On one occasion he destroyed a bed of imported tulips planted in front of the Zanesville Historical and Art Institute. The name Pearl, especially in conjunction with the name Gray, apparently bothered him considerably. The only time he ever liked it was during his adolescent years, when he strove to dramatize himself by dressing in pearl-gray suits.

He was six when he saw his first fish. "Looking down from my high perch into the clear pool directly under me, I saw something that transfixed me with a strange rapture. Against the sunlit amber depths of the little pool shone a wondrous fish creature that came to the surface and snapped at a bug. It flashed silver and rose." The experience stayed with him. In school and church Pearl Gray was a dreamer. "I dreamed, mostly of fields, hills and streams. . . . As I grew older, and learned the joys of angling, I used to run away on Sunday afternoons. Many a time have I come home late, wet and weary after a thrilling time along the river or stream, to meet with severe punishment from my outraged father. But it never cured me. I always went fishing on Sunday. It seemed the luckiest day." Dr. Gray told Pearl the only good fishermen who had ever lived were Christ's disciples, but the boy paid no heed, and he became the admirer of a local bum named Muddy Mizer who was always fishing on the Muskingum River.

Besides fishing, Pearl's other love was baseball, a sport at which he and his brother Romer, called R.C., excelled. Pearl was a pitcher, and he and R.C. played semipro ball around Ohio. Dr. Gray wanted Pearl to become a dentist, and he had him start by polishing sets of false teeth on a lathe. His pitching arm stood him in good stead. When the family moved to Columbus, Pearl unofficially went into practice on his own, pulling teeth in Frazeysburg until the Ohio Dental Association compelled him to stop. He continued playing baseball, and after one game a scout from the University of Pennsylvania offered him a scholarship. His father allowed him to accept it on the condition that he major in dentistry.

At Penn, Grey was at first highly unpopular. Ignorant of student traditions, he accidentally entered the upper class section of a lecture hall one day and triggered a riot in which his clothes were torn off and the room wrecked. After another contretemps he was chased by sophomores into a stairwell, where he managed to hold them off by hurling potatoes. His name and his refusal to go along with the crowd, to smoke, to drink or to gamble, made him the butt of jokes, and he escaped by spending most of his time reading in the library and playing baseball. He proved to be so good a ballplayer that, as he wrote later, "The bitter loneliness of my college days seemed to change. Wilborn, captain of the track team, took me up; Danny Coogan, the great varsity catcher, made me a member of Sigma Nu; Al Bull, the center on the famous football team that beat Yale and Princeton and Harvard, took me as a roommate."

Grey played left field for Penn. His one lapse came in a game against Harvard, when he accidentally stepped into a hole and a fly ball hit him on the head, allowing the winning run to score. Ordinarily his fielding was excellent. He once made a catch that helped Penn beat the Giants at the Polo Grounds. In his senior year he came to bat in the ninth inning against the University of Virginia with Penn trailing by a run. There were two out and a man on second. A verbose professor shouted, "Grey, the honor of the University of Pennsylvania rests with you!" Grey homered to win the game.

Grey was graduated with a diploma in dentistry in 1896. He opened an office in Manhattan on the West Side, and there he languished. He did not like the city, and he got away whenever possible. He played baseball for the Orange Athletic Club in New Jersey, and he became the youngest member of the Camp Fire Club. There a fellow member suggested that Grey write a story about his bass fishing on the Delaware. He did, and the story—his first effort—was published in *Recreation* in May 1902. The appearance of the article gave him direction, and he began writing an historical novel about his ancestor, Betty Zane, who carried gunpowder to her brother, Colonel Zane, during the siege of Fort Henry in the Revolution. All winter Grey labored over the book in a dingy flat. Upon completing it he drew the cover and inside illustrations. No publisher would accept *Betty Zane*, and, after a wealthy patient offered to back it, Grey had it printed privately. Sales were nil, but in a visit to Zanesville in 1904, Grey grandly announced that he had given up dentistry to devote himself "exclusively to literature."

In 1905 Grey married Lina Roth of New York, whom he had met a few years earlier while he was canoeing down the Delaware in one of his escapes from dentistry. She had faith in her husband and a bit of money to boot, and he gave up his practice to write while living in a house overlooking the Delaware in Lackawaxen, Pennsylvania. There he wrote, hunted, fished and savored "the happiness that dwells in wilderness alone." R.C., by now a professional ballplayer, chipped in with an occasional dollar, and Zane later repaid him by making him his official secretary and constant fishing companion.

Grey followed up *Betty Zane* by writing a couple of other books about the Ohio frontier, *The Spirit of the Border* and *The Last Trail*, which the A. L. Burt Company eventually published. They were flops. But Grey hung on, and in 1907 he went west with one Buffalo Jones, visiting the wilder parts of Utah and Arizona. Jones had a ranch on the rim of the Grand Canyon, where he was hybridizing black Galloway cattle with buffalo and calling the offspring cattalo. In his spare time he liked to lasso mountain lions. Grey loved it all, and, upon returning to the East, he wrote a book about Jones, *The Last of the Plainsmen*, which he took to Harper, a firm that had rebuffed him previously. Eagerly he awaited word and, hearing none, he visited the publishing house, where an editor coldly informed him, "I don't see anything in this to convince me that you can write either narrative or fiction." It was the bleakest moment in Grey's life. He was 36 years old, he had abandoned dentistry, his wife was pregnant with their first child and he had failed again. "When I staggered down the old stairway and out into Pearl Street I could not see," he later recalled. "I had to hold on to an iron post at the corner, and there I hung fighting such misery as I had never known. Something came to me there. They had all missed it. They did not know . . . and I went back to Lackawaxen to the smile and encouragement that never failed me."

He promptly wrote his first Western novel, *The Heritage of the Desert*. Harper yielded and published it in 1910—the year of the birth of his first son, Romer—and Grey thought he was at last on his way. Quickly he wrote *Riders of the Purple Sage*, but Harper rejected it as too "bulgy." Grey asked a vice-president of the firm to read the manuscript. He liked the novel, and so did his wife, who stayed up until three in the morning to finish it. The book was published, and Grey was permanently established. In fifteen years *Riders of the Purple Sage* sold two million copies. Grey also turned out half a dozen juveniles, many of them dealing with his baseball experiences. In *The Young Pitcher* he wrote of the potato episode at Penn and drew himself as Ken Ward, the hero. His brother, R.C., also called Reddy, was Reddy Ray, spark plug of the team. In *The Shortstop*, Grey named the hero after Chase Alloway, a professional player he had known in Ohio. (In the Western *The Lone Star Ranger* Grey named one of the villains Chess Alloway.)

Although comfortably off, Grey continued to write feverishly. He could not abide waste of time. As a writer and as an angler Grey was a finisher, and he followed both callings to the hilt. "It is so easy to start anything, a fishing jaunt or a career," he wrote, "but it is an entirely different matter to finish. The men who fail to finish in any walk of life, men who have had every opportunity . . . can be numbered by the millions." At top speed, Grey found he could write 100,000 words a month. He would pen himself up in his study, where he would sit in a Morris chair, writing in longhand on a lapboard, furiously chewing the top of a soft No. 1 pencil when a sentence failed him. He compiled notebooks of vivid phrases and expressions, and he often thumbed a worn copy of a book, *Materials and Methods of Fiction*, by Clayton Hamilton. Grey's son Romer, now president of Zane Grey, Inc., says, "That was father's bible. It had a greater influence on his writing than any other work." Grey wrote only one draft of a book; he left the finishing of the manuscript to his wife. When not writing he fished. He knew a long stretch of the Delaware by memory. "I own nearly a thousand acres of land on it," he wrote. "I have fished it for ten years. I know every rapid, every eddy, almost, I might say, every stone from Callicoon to Port Jervis. This fifty-mile stretch of fast water I consider the finest bass ground I have ever fished." In July, when the river was low, he would scout the water for big bass by going upstream and drifting face down on a raft. "I see the bottom everywhere, except in rough water. I see the rocks, the shelves, the caverns. I see where the big bass live. And I remember." When the time came to fish, Grey became part of the landscape; he trod the slippery stones "as if I were a stalking Indian. I knew that a glimpse of me, or a faint jar vibrating under the water, or an unnatural ripple on its surface, would be fatal to my enterprise." Not every visiting angler exalted the fishing; some referred to Lackawaxen Creek as the Lackanothing or Lackarotten.

With money coming in, Grey and R.C. began fishing in Florida. They went after bonefish, snook and tarpon. Grey was among the first to go after sailfish, and he did so well that other fishermen flocked to the Gulf Stream. He was intrigued by wahoo, then seldom caught, reasoning that they could be taken because "all fish have to eat." He caught wahoo, and he helped put the Keys on the map. Wherever he went, he fished. On a trip to Mexico to gather material for a novel, his train chanced to pass by a jungle river, the Santa Rosa. Immediately Grey wondered, "Where did that river go? How many waterfalls and rapids hastened its journey to the Gulf? What teeming life inhabited its rich banks? How wild was the prospect! It haunted me!" In time he made the trip in a flat-bottom boat. On a trip to Yucatán, he happened to hear of "the wild and lonely Alacranes Reef where lighthouse keepers went insane from solitude, and where wonderful fishes inhabited the lagoons. That was enough for me. Forthwith I meant to go to Alacranes." Forthwith he did. There he met a little Englishman, Lord L., and "it was from him I got my type for Castleton, the Englishman, in *The Light of the Western Stars*. I have been told that never was there an Englishman on earth like the one I portrayed in my novel. But my critics never fished with Lord L."

Grey never lost any time. On a fishing trip he was up before everyone at four in the morning, transcribing the adventures of the previous day. If fishing was slack, he worked on a book until breakfast. He wrote much of *The Drift Fence* and *Robbers' Roost* at sea, and he piled up such a backlog of books that *Boulder Dam*, which he wrote while off on a trip in the 1930s, was not published by Harper until 1963.

In 1914 Grey started going west to Catalina each summer, where he tried swordfishing. In his first year he spent over three weeks at sea, trolling a total of 1,500 miles. Grey saw nineteen swordfish but did not get one strike. Instead of becoming discouraged, he was pleased. "By this time," he wrote, "I had realized something of the difficult nature of the game, and I had begun to have an inkling of what sport it might be." On the twenty-fifth day Grey sighted a swordfish, which he hooked. But the fish broke away, and Grey was sick at heart. The following summer found him back in Catalina. "I was crazy on swordfish," he admitted. To get his arms, hands and back into fighting trim, he rowed a boat for weeks on end. His patience and training were rewarded—he set a record by catching four swordfish in one day.

Between gathering material for novels and advising on movies and fishing, Grey began to visit Southern California so frequently that he moved his family to Los Angeles in 1918. Two years later he bought the small estate in Altadena that now serves as the headquarters of Zane Grey, Inc. Once established on the West Coast, Grey took up steelhead fishing in Oregon, and on a trip down the Rogue River he ran into a prospector who offered to sell his shack and land. Grey bought the place at Winkle Bar as offhandedly as he would buy a dozen new rods. He also owned some land and a small hunting lodge in Arizona. He shuttled from one place to another, writing, fishing, hunting, and gathering material. "[The year] 1923 was typical of what I do in the way of work and play," he replied to an admirer who had asked what a typical year was like.

The pleasant paradox, however, is that my play turns out to be valuable work. January and February I spent at Long Key, Florida, where I wrote, read, fished and wandered along the beach. The spring I spent with my family in Altadena, California, where I wrote and studied, and played with my family. Tennis is my favorite game. During this season I motored with Mrs. Grey down to San Diego and across the mountains to El Centro and Yuma, through the wonderful desert land of Southern California. June found me at Avalon, Catalina Island, a place I have found as inspiring as Long Key, and infinitely different. Here I finished a novel, and then began my sword-fishing on the Pacific. My brother, R.C., and I roamed the sea searching for giant sword-fish. Sometimes we ran a hundred miles in a day. The sea presents a marvelous contrast to the desert. It inspires, teaches, subdues, uplifts, appalls and remakes me. There I learned more of nature than on land. Birds and fishes, strange sea creatures, are always in evidence. In September I took Mr. [Jesse] Lasky and his [Paramount] staff to Arizona to pick out locations for the motion picture, *The Vanishing American*. Upon the return I parted with the Lasky outfit at the foot of Navajo Mountains. . . . I, with my guide Wetherill, with selected cowboys and horses, tried for the third time to reach Wild Horse Mesa. In October I went to my hunting lodge in the Tonto Basin, where the magnificent forests of green pine and silver spruce and golden aspen soothed my eyes after the long weeks on sea and desert. Here I hunted and rode the lonely leaf-covered trails, lay for hours on the Rim, listening to the bay of hounds, and spent many a pleasant evening round the camp-fire, listening to my men, the gaunt long-legged and lead-faced backwoodsmen of the Tonto Basin. November and December found me back again at Altadena, hard as nails, brown as an Indian, happy to be home with my family, keen for my study with its books and pictures, and for the long spell of writing calling me to its fulfillment.

Grey always had some new adventure going. A Norwegian named Sievert Nielsen, a sailor turned prospector, read Grey's novel *Desert Gold* and wrote to him under the misapprehension that the story of the lost treasure in the farfetched plot was true. Grey was so charmed with the letter that he invited Nielsen to see him. They became friends and together hiked across Death Valley for the thrill of it.

Grey's success at landing big fish prompted a correspondence with Captain Laurie Mitchell of Liverpool, Nova Scotia. Mitchell, who was to become one of Grey's fishing companions, was enthusiastic about giant bluefin tuna off Nova Scotia. He himself had landed only one—it happened to be a world-record 710 pounds—and had lost between fifty and sixty of the big fish. Other anglers had caught perhaps a total of ten. The fish were simply too tough for ordinary tackle. This was just the sort of challenge that appealed to Grey, who promptly began laying plans to fish in Nova Scotia. He reasoned that his swordfish tackle would be adequate for the tuna, provided that the boat from which he was fishing was fast and maneuverable. He had two light skiffs built in Nova Scotia, and from Florida he ordered a special launch, twenty-five feet long and equipped with two engines capable of doing eighteen miles an hour. The launch was so designed that at full speed it could turn on its own length. Grey installed Catalina fighting chairs in each boat.

Within a couple of weeks Grey proved his strategy to be right. He hooked three tuna and landed two, one of which was a world-record 758 pounds and the largest fish of any species ever caught on rod and reel.

Before leaving Nova Scotia, Grey fulfilled a boyhood dream of buying "a beautiful white ship with sails like wings to sail into tropic seas." The three-masted schooner, which he called *Fisherman*, held the record for the run from Halifax to New York City. Grey scrupulously made certain she never had been used as a rumrunner; ever the teetotaler, he would not have a bootlegger's boat as a gift. He had *Fisherman* outfitted with all the tackle that "money could buy and ingenuity devise," and, with R.C. and Romer, he set sail for Galápagos, Cocos Island, the Gulf of Panama and the Pacific coast of Mexico. On this trip he caught a 135-pound Pacific sailfish, the first known to science, but otherwise fishing conditions were not good because of an abundance of sharks.

Broadbill swordfish remained Grey's great love. In 1926 at Catalina, he and his brother caught a total of 10, including Zane's world-record 582-pounder. In that same year R.C. caught five marlin, all weighing more than 300 pounds. No other angler had then caught more than one 300-pound fish, and the 354-pounder taken by R.C. was a world record. It was a great year for the brothers, and, as Grey wrote, "Not the least pleasure in our success was to run back to Avalon with the red flag flying at the masthead, to blow a clarion blast from the boat's whistle, and to see the pier filled with excited spectators. Sometimes thousands of visitors massed at the end of the pier to see the swordfish weighed and photographed. On these occasions R.C. and I would have to stand the battery of hundreds of cameras and shake hands until we broke away from the pier."

Not everyone cheered Grey. He and R.C. broke early with members of the Catalina Tuna Club over Grey's choice of tackle. Although a light-tackle man in freshwater, Grey used very heavy tackle for big-game fish. He argued that fish that broke off light tackle either became prey to sharks or died.

Grey accepted the invitation of the New Zealand government to investigate the big-game fishing possibilities in that country. Captain Mitchell and R.C. went with him. They revolutionized local practices; instead of fishing with bait deep down, they took fish by trolling. Grey caught a world-record 450-pound striped marlin and a record 111-pound yellowtail, while Captain Mitchell set a record with a 976-pound black marlin. Grey's greatest pleasure, however, was finding copies of his Westerns in even the remotest homes he visited. "This was surely the sweetest and most moving of all the experiences I had; and it faced me again with the appalling responsibility of a novelist who in these modern days of materialism dares to foster idealism and love of nature, chivalry in men and chastity in women."

Back home, Grey had difficulties in Arizona. In 1930 the state passed game laws and established seasons, and Grey, accustomed to hunting bears whenever the mood was on him, was angered. He felt that he was entitled to hunt year round, because he had put Arizona on the map. When a warden refused to issue him a resident license Grey was "grossly insulted," and he gave up his lodge in the Tonto Basin. "In twelve years my whole bag of game has been five bears, three bucks and a few turkeys," he said. "I have written fifteen novels with Arizona background. Personally it cost me $30,000 to get material for one book alone, *To the Last Man*. My many trips all over the state have cost me $100,000. So in every way I have not been exactly an undesirable visitor." He was so indignant he said he would never return and, as a parting shot, he said that the game commission and the Forest Service had sold out to "the commercial interest." As a case in point, he cited the north rim of the Grand Canyon as nothing more than a "tin-can gasoline joint." Grey felt strongly about the Grand Canyon, so much so that he could not bring himself to write about it. It was simply too marvelous to describe.

Fishing in the Pacific lured him more and more. He revisited New

Zealand and Tahiti, where he caught his record 1,040-pound striped marlin. The fish was mutilated by sharks; had it not been, it would have weighed 200 pounds more. When the Australian government asked him to explore big-game fishing there, Grey went to Australia and landed his record tiger shark off Sydney Heads. Always the unknown beckoned. He spent $40,000 for a steel-hulled schooner originally built for the Kaiser, and another $270,000 went into refurbishing the ship, which he named *Fisherman II*. His dream of dreams was to fish the waters of Christmas Island off Madagascar, where there were reports of sailfish twenty-two feet long. Equipped with six launches, *Fisherman II* embarked for Christmas Island on a round-the-world cruise. The ship was 195 feet long, but she had a narrow twenty-eight-foot beam and she rolled, even in a calm sea. Even Grey got sick. "We had so much trouble it was unbelievable," says his younger son, Loren. "We got as far as Totoya in the Fijis. The captain was ill. The chief engineer had appendicitis. We were there for over a month or more with costly repairs. Father finally called the trip off because of a pressing business matter with his publisher." Eventually Grey gave up on the ship, and she ended her days as a cannery tender for a West Coast tuna fleet.

While steelhead fishing in Oregon in 1937 Grey suffered a stroke. Romer and a guide carried him to a car and got him home, where he recuperated. Within a year he seemed recovered. He went to Australia to fish and then back to Altadena to write, before going on to Oregon for steelhead. There he insisted that Loren and three friends fish "not only all day, but every day in the week," says Loren, now a professor of education at San Fernado Valley State College. "We finally had a big fight with him and said we wanted to go home. If he wouldn't let us go home, would he at least let us go into town on weekends and live it up a little bit? He finally gave in, so we'd fish just five days a week."

Determined to make a complete recovery, Grey worked out with a rod in a fighting chair set on the porch of the west wing of his house. Every day Grey would battle imaginary fish, pumping the rod perhaps 200 times before calling it quits. He was getting ready for the next expedition. It never came. On October 23, 1939 Zane Grey died. His workouts in the fighting chair apparently had been too much for him. He once wrote, in his younger days, "There is only one thing wrong with a fishing day—its staggering brevity. If a man spent all his days fishing, life would seem to be a swift dream." For Zane Grey, compulsive angler, the swift dream was over.

KIND AND CANNY CANINES

ALBERT PAYSON TERHUNE

January 18, 1968

E VERY AGE has its heroes, and to goggle-eyed young-sters of the 1920s, '30s and even into the '40s, '50s and '60s, Albert Payson Terhune was a godlike figure. Terhune, who died in 1942, wrote dog stories—most often about collies—by the score, and the influence they had has been tremendous, if not traumatic. "I must have read every one of his books when I was a kid," says Merrill Pollack, an editor at a New York publishing house. "I wanted to be a collie when I grew up. Mention Terhune's name and I go to pieces." Most of the collie breeders going today got into the sport of dogs because of Terhune. "I grew up on Terhune's stories and cried salty tears over them," says Mrs. Peggy Young, a collie breeder in Finleyville, Pennsylvania. "I still cry," says Mrs. Eugene Price, a collie fancier in Croton-on-Hudson, New York. "My husband cries, too. We're both sloppy that way." By working eleven hours a day, six days a week, Terhune was able to meet the demands of his public. In fact, his productivity was such that one critic remarked, "It is easy to imagine the printer of

65

any one of a half dozen magazines returning a dummy of the month's issue to the editor and saying: 'There's some mistake. You've left out the Albert Payson Terhune story!' "

Terhune buffs can quote phrases or recite plots from the stories and books, much in the manner of the Baker Street Irregulars reeling off Holmesian lore. There is Lad, Terhune wrote, "such a dog as is found perhaps once in a generation." Lad had "absurdly tiny silver white forepaws," which he was always licking clean when the action got dull. There was Lad's mate, Lady, "an imperious and temperamental wisp of thoroughbred caninity," and then there was Bruce, "the dog without a fault," or, to put it Terhune's way, "Bruce is not just a 'mere dog.' He is—he is *Bruce*."

Bruce, Lad, Lady, Gray Dawn, Thane, Athos, Buff—the mind reels at this roster of the great. They herded sheep, caught robbers, saved babies and cheerfully charged into battle against maddened bulls, angry hawks, lurking snakes and stags in rut. Almost every story had at least one rousing fight, and no matter how bad things went at first, "a collie down is not a collie beaten," for "the collie brain—though never the collie heart—is wont to flash back in moments of mortal stress, to the ancestral wolf." The piles of tumbled ruff hair gave "a protection no other breed of dog can boast," and the unfortunate opponent soon found that the collie "may bite or slash a dozen times in as many seconds and in as many parts of the body. He is everywhere at once—he is nowhere in particular."

Like knights-errant of old, collies roamed through Terhune's stories with big hearts that "ever went out to the weak and defenseless."

Terhune claimed he based most of his stories on actual dogs, often his own, and on occasion fact outdid fiction. When his Sunnybank Wolf was killed saving a cur from being struck by a train, *The New York Times* ran a long obituary, and the American Kennel Club *Gazette* reported that "the world paused for more than a moment." Unlike Lassie, the TV collie inspired by a novel by Eric Knight, Terhune's dogs did not have perpetual youth. They led epic lives, and they had epic deaths, worthy of Beowulf, Little Nell or Mimi. Thus, "Over a magnificent lifeless body on the veranda bent the two who had loved Lad best and whom he had served so worshipfully for sixteen years. The Mistress's face was wet with tears she did not try to check. In the Master's throat was a lump that made speech painful. For the tenth time he leaned down and laid his fingers above the still heart of the dog, seeking vainly for sign of fluttering.

" 'No use!' he said thickly, bowing his head, harking back by instinct to a half-remembered phrase. 'The engine has broken down.'

" 'No,' quoted the sobbing Mistress, wiser than he. 'The engineer has left it.' "

Terhune, an admitted rank sentimentalist, made a practice of burying many of his canine heroes on his estate, Sunnybank Farm, in Pompton Lakes, New Jersey. Lad was the first collie to be interred, and a granite block was placed over the grave with the carved words: "Lad, Thoroughbred in Body and Soul."

Unfortunately for Terhune, his readers were not content with simply reading about the dogs. They wanted to see them, dead or alive; they wanted to visit "The Place," as Terhune called Sunnybank in his stories; they wanted to chat with "the Master" himself. "The public at large seems afflicted with the belief that Sunnybank is a zoo; and that I am a freak of sorts," he complained in his autobiography, *To the Best of My Memory*. "This I judge from the hordes of motor tourists who swarm into the grounds to see our collies and to waste my own time." This intrusion of visitors "rips at my nerves and temper," he declared, and after counting more than 1,700 strangers in one season who came to see Lad's grave, he shut the iron gates to The Place and posted a sign which read NO ADMITTANCE TODAY.

Despite Terhune's distaste for welcoming his readers to his home, he relished personal publicity, and at the height of his career his every coming and going was news.

Though the press constantly followed him, Terhune began to fear that he had been around so long that he was being neglected, and in the mid-1930s he hired a press agent, Amy Vanderbilt, at the time a young writer in New York. Miss Vanderbilt recalls that Terhune was a big, bumbly grandfather type, who "couldn't stand dirty stories about dogs." She wangled him reams of publicity; he was especially delighted with the worldwide play he got when he announced that cats were smarter than dogs.

Terhune had the build of a lumberjack—he was six feet three inches tall and weighed 220 pounds—and his head was almost heroic. His hair usually hung over his forehead, making him look like a brooder, and he had a massive, determined chin. Most of the time he dressed like an English squire and was fond of striding through the countryside accompanied by thirty or forty of his collies. A capacious drinker, he had a great fondness for Swiss S, a cocktail that is made with Pernod, and he ordinarily began lunch by ordering a pair of doubles.

Physical strength, a talent for writing and a love of sports ran in the family. His great-grandfather, Abram Terhune, served in George Washington's bodyguard, and, according to family tradition, Abram is shown in the painting *Washington Crossing the Delaware* pulling the starboard bow oar. Terhune's father, the Reverend Doctor Edward Payson Terhune, a Dutch Reformed minister, occasionally shocked his congregations by his fondness for fast horses, billiards, shooting and fishing. Terhune's mother came from Richmond, where she had known Edgar Allan Poe. Under the pen name of Marion Harland, she wrote bestselling romantic novels and a cookbook, *Common Sense in the Household*, which sold almost half a million copies.

Terhune was born in Newark, New Jersey on December 21, 1872. His father later accepted calls to Springfield, Massachusetts and Brooklyn, New York, but home was always Sunnybank, a forty-acre estate on the shore of Pompton Lake in north Jersey. Terhune attended Columbia College, and to earn money during his senior year he boxed professionally under an assumed name. He was fond of fencing, too, and one of his favorite opponents at Sunnybank was a neighbor, Cecil B. De Mille. Upon graduating from Columbia, Terhune visited the Middle East and wrote his first book, *Syria from the Saddle*, which earned him a fifty-dollar advance and a few good reviews. Then twenty-one and in need of a job, he became a reporter for the New York *Evening World*, published by Joseph Pulitzer. Terhune stayed at the *World* until 1916. "I did not like newspaper work," he wrote later. "I loathed it. During my entire twenty-one and one-half years on the *World* I never once ceased to detest my various jobs there and the newspaper game in general." Yet Terhune had a nose for news and a zest for work, so much so that he was nicknamed the "Iron Man" by his colleagues. One morning, upon observing a pile of broken chains in front of the *World* building, Irvin S. Cobb exclaimed, "Terhune must be taking a day off!" Terhune liked to make light of his labors, but he was proud that when he quit, the *World* hired two men to replace him.

While Terhune was on the *World*, he had a hand in everything. He did rewriting and reporting; he wrote editorials and edited letters and features. For a while he wrote a feature column, "Up and Down with the Elevator Man." But his forte was long serials, such as *Ten Beautiful Shopgirls* and *Ten Popular Actresses*, whose stories he concocted himself. He did another series, supposedly by Lillian Russell who wrote to the *World*, "I wish it to be understood by all my friends that I am not in any way responsible for the incoherent drivel appearing in your pages under my name." For another series, an editor assigned Terhune to box with the leading prizefighters of the day. Terhune got in the ring with Jim Jeffries, Bob Fitzsimmons, Jim Corbett, Tom Sharkey, Gus Ruhlin and Kid McCoy. He had sparred with all of them on his own, but for the readers of the *World* he went through an ordeal, emerging with two missing teeth and a broken left hand. Later he discovered that the editor had secretly offered a special half-page story in the Saturday paper to the boxer who kayoed him. Terhune was on friendly terms with Corbett and Fitzsimmons, but "John L. Sullivan was the only fighter I knew well whom I did not like . . . he was a bully, a sodden beast, a hog. He has been handed down to posterity as a ring hero. He was nothing of the kind. He had the intelligence of a louse—if any." Terhune was often apologetic about his writings, but he was proud of a now long-vanished novel *The Fighter*, which he called "my nearest fictional approach to literature."

In 1901 Terhune married Anice Stockton, whom he had known as a child. Terhune had one daughter from a previous marriage, Lorraine, who died in 1946. In 1905 Anice Terhune became gravely ill, and Terhune, unable to afford a nurse, had to take time off from the *World* to look after her. She recovered, but it was a turning point of his life. "I realized I was a lazy failure," he wrote. "I was thirty-two years old. I had not one hundred dollars in the world, above my weekly pay. I was several thousand dollars in debt. I had no reasonable hope of doing better along the lines I was following.

"I saw no way to get ahead in the world except by forcing some kind of opening for myself as a fiction writer. Thenceforth, for several years, I set aside five hours a night, five nights a week, for this kind of work. I came home, got a shower and a rubdown; and, as soon as dinner was ended, I went to my desk and began writing. At first it was torment, to attack fresh toil at the jaded end of a nine-hour work period. But, bit by bit, I got into my stride."

Most of the stories were cheap melodrama without the slightest pretensions to literature—"I knew that better than did anyone else; and I grieved bitterly over the knowledge," he admitted, but he did well financially. By 1912 he was getting $100 for a story and $1,400 for a serial, and in a typical year he was writing twenty short stories and five 60,000-word serials. He was able to spend more and more time at Sunnybank with his wife and dogs. He had for some time tried to persuade editors to buy dog stories, but he was told that the reading public was not interested. One weekend in 1914 Ray Long, editor of *Redbook*, happened to be at Sunnybank. Long, who had taken a fancy to Lad, suggested Terhune do a story about the dog. Terhune wrote *His Mate*, about Lad and Lady, and it was such a success that other editors began clamoring for Lad stories. Terhune left the *World* and quickly turned out a dozen stories, all revolving around this "eighty-pound collie, thoroughbred in spirit as well as in blood." In real life Lad was not registered with the AKC, yet in print he had a "benign dignity that was a heritage from endless generations of high-strain ancestors." Moreover, Lad had "the gay courage of a d'Artagnan, and an uncanny wisdom. Also—who could doubt it, after a look into his mournful brown eyes—he had a Soul."

Lad, obviously, was a dog of destiny, and in successive stories, or "yarns," as Terhune called them, Lad captures a thief in the night; rescues the Mistress from drowning; saves a baby from a copperhead snake; rescues his offspring, Wolf, from drowning; wins two blue ribbons at the Westminster Kennel Club Show; gets lost in New York but makes it back home to Sunnybank by swimming the Hudson River. (In a later epic, *Gray Dawn*, the collie of the title name also becomes lost on the east bank of the Hudson but, instead of swimming the river, he wisely takes the Tarrytown-Nyack ferry.) There is little that Lad cannot do. Perhaps the best remembered Lad stories involve the nasty Hamilcar Q. Glure, who "had made much money in Wall Street—a crooked little street that begins with a graveyard and ends in a river." Having "waxed indecently rich," Glure buys "a hideously expensive estate" and settles down as a gentleman farmer in the north Jersey hills, where he dresses like "a blend of Landseer's *Edinburgh Drover* and a theater program picture of *What the Man Will Wear*." Anxious to accumulate prizes for his dogs, Glure offers a $1,600 gold trophy in the shape of a hat for the dog that wins a specialty competition, conditions to be announced later. They are not announced until the day of the show at Glure's estate, and it turns out that Lad is the only visiting dog that can qualify to compete for the trophy. He has won at least one blue ribbon at a licensed American or British Kennel Club show, and he has a certified five-generation pedigree with at least ten champions. Now all he need do to win the trophy is to complete an obscure and tricky competition prescribed by the Kirkaldie Association, Inc., of Great Britain for Working Sheepdog Trials. But Lad really doesn't have a chance. He has never gone through such a competition, while the sly

Glure has paid $7,000 to the Duke of Hereford for Champion Lochinvar III, the only dog in the world that can possibly qualify and win. But the Mistress, "like Lad, was of the breed that goes down fighting," and surely but very slowly Lad responds to her commands to complete the course. Full of confidence, Glure dismisses his dog's Scottish trainer to give Lochinvar hand signals. The dog bounds off to do the course, but Glure, who has been smoking a cigar, burns his fingers. He shakes his hand in pain, then sticks his fingers in his mouth. Baffled by these strange movements, Lochinvar stops and refuses to move. In a rage, Glure tries to kick the dog and thereby forfeits the match by moving from the central post. Lad wins the Gold Hat, and the Master sends it to the Red Cross to have it melted down and sold to buy hospital supplies, explaining, "If that doesn't take off its curse of unsportsmanliness, nothing will."

Nouveaux riches such as Glure were among Terhune's favorite villians. Others were tramps, any trespassers on The Place, "the professional dog catcher in quest of his dirty fee," and vivisectionists. The last flourished because "There seems to be no law to prevent human devils from strapping helpless dogs to a table and torturing them to death in the unholy name of Science." The vivisectionists were usually Germans, or, to put it another way, Germans were usually vivisectionists. Thus, in *Bruce*, written during the heat of World War I, the sinister Dr. Halding furtively goes around buying dogs at shows. "The bigger and stronger they are, the more he pays for them. He seems to think pedigreed dogs are better for his filthy purposes than street curs. They have a higher nervous organism, I suppose. The swine!" In time Dr. Halding is arrested as a dangerous alien. In addition to an ample trove of "treasonable documents," the arresting officers discover "no fewer than five dogs, in varying stages of hideous torture . . . strapped to tables or hanging to wall hooks." Upon being seized, Dr. Halding bewails "loudly and gutturally, this cruel interruption to his researches in Science's behalf."

When the Master and the Mistress later offer Bruce for service as a courier dog in France to rid the world of the Hun pestilence, the Master suddenly has second thoughts about his dog: "To think of him lying smashed and helpless, somewhere in No Man's Land, waiting for death, or caught by the enemy and eaten . . . ! Or else to be captured and then cut up by some German vivisector-surgeon in the sacred interests of Science!"

Not even devotees of the dog game were exempt from Terhune's wrath. Woe to the breeder who foisted off a poor pup, or "purp," as Terhune wrote, on some innocent buyer. Woe, too, to fanciers who cared only to exhibit dogs at shows. Terhune was repelled by the anguish bull terriers underwent for shows "by the harsh rubbing of pipe clay into the tender skin. Sensitive tails, and still more sensitive ears were sandpapered, for the victim's greater beauty—and agony. Ear-interiors also were shaved close with safety razors." Even collies were hurt by "murderous little 'knife combs' " that transformed "natural furriness into painful and unnatural trimness. Ears were 'scrunched' until their wearers quivered with stark anguish—to impart the perfect tulip-shape; ordained by fashion for collies. . . .

"Few of these ruthlessly 'prepared' dogs were personal pets. The bulk of them were 'kennel dogs'—dogs bred and raised after the formula for raising and breeding prize hogs or chickens, and with little more of the individual element in it.

"Brain, fidelity, devotion, the *human* side of a dog—these were totally ignored in the effort to breed the perfect physical animal. . . . The body was everything; the heart, the mind, the namelessly delightful quality of the master-raised dog—these were nothing. Such traits do not win prizes at a bench-show. Therefore fanciers, whose sole aim is to win ribbons and cups, do not bother to cultivate them." But for all this, Terhune was ready, willing and able to enter his own dogs at a show, provided the show was not too taxing. After all, showing dogs was "the straightest show on earth. Not an atom of graft in it, and seldom any profit." For four years Terhune served on the board of the American Kennel Club, the ruling body of dogdom.

When the Lad stories were done, Terhune looked around for a publisher. John Macrae of Dutton offered to gamble on a book about Lad, and it was a success at once. Published in 1919, it went through thirty-eight printings in ten years. *Lad* has now sold so many copies the publisher has lost count. The same is true of any number of other Terhune books, some of which are still in print.

After Lad, Terhune went on to Bruce, Buff, Gray Dawn and a host of other canine do-gooders. One theme common to many stories is the dog as an instrument of salvation. Thus it is in the story, *The Foul Fighter*, with Champ, a collie adopted by Dan Rorke, a dirty fighter who wins by fouling. "That was how he made his living—by tactics his own dog would not stoop to." After seeing Champ fight clean against a mongrel, Rorke vows to do the same in his next bout. He does, and he wins. In

His Dog, Link Ferris finds a collie purp by the side of a road. Because of
the dog, named Chum, Ferris gives up booze. "I stopped drinking
because I got to seeing how much more of a beast I was than the fine
clean dog that was living with me." With Chum's instincts for herding
sheep and cattle, the sober Ferris pays off the mortgage on his farm,
prospers and marries the beautiful Dorcas Chatham, daughter of the
postmaster.

Ferris, incidentally, found Chum when the dog was tossed from a
speeding car going around a curve. A curve in the road was one of
Terhune's favorite plot devices. Screeching cars threw forth a veritable
army of collies, babies, stolen goods and picnic hampers, all grist for
stories. It so happened that The Place fronted, and still fronts, a wicked
curve on Route 202, a fact impressed on Terhune himself, who was
once struck there by a car. As a result of the accident, Terhune lost
much of the use of his right hand and had to give up longhand for
typing, a chore he disliked.

Another Terhune device was to have two characters explain the
whole background and point of the story in the opening dialogue.
There are even times when the leading character does this in a solilo-
quy to a dog, as in the novel *Buff*, where a maltreated purp is rescued
by a man named Michael Trent. As Trent drives off with the dog, he
says, "I'm an outcast, you know, Buff. An Ishmaelite. And I'm on my
way back to my home-place to live things down. It'll be a tough job,
Buff. All kinds of rotten times ahead. Want to face it with me? . . . Not
to take up too much of your time, Buff, here's the main idea: I'd just got
that farm of mine on a paying basis, and changed it from a liability to
something like an asset, when the smash-up came. Just because I chose
to play the fool. It was down at the Boone Lake store one night . . ."
After Trent goes on for another two pages and tells the dog about his
being wrongly sentenced to prison, he pauses. Buff snuggles close and
licks his hand. "Good little pal!" exclaims Trent as he heads home to
attempt to clear his name. Does he succeed? Of course. And he wins the
heroine, too, winsome Ruth Hammerton, daughter of the local judge—
but none of this would have happened were it not for the collie, Buff,
who pursues his kidnapped master with all the eagerness of a man from
a bill-collection agency. "Dizzy from his wound, faint from loss of
blood, heart-broken and frantic at the vanishing of his master, the collie
sped in pursuit . . ."

Faithful collies! Tireless collies! Psychic collies! They ever carry

onward. "A dog is a dog, but a collie is—a collie." Some of what
Terhune wrote is outdated or flimsy cardboard, but much still has a
certain magic. Terhune was perhaps at his best in some of his Lad
stories or stories where collies revert to the wild, such as in *Fox!* and
Lochinvar Bobby. The writing, at least for children, is highly effective, as
in this passage from *Fox!* where Whitefoot, the registered silver fox,
escapes from the fur farm:

> Wriggling out of his tunnel, he shook himself daintily to rid his
> shimmering silver-flecked black coat of such dirt as clung to it.
> Then he glanced around him. From the nearby wire runs,
> twenty-three pairs of slitted topaz eyes flamed avidly at him.
> Twenty-three ebony bodies crouched moveless; the moon glinting
> on their silver stipples and snowy tailtips.
>
> The eyes of the world were on the fugitive. The nerves of his
> world were taut and vibrant with thrill at his escapade. But they
> were sportsmen in their own way, these twenty-three prisoners
> who looked on while their skilled fellow won his way to liberty.
> Not a whine, not so much as a deep-drawn breath gave token of
> the excitement that was theirs. No yelping bark brought the
> partners out to investigate. These captives could help their com-
> rade only by silence. And they gave him silence to a suffocating
> degree.

Terhune always had doubts about his writing, stating at one point,
"I found I could make more money as a scrawler of second- and third-
rate stuff. While it is a noble thing to starve in a garret and to leave to
posterity a few precious volumes which all folk praise and a few read,
yet to me there was something better worthwhile in grinding out work
which brought me plenty of cash, if no high repute." In an even darker
moment he wrote, "I have become an Apostle of the Obvious, a writer
for the Very Young."

In the 1930s Terhune discovered he had cancer. He bore the illness
as would Bruce or Lad or Buff—stoically. Bruce Chapman, producer of
Terhune's radio show, says that Terhune would tell the doctors, "Take
out enough so I can be on the air next Sunday." Always close to his
wife, his dear "chum," he loved their hours together at Sunnybank.
"He was happy in the simple sense," says Chapman. On February 18,
1942 Terhune died at The Place. A religious man, his last words to his
wife were, "I know the Dear Savior will help me across."

The story of Albert Payson Terhune does not end there. Mrs. Terhune survived him for twenty-two years. A gentle, old-fashioned Victorian sort of lady, Anice Terhune continued to set her beloved Bert's place at the dinner table. For solace, she wrote music. She wore flowery hats, and she was upset by women in slacks. Before his death, Terhune had prepared rough notes for an article, "Across the Line", in which he speculated on life in the hereafter and which he ended, "It is not ridiculous to believe—to KNOW—there is something very definite Across the Line. It is ridiculous to believe there is not." The psychic had always held an interest for him. Indeed, he touches on this in a couple of stories, most notably *Something*, where a collie howls at his master's death far away.

Mrs. Terhune's loneliness did not last for long. According to a book she wrote and which she called *Across the Line*, Bert first manifested himself to her while she was searching in his untidy study for the pedigree papers for their dogs. "Bert's voice—dear and familiar— suddenly startled me. It came clear, distinct and natural." He told her where to find the missing papers. "Look *behind* you, little girl!" he said. "Look right *behind* you! They're *all* there! Everything! Look! Look right *behind* you! Turn around!"

In time, she wrote, she was able to take dictation from her husband, a celestial being who, through electrical impulse, manipulated a pencil she held. He reported, "Laddie and Wolf knew me at once. It was so good to have them bounding around me again!" He still loved her and Sunnybank. He gave her advice òn how to handle a mischievous dog. She once asked, "How about swearing? Do you still do it?" Terhune replied, "No, Annie; I no longer swear. I had to clean all of that out of my heart at once." When she asked Terhune about John the Baptist, she reported that her husband replied, "He is here. In a droning, resounding voice he tells us the Eternal Truths." She then asked, "Why does he do it in a droning voice?" To which Terhune replied, "Because he is the same soul he was on earth."

In the old house by the lake the servants grew fewer, and in 1964 Anice Terhune died. Under wills set up by her husband and herself, the Albert Payson Terhune Foundation, Inc. came into being. Terhune, Inc. earns money to give to the Terhune Foundation, which dispenses largess to charity. Sunnybank was sold to earn money. A housing developer ended up with the final ten acres, including the house, the kennels, the barn and the gazebo. In 1967 Wayne township condemned

The Place. Weeds grew around the graves of Lad and Bruce, and vandals pillaged the house for souvenirs. Soon thereafter the township dedicated The Place as a park. The house stands, in need of repair. From time to time collie fanciers, dog lovers and people who remember the stories and books with affection drive in to look around. They come from all over the country, and one of them who lives nearby, Mrs. Claire Leishman, of Paramus, New Jersey, has started a drive to restore the house as a shrine. She has written about her efforts in the monthly *Collie Cues*, and the response has been excellent. One lady in California pledged $1,000 and wrote, "Everything I am and ever have been in collies is because of the Terhune books."

Apostle of the Obvious, writer to the Very Young, Albert Payson Terhune is still very much alive.

*   *   *

Indeed he is, according to spiritualists who hold séances at The Place, especially on the anniversaries of Terhune's birth and death. Other admirers from all over the country and abroad also visit the park. Although Wayne Township bulldozed the house in the mid-1970s—despite the best efforts of Mrs. Claire Leishman and other collie fanciers who sought to preserve it—there is a small monument to the Master of Sunnybank at The Place. Each year the park is host to the Sunnybank Festival, a flower, crafts and arts show, and during it Mrs. Leishman, who writes a monthly feature article on Terhune for Collie Cues, *displays pictures illustrating the history of Sunnybank.*

NOBODY TOUCHES ME
WITH IMPUNITY

ROBERT ABADY

March 15, 1971

Whenever Robert Abady, a slender, intense artist
and breeder of immense working dogs known as bouviers des Flandres,
appears at a dog show, no one knows what to expect. Once, when
Abady feared he would be late with a dog at an outdoor show, he shot
his car around the admissions gate, swept by several rows of startled
officials, gunned across an open field, bounced over a log—nearly
demolishing the *Popular Dogs* stand in transit—and slammed on the
brakes at ringside. After giving his dog, Ch. Marc de la Thudinie, to an
embarrassed handler, Abady raced the car around the ring, parked in
front of the *Popular Dogs* stand and coped with the army of angry people
descending upon him by cautioning, "If you have something to say, say
it in gentlemanly fashion. Otherwise I'll report you to the bench-show
committee."

Abady, appropriately, lives in Stormville, New York, but he was
educated in French schools and is all gall. "Dog people" either love

him or loathe him. The latter group includes the American Bouvier des Flandres Club, which steadfastly refuses him membership. "They won't let me in because they know I'd wipe the floor with them," Abady says.

To just about everyone in dogdom, the American Kennel Club is the ultimate power seat, the White House, the Vatican and the Kremlin rolled into one, but to Abady the AKC is "a dilettante organization" composed of "pompous idiots" who do not have the true advancement of the breeds at heart. In 1965 the AKC suspended him for life for allegedly striking a woman handler and kicking her dog during a show in Connecticut. Among other things, this penalty made dogs from his kennel, Vuilbaard Bouviers, ineligible for AKC registration, but Abady sued in federal court and won reinstatement—an unprecedented victory.

Abady gives unhesitating voice to his opinion that the dog-show game is shot through with stupidity and politics. In his gentler moments, he says that most judges are "semi-Mongolian idiots." Once, when a judge who had been brought over from Europe rendered what Abady (who speaks eleven languages including Arabic) deemed an absolutely rotten decision, he offered to debate the judge on all the points involved. "I challenged him in French, in Flemish or in any language he wanted," says Abady, afire at the memory of it. "It didn't make any difference to me. The guy backed down. I told him he was obviously an incompetent. When I get an audience, I am really at my best." But all Abady got that day was a kick in the shins from one of the judge's supporters.

Abady's controversial convictions reach beyond the show ring. It is his deep belief that "most people involved in dogs are fruitcakes," and he adds that the average American dog, be it family pet, show dog or field dog, is in "miserable condition." Abady's admirers, though they may cringe at his outspoken assaults on the canine establishment, hail him as a great guru of dogs, a true authority on the breeding of dogs, the health of dogs and dog nutrition. "I think Abady is the most important thing that has happened in the dog business in the last ten years," says Jacquin Sanders, a breeder of bull mastiffs. "His nutritional ideas are extremely advanced. His dogs are in fantastic condition. The breed looks completely changed from five years ago when I saw bouviers limping around the ring."

A number of guard- and attack-dog enthusiasts regard Abady as a seer, and his attack-trained bouviers fetch several thousands of dollars each. "Every time there is a murder in New York City, Cleveland or Chicago, we're inundated with phone calls," Abady says. "So that's good for business."

The bouvier des Flandres, native to Belgium, the Netherlands and northern France, is a shaggy, bearlike dog with cropped ears and tail and a heavy beard. In Belgium a show championship cannot be awarded to a bouvier unless it has won a prize for tracking or as an army, police or guard dog. The male is big, up to 140 pounds, very strong and agile. It is a good jumping breed. A bouvier holds the world record for scaling a wall—sixteen feet. Originally bred in Flanders to herd cattle—bouvier literally means cattle dog—the dog is supposed to be of calm temperament. "The bouvier does not have a chip on his shoulder," says Abady's wife, Isabel, an assistant professor of French at Vassar. "He does not want to be nasty. He is gentle and friendly and marvelous with children. He is only aggressive when someone threatens his people or his property. Our kennel motto is *Nemo me impune lacessit* (Nobody touches me with impunity). The bouvier protects not because he's vicious, but because he is your dog. He does what is needed."

As an example of the dog's measured response to a situation, Abady cites the time a plumber came to his house a day late when no one was at home. "There were seven dogs in the house," Abady recalls, "and the plumber was pinned to the living-room wall for eight or nine hours. When we came in, he was ashen. The dogs didn't hurt him, they just wouldn't let him move even though he was only a foot and a half away from the door. Of course, he should have come the day he said he would."

Then there was the time Abady went into Manhattan with Picot, an untrained year-old male. "I took him into the Figaro, a coffeehouse in Greenwich Village," Abady says. "You could take a dog in there, eat, drink coffee and play chess in a relaxed atmosphere. A guy who seemed about eight feet tall and wearing an orange motorcycle suit came in and sat at the next table. He ordered a hamburger and French fries. Picot was curled up at my feet. When this guy's order came, he got up and leaned across me to get the ketchup. It was a very irritating and insolent gesture, as though he wanted to pick a fight. I did nothing. Shortly after that, he came back for the pepper and salt. I did nothing. As he was eating, he dropped one of his French fries on the floor and kicked it toward Picot. I kicked it back. He kicked again. I picked it up and said, 'Don't feed the dog without the owner's permission.' I threw the French fry back at him and, by accident, it landed on his plate. Get the picture? He stands up and pushes the table aside. I stand, and suddenly I hear this high-pitched shriek from this huge guy. I didn't know what was going on. The place was absolutely still, and all I wondered was how a big guy, an enormous guy like this, could scream in such a high voice.

"What had happened was that Picot had grabbed the guy by the hand. The guy fell over a bannister, his hand bleeding, rushed into the bathroom and then shot out of the Figaro. There wasn't a sound in the restaurant. Not a sound. It was eerie. I didn't know what to say. Should I offer to pay his check? The waitress comes over, silently gives me my check, I pay and I leave with Picot. I didn't know whether I could ever go back, but a few weeks later a friend of mine went in there and he told me, 'Hey, there's this legend about this guy who went into the Figaro with a bear! And the bear tore this motorcyclist guy apart! The guy was all covered with blood after the bear chewed him up, and they had to carry him on a stretcher to an ambulance.' It turned out the manager was delighted, because motorcyclists had made the place a hangout and annoyed his customers."

Abady, who is 32, was born in Curaçao in the West Indies. He is of Dutch, French and English extraction. His father was a wealthy entrepreneur who invested in various enterprises ranging from ranches and department stores in Latin America to tea in India. Abady spent part of his childhood in Egypt; later his family moved to France and then to Italy. But wherever they went, Abady had horses and dogs. He credits a great deal of his knowledge of dog anatomy and structure to his experience with horses and also to his artistic training. "Robert's forte is his artist's eye," says Isabel. "He is extremely visual."

Abady's education was classically French, and when the family moved to New York he attended the Lycée Français, which was for him "a terrible school. It was too rigid and I was basically rebellious." Once when he was briefly living on his own after a spat with his father, he was called in by the headmaster and informed he was going to be expelled. "I said, 'Okay, I won't pay the bill.' " He remained in school.

When Abady was 16, he had his final break with his family. "My father told me there was a big place waiting for me if I wanted to get involved in his affairs. He told me what they were, but they were not too engaging to me at the time. I was torn between medicine and art. My father didn't think very much of physicians generally, and when I told him I wanted to be a painter he thought I was insane. I packed my bags, rented an apartment and took a job as a salesman. I wasn't much of a salesman so they suggested I look for other work. Those were troubled years for me. I didn't know how hard it was to make one's own way in the world. I worked at various jobs and gradually I started to sell paintings. Little by little I didn't have to work part-time."

Abady studied with Maximilian Aurel Rasko, whom he regards as "one of the last great masters of the century." From him Abady absorbed the principles of harmony, composition and design, elements that are lacking, he says, in modern art, which he considers a "hoax." When Abady was eighteen, his work was presented at a number of big shows, including a show at the National Academy.

Abady's father died shortly after Abady had left home, and a quarter of a million dollars was placed in trust for him until he reached twenty-one. Fearing that the trust fund was being mishandled, he sought to get his money. "I got a few thousand here and there to keep me quiet," he says. "Then I was told that's it." Knowing that he was due a considerable sum from one of his father's former business associates in Curaçao, Abady went there. "I realized there was no way I could get the money legally," Abady says, "but I knew that this man was tremendously superstitious, so I began a campaign of terror. In the evenings I planted speakers in his garden just outside his bedroom, and I would hide in the shrubbery with a mike and say, 'This is the great spirit speaking.' He was a Rosicrucianist or something. I would speak in Papiamento, which is a dialect I picked up at the time, and I would say, 'You've been a very bad man. That fellow Robert is such a nice boy, a young man at the beginning of life, and you're taking his money. He's really trying to work hard, and he's going to school. Do you realize your soul is going to burn?' This got him so scared he capitulated."

Comfortably fixed, Abady went to Germany and to Holland. He studied and painted and came to know the bouvier. In 1963 he returned to the United States, where he met Isabel in a Philadelphia junk shop while he was seeking objects for a still life. Isabel, who had studied for her doctorate at the University of Montreal, was then teaching at St. Joseph's College. They bought bouviers, got married and purchased a farm in Quebec.

"Soon the whole place was crawling with bouviers," Abady recalls.

"They were all terrible. I was very disenchanted. I had started to learn about bouviers in a creative way. They were supposed to be courageous. These were very shy. I was determined to find out if the dog really had the character that his heritage suggested. We sold the farm, sold all our dogs or gave them away and started from scratch."

The Abadys moved back to the United States and settled in Stormville, fifty miles north of New York City. Passionately committed to raising better bouviers, Abady got in touch with breeders in Belgium and he went there to buy dogs. He was discouraged at the first kennel he visited. "The dogs were much handsomer than the ones here, but they were very, very timid," he says. "I looked at them in complete disgust and just walked away." At the next kennel he visited, Posty Arlequin, he paid several thousand dollars for three handsome bitches, and then he saw Marc, a two-year-old male at the Thudinie kennel of Justin Chastel. To see if the dog had courage, Abady donned a protective suit of heavy canvas and leather and asked Chastel to send the dog on the attack. "Marc barreled into me, knocked me over and tried to kill me," says Abady. "I knew this was the dog I wanted. This was the beginning of a new strain." Chastel did not want to sell Marc, who was the sensation of show rings in Belgium and France. But after five cognacs he agreed to let the dog go for a bit less than $6,000, including shipping.

In the United States Marc promptly won his show championship. "Marc won a lot," Abady says. "But not until *Dog World* ran a story on Marc did he get the recognition he deserved. When the article appeared, he started winning working groups almost overnight. That is how susceptible many judges are to publicity. Before that, no one looked at him much because he was a bouvier and bouviers hadn't won in many, many years. Marc is a great dog and he should have won on his own merits." Marc, along with other Vuilbaard Bouviers, has been handled in the ring by J. Monroe Stebbins, Jr. "He's an excellent handler," says Abady, "but he wishes we wouldn't show up at ringside. He has no desire to be associated with the dramatic side of our kennel."

Although Abady has bred a dozen champions since he bought Marc, he remains skeptical of the show circuit. "It is obvious to me," he says, "that is it impossible to make judgments that are absolutely concrete because of the system. Judges are not really trained, they're not schooled in esthetics and they're not schooled in structure. There are no classes to explain dynamics and all the principles that exist in dogs.

To become a dog judge, you have to become a busybody and get involved with a breed club. Eventually you get assignments and are considered an expert by a lot of other nonexperts. There are no standards that are really plausible. There are some good judges, judges who seem extremely knowledgeable. These are people who have done a great deal of research on their own. A lot of handlers become judges. Some know something here or something there, but they usually do not have the cohesive overall ability to go over a dog in detail. We've seen some outrageous things happen; top ranking dogs that have been lame, lame for years, some judges will throw out of the ring and other judges will confer the highest awards on them.

"The whole dog game should be reorganized. The American Kennel Club should be completely divested of its autocratic power. The AKC treats everyone like little children. There should be rules of conduct at shows, I agree with that. But there should also be the possibility for people who have serious grievances to bring them to a board that is independent.

"People want to know that the winning dog is the one after which the breed should be patterned. That's essentially what showing should be all about. But breeds take turns for the worse because winning dogs sometimes shouldn't win. People read that this dog has six best-in-shows or fifty group wins, and they'll send their bitch over to be bred and the dog could have 10,000 faults. This does a tremendous disservice to purebred dogs. It is perpetuating dogs for reasons that have nothing to do with dogs. It has to do with politics. It has to do with money. It has to do with influence. So dogs don't make the progress they should."

Although Abady has a poor opinion of the show ring, he regards attack training as superb sport. His only difficulty is finding a steady supply of "villains." A villain is the fellow who serves as the bouvier's object of attack. He should weigh at least 200 pounds, because a charging bouvier can easily knock down a lighter man. Once the villain is knocked flat, the dog can burrow underneath the protective suit and do severe damage. "You find villains anywhere you can get them," Abady says. "Anyone who talks big and thinks he has guts. We pay four dollars an hour, but when a villain sees an enraged dog coming at him for the first time, he wants to raise the price."

It takes about a year to train an attack bouvier, and only the most stable dogs are taught. The first thing that the bouvier must learn is how to bite properly. Abady trains his dogs to bite the calf, the thigh, the arm and the crotch. "When we say a bouvier bites," says Abady, "it doesn't mean the dog just puts his teeth into someone. A bite is a trained procedure. A bite is a lethal assault. For a dog to bite, it is not enough to slash or nip. A dog is not really effective that way. For a dog to bite effectively, he must apply pressure and break bones and tear muscles and not let go and quit. When you first start training a dog to bite, he may exert one hundred pounds of pressure. That's meaningless. A bouvier that has been taught to bite will exert up to 1,000 pounds of pressure per square inch, and it takes only about 300 or 350 to break the average human forearm. The bouvier has to learn to throw his weight into the bite, his shoulders into it, his neck into it. And he really has to tear. The first time he shakes his head, everything goes with it. This is our whole concept. If a bouvier gets you in the thigh, you'll be unconscious in about five seconds. You couldn't stand the pain. If a dog comes in and slashes, you have a chance to break his head, but if a dog comes in and holds and starts tearing and breaking things, then it's all over, because you can't get him off you.

"A bouvier bite is a studied thing. It really doesn't matter where he bites you. If he's got you on the big toe, you'd probably lose consciousness. Shepherds and Dobermans are slashers; they have a longer jaw, so instinctively they want to let go. They do not have the same jaw structure as the bouvier." Abady speaks from experience about the bouvier bite. While photographing an attack lesson in France, he got a little too close to the villain. The bouvier wheeled off target and grabbed Abady in the thigh. A doctor used twenty-seven stitches on the wound and Abady limped for months.

In the early stages of training, the bouvier is held on a special leash made of whale hide. "The leash is very pliable," says Abady, "and its vibrations will give you an idea of what's going on in a potential attack situation. You can feel the bouvier quiver and tense up. It's as though an electrical signal is given through the leash. He should do nothing unless there is a direct assault on you or unless he is commanded. I don't use complicated verbal commands. The command to be on guard, the last step before an all-out assault, is 'Cha,' which is said just under my breath. It means nothing in any language. 'Cha' is enough, and the dog is like a live wire. The command to attack, very good insofar as it's so subtle that no one would ever know what is happening is 'Tsk, tsk.' That's it. Suddenly the dog turns into a cannonball."

Dr. Stephen Wilder, a Manhattan psychologist, lives on the West Side and practices on the East Side. He has to walk through Central Park twice a day, and so he has two Abady-bred bouviers accompany him for protection. "Bouviers are very much a part of my life in the city," Wilder says. "I think Robert's bouviers are the best of all the dogs I've seen, and I've tried shepherds, Dobermans, rottweilers, and Rhodesian Ridgebacks. None has the stability or temperament of my two bouviers. You have to have a dog that is very calm. City living is complicated. If the dog went at everyone who looked or acted strange, he'd get you into an awful lot of trouble very easily.

"Bouvier attack training requires a very complex set of discriminations. Why should the dog attack the 101st stranger and not the first one-hundred? The bouvier has two attributes that are seemingly contradictory. One, a tremendous amount of stability, and two, a predisposition to protect, to bite without hesitation when required. These dogs have a deep sense of territory. When I let them off the leash, they're never more than forty feet away from me. With my wife, the dogs are never more than ten feet away."

A year ago, while walking home through the park one evening, Dr. Wilder found himself being followed by a group of teenagers. They caught up to him and demanded money. "When I refused, one kid reached into his pocket and flicked out a switchblade knife," Wilder recalls. "It was like a signal and they started to surround me. I had Rocco, my trained bouvier, a bouvier pup and another dog with me. I didn't want to challenge these kids, but I suggested that the first one who came at me probably would die and that three or four others wouldn't go through life looking the same. Rocco had oriented himself in a certain way. He doesn't rave or jump around. These dogs have an understated way that people don't understand. Rocco's neck arches, his ears stand, his gait changes. I started walking backward, and Rocco kept doing figure eights around me to make sure no one came close. No one did."

Abady recalls the occasion on which he drove to the East Side of Manhattan to deliver a painting, leaving a bouvier bitch to guard the car. "I parked the car about a third of a block away," he says. "It was a warm evening, and I left the dog inside with another painting and a few odds and ends on the front seat. I delivered my painting and it was getting dark when I came out. I remember passing a row of cars and seeing a man trying to get into a car that I had thought at first was mine, but in the dusk I figured I had made a mistake. I tried to remember exactly where I had parked. I knew it was on this street, and I went back again.

"All of a sudden it dawned on me that the guy had been getting into my car. I looked, and he seemed to be in the same position he had been three or four minutes before when I first passed him. I was very puzzled. All of a sudden the terrible thought occurred to me that something was going on with this guy's arm. The car was shaking and quivering. Here was this guy moaning as though he was in pretty bad shape. The dog had nailed him right in the shoulder. I tried to extricate him, but I couldn't get him out. I went inside and tried to get her to release him, but she wouldn't. She was just braced in there.

"I figured I better get a cop. After a good five or six minutes, I finally got the police. Here they came in a patrol car. They get out as big as life. 'Okay, where's the guy?' they asked. I said, 'He's in there.' So a cop opened the door, grabbed him and said 'Okay, c'mon, buddy.' Then the cop said, 'God, what's in there?' I said, 'That's my dog.' One cop said, 'That ain't no dog, that's a bear!' The familiar bear nonsense. I said, 'You just hold him and drag, and I'll get in the car and release him.' But the cops jumped in the patrol car, slammed the door and rolled up their windows a little bit and said, 'When you get him out, call us.'

"Finally I got the guy's arm loose. It was an ordeal. I had to pry her and coax her and tell her she was a good girl. She was very blood-thirsty, this dog, in any case. Finally, the cops got the guy and took him away. He was delighted to be arrested."

In the course of the last six years, Abady has spent almost $250,000 on his kennel and now makes a good living from dogs. "Most of the money is from the peripheral activities that concern dogs," he says. "Training, of course, is very lucrative, and word of good training spreads fast. Up to now we have trained only bouviers, but we are expanding to take in any dogs. Boarding is very important. We have a lot of consultations on nutritional problems, and we have a small mail-order business selling nutritional supplements."

To a growing number of dog fanciers, Abady is a recognized expert on condition and nutrition. Not long ago he visited an acquaintance, who was very proud of his Labrador retriever. Abady looked at the dog, felt the stomach, checked the coat and peered down the throat as the owner beamed. "Your dog is not well," Abady said. "He has tonsillitis, the gums look pale, the coat is terrible and he lacks vigor. Have your vet check for worms." The veterinarian reported that the dog had the start of an infestation of hookworms.

"You hear this country has the best nourished people and everyone is healthy," says Abady. "Then you see people who are nervous wrecks, they tire easily, they're not healthy. It's the same thing with dogs. Dogs are not always in top shape. For the most part they are in awful shape. They are eating rations that are inadequate. Dog owners and veterinarians are brainwashed by big companies. The rations are helpful in the sense that they are balanced, but over a long period of time I would say no dog can really do well on them. Let's assume that a dog has worms. The intestine is upset, and the dog can't synthesize vitamin C normally. So he starts to develop certain serious symptoms that are not picked up by a vet because he is not nutritionally oriented. The B complex is interfered with. This becomes chronic, and you start to see the results: wear on the inside of the gum, pigment is lacking, the dog lacks luster, he starts to have bad breath, which is mostly caused by niacin deficiency.

"Because the dog has bad breath, the modern notion is to give him chlorophyll. No one bothers to think that maybe the dog has some trouble with his intestinal tract. Then the dog becomes susceptible to certain diseases and infections. This is automatic. Say the dog picks up a mixed bacterial infection. Essentially dogs are very hardy, and they generally have much better defenses than people do. But unless the dog has enough proper nutrition in his rations, the infection is going to take hold and attack various organs. Say he gets tonsillitis. You go to the vet, and he says, 'Okay, your dog has tonsillitis.' He may not realize it's an ascending infection coming up from the intestines. So he treats the dog for tonsillitis, the symptoms disappear temporarily and the dog is still in as lousy shape as before."

Abady has his own laboratory. "I was forced by circumstances to become my own vet," he says. "Our mortality of newborn puppies is maybe two percent. It was sixty percent when I didn't do the work and when I wasn't my own vet." There has been such a demand for Abady's nutritional supplements that he is planning to start a company to sell them in packaged form. The first half dozen kennel-tested supplements are specifically formulated to meet various needs or problems. There is a supplement to increase the stamina of hunting dogs, another for pups of large breeds ("to give them the chance to grow up to their genetic potential"), supplements for breeding dogs, a supplement for lactating bitches of all breeds and supplements for dogs under stress or in a diseased condition.

"We're not interested in making money for money's sake," Abady says. "We want to break new ground. We are always looking for things that will work better than anything has before."

Meanwhile, no one had better give Abady any trouble—his bark is just as bad as his bite.

* * *

Robert Abady still raises bouviers, but he no longer shows. He keeps himself busy in Poughkeepsie, New York, running the Robert Abady Dog Food Company Ltd. and the Nutra Vet Research Corporation, which sells nutritional supplements for animals.

REALLY THE GREATEST

JIMMY JACOBS

March 7, 1966

T HERE IS no athlete in the world who dominates his sport with the supremacy that Jimmy Jacobs of Los Angeles and New York enjoys in four-wall handball. Handball is a demanding sport that requires endurance, speed, power and dexterity, all of which the muscular Jacobs, who stands five feet nine inches tall and weighs 175 pounds, has in abundance. In handball, which has more than five million devotees in the United States, Jacobs is generally hailed as the finest player of all time. Indeed, there are those who say Jacobs is the best athlete in this country. So far, Jacobs has won six United States Handball Association singles championships and has shared in four USHA doubles titles. With Marty Decatur, a fellow player from the 92nd Street YMHA in New York, he forms the strongest doubles team ever seen. They are unbeatable. In four years of competition they not only have never lost a match, they have never lost a game. Even by himself, Jacobs is a great doubles player. Several years ago, for instance, he played alone against Rudy and Carl Obert, two nationally ranked players, and whipped them in a 31-point game, taking only one serve to their two. But playing alone in a doubles game is nothing new for Jacobs. In the 1960 USHA doubles final he and his partner, Dick Weisman, had lost the first game and were losing the second fifteen to three, when Jacobs had Weisman stand in the rear of the court. Jacobs then won the second game alone and, with Weisman's help, the third.

In Jacob's younger days (he is now thirty-five) he also competed in other sports. As a teenager he played football, baseball and basketball. He was a good enough basketball player to be invited to an Olympic tryout. He ran the 100-yard dash in 9.8, and he was a skeet shot of championship caliber. Then and now his physical and mental abilities are such that professional athletes who know Jacobs well claim he could be a superstar in any sport. Jim Bouton, the Yankee pitcher, flatly says that Jacobs is the best athlete he has ever seen and adds, in moments of exultation, that if Jacobs played big-league ball "he would hit .500." In calmer moments Bouton merely says that Jacobs would be "the last of the .400 hitters." Cus D'Amato, the fight manager and a man ordinarily given to a squinty-eyed view of athletes, says that he has met only two men who had the aura of a champion that Jacobs has. Those men were Joe Louis and Sugar Ray Robinson. And Bob Waterfield, the old quarterback who is known to reporters as the Sphinx and the Great Stone Face because he ordinarily never says anything, becomes a gushing chatterbox when it comes to Jacobs, his onetime handball partner. "Jimmy is by far the most coordinated athlete I've ever seen," says Waterfield. "I don't see how anyone could be better. I've never seen an athlete like him. He is so coordinated it is impossible to tell whether he is left- or right-handed. He could be the best athlete in the world."

Away from handball, Jacobs has achieved a certain amount of standing as a collector of comic books and fight films. He has the largest collection of both kinds in the world, and both have fitted into his sporting endeavors. As a youngster, Jacobs got added inspiration in sports by pretending that he was Dick Grayson, alias Robin, the Boy Wonder, combater of crime with Bruce Wayne, millionaire Gotham City playboy, secretly Batman. In partnership with Bill Cayton, owner of an advertising agency and a New York producer, Jacobs has put out any number of films of famous fights. Their latest offering, *Knockout,* is a brisk compilation of the most savage bouts available on film. As a writer, editor and producer of this and similar fight films, Jacobs earns an impressive annual income. He is in fight films not for the money, however, but because he is simply nuts about boxing. He watches films of old fights by the hour, and he can practically recite the punches thrown in any title bout. While barroom habitués might wrangle forever in arguments over who was the greatest heavyweight champion, Jacobs declares for Joe Louis, and he has the films to prove it.

When Norman Mailer, the contentious novelist, first met Jacobs they got into an argument about boxing. Jacobs drubbed him so that Mailer was moved to include an account of their debate in his book, *The Presidential Papers*, where he confessed that Jacobs "ran me all over the court." In turn, *Strength and Health*, the physical culture journal, was so taken with Jacobs' build that it ran a long feature on his muscles and how they got that way.

Jacobs is busy every day, practicing handball or editing films. He leaves absolutely nothing to chance. During political campaigns he writes down the promises of every candidate, and when a politician comes up for reelection Jacobs consults his notes to see how the man has done. Friends and followers beseech Jacobs for advice on all sorts of matters, and his conversations with D'Amato, with whom he shares an apartment in New York, sometimes run very deep. "We discuss my favorite subject—fear," says D'Amato. Jacobs' interest in fear and the role it plays in winning or losing is one of the subjects he covers when giving clinics for the U.S. Handball Association. When Jacobs talks about handball he has overtones of Freud and Von Clausewitz. His listeners lap it up.

Jacobs is not the sobersides young man this would suggest. He is, in fact, a practical joker of some attainment. When he was living regularly in Los Angeles, his apartment was around the corner from a memory school. He found out the name of the director, and one day he dropped into the school, where he greeted the director with the excited cry, "George, how are you!" Flustered and embarrassed at being unable to remember Jacobs, the director fumbled for a reply. "George!" Jacobs exclaimed. "You've forgotten!" Then he left.

Once, when Jacobs took a boat to England in search of rare fight films, he signed up for lessons with a steward in the ship's three-wall handball court. He made no mention of his handball experience, and every morning at 10 he presented himself for an hour's instruction. Each day Jacobs permitted his game to improve, and after the last lesson the steward told him, "You're by far the best student I've ever had. For the first time I really feel like a teacher."

As a boy, Jacobs lived largely in his imagination. Born in St. Louis, he moved to Los Angeles with his parents when he was five. Shortly afterward his parents were divorced, and he was raised by his mother. Always intense, he became the tetherball champion of his grade school. Until the age of fifteen he was under the spell of comic books. He bought and devoured hundreds of them, and among his heroes were The Atom, Aquaman, Batman and Robin, of course, Black Hawk, Black-X, Blue Beetle, Boy Commandoes, Captain America, Captain Marvel and on and on through the alphabet. Jacobs was so exhilarated by his heroes that he began acquiring as many as ten copies of every issue that dealt with their adventures. He read and thumbed one copy and put the other nine aside in glassine envelopes to keep them in mint condition. When Jacobs went into the Army he had subscriptions to a couple of dozen comic books, but he still asked his mother to buy additional copies at newsstands because the subscription copies came creased in the mail. To the permanent astonishment of his mother, Jacobs keeps an apartment in Los Angeles that is stacked with comic books, but she does not know that he also rents a storage room in a warehouse to hold the bulk of the collection. On a recent visit to Los Angeles, Jacobs spent an afternoon sifting through his comic books, recalling where and under what circumstances he had bought certain memorable issues. Off the top of his head, Jacobs has no difficulty remembering, for instance, that Batman first appeared in issue No. 27 of Detective Comics and that Robin happened along in issue No. 38. He is an avid reader of the eighty-page *Giant Batman* issued now, but he despises the television version of *Batman*. "It's a comedy," he says. "It's something to laugh at, and that hurts me."

The fine points of Batman's and Robin's adventures are so engraved on Jacobs' mind that he was outraged when their initial meeting was redrawn for an issue fifteen years later. Instead of meeting with a trapeze ladder in the background, as was the case in the original episode, Batman and Robin were portrayed in a room. Jacobs was so vexed by this tampering with history that he told other Batman fans to disregard the blatant fraud, and he wrote an angry letter to the publisher.

"You see," Jacobs says, "I always pretended that I was Robin, the Boy Wonder. Superman I admired, but Batman and Robin were human, and everything athletic that Robin did, I tried to do. He threw a boomerang. I learned how to throw a boomerang. Robin was an excellent tumbler, and so I would run off diving boards to practice double flips. Robin knew jujitsu, so I took lessons. In one issue Robin swam underwater for two minutes. I didn't know if a kid could swim underwater for a minute. So I tried. I learned first that when you swim underwater you use up oxygen. So then I learned how to hold my breath underwater. Before long I could swim underwater for two minutes. I didn't want to admit that Robin could do something I couldn't do. I always envisioned myself as Robin, the Boy Wonder, or else as Dick Grayson, who had to keep himself under wraps. When I did something extraordinary in athletics I would think to myself, 'Well, I took off the wraps just to show what I could do.'

"Being Robin, the Boy Wonder, was a tremendous help to me in sports. All of us are susceptible to our emotions when under stress, and when I was younger I would think: What would Robin do? Instead of succumbing to nervous apprehension, I would transform myself into this other character who was emotionally unaffected."

At Los Angeles High School, Jacobs was rarely eligible for sports because of poor grades, especially in English. He looks back upon his academic career with regret, but at the time he simply was not interested. "He wasn't happy in anything except sports," says his mother. Instead of competing at school, he played halfback in football, shortstop in baseball and forward in basketball for the George Gershwin Chapter of AZA, a branch of the B'nai B'rith, a national Jewish organization. The competition was keen, because any youngster, regardless of religion, could play. While Jacobs played football, the Gershwin chapter won the AZA championship three years in a row, and one year it won all three major team championships.

At fifteen, Jacobs had largely given up pretending that he was Robin, the Boy Wonder, and began searching for new mental approaches to victory. He tried various techniques. In the AZA basketball finals one year Jacobs scored on a lay-up to tie the game just before the buzzer sounded. However, he had been fouled making the shot and was given one free throw. If he made it his team would win the championship; if he missed, the game would go into overtime.

"I asked for a time-out" Jacobs says. "I wanted to know how I was going to conduct myself mentally. The fellows thought I had called time to catch my breath, but I was trying to select which mental image

I wanted at the foul line. My coach had once told me that in an important situation on the free-throw line the thing that will destroy you is overconcentration. He always impressed on us that a free throw was easy, and that you should conduct yourself as though you were in practice. So I decided on my mental image in this case. I was going to walk up to the line and shoot the shot just as if it were a warm-up, as though the referee said I had one to practice before shooting the real one. I went up to the line, the referee gave me the ball and I made the shot."

When Jacobs was nineteen he began playing four-wall handball at the Hollywood YMCA. Art Linkletter, the TV master of ceremonies, had been playing the sport at the Y for a number of years, and when Jacobs first started, Linkletter had no trouble beating him. But Jacobs was determined to be the best. Since the courts were closed on Sundays, he got in to practice by himself by leaping from the gallery. Naturally right-handed, he spent hours in front of a mirror at home practicing left-hand returns. "I don't know where he got it from," says his mother, "but he has an ungodly amount of drive, enthusiasm and determination."

Whenever Jacobs passed the May Company department store he would stop for five minutes to check his handball form in the reflection of a large window. "People used to think I was kooky," he says. Within several months, however, he had no trouble thrashing Linkletter or anyone else in Los Angeles. Linkletter and several other enthusiasts, sensing that they had a prodigy in their midst, raised money and sent Jacobs to the junior nationals in Bremerton, Washington, where he won the singles title. At the time Jacobs was also playing AAU basketball for a printing company, and he was good enough to be invited to try out for the Olympic team. He declined, to concentrate on handball.

While on a trip to Chicago with the AAU basketball team in 1950, Jacobs managed to wangle a singles game against Gus Lewis, the former national champion. Then and now, Chicago is the spiritual capital of handball in the United States because of the efforts of Robert Kendler, a multimillionaire home remodeler. Kendler was (and is) so crazy about handball that he had a dozen of the best players in the country working for him, including Lewis, and he had built the Town Club of Chicago as a place for them to practice. After Lewis played Jacobs at the club he called his boss, Kendler, and said, "I've just played a kid who doesn't know what he's doing, and for a kid who doesn't know what he's doing he's a hell of a handball player."

Kendler immediately hired Jacobs as a home-remodeling salesman, put him into an apartment with Billy Baier, coholder of the national doubles title, and had him practice at the club with the rest of the handball players in his off hours. "My real schooling was with this group," Jacobs says. "There were ten to fifteen guys I couldn't get ten points off of, and they all taught me. Gus Lewis taught me about anticipation. Ken Schneider, the national singles champ, taught me a lot about the danger of letting up in a game. Frank Coyle, who had dethroned Joe Platak, one of the top players in the history of the sport, gave me a real lesson. When I was young I hit the ball like a son of a gun. Frank came in. He was much older, and he let his brain and soft play completely neutralize my power. He just brained me to death, and he opened up an area in handball I had never explored."

Jacobs spent a year and a half in Chicago, then he was drafted. He served as a rifleman with the First Cavalry Division in Japan and in Korea. In his younger days he used to get involved in fights, and he had the most memorable one of his life in Japan with the company bully. "He was huge," Jacobs says. "But when I saw what kind of a guy he was I had to get him." When the fight was over Jacobs had lost his two front teeth, but the bully spent a month in the hospital with a broken jaw and collarbone. Nowadays Jacobs avoids fights. Not long ago, when he got into an exchange with a motorist in New York, the stranger jumped from his car and offered to punch Jacobs in the mouth. "Gee, mister," Jacobs pleaded, "don't hit me. I've got a heart condition. You might kill me." The stranger was all apologies.

After his discharge, Jacobs returned to Los Angeles, where he worked as a salesman for a business-machine company. When he applied for the job he told the owner of the firm, Murray Spivak, that he wanted to be the sales chief. Spivak made him a salesman. To prove his worth, Jacobs spent the first couple of weeks learning the business and then went out and made eighteen sales in one day, topping the company's record. What astounded Spivak was that Jacobs made the sales during a hailstorm. "With the hail, I couldn't see how he could even make eighteen calls," says Spivak. "With his personality, he was perfect for sales."

At the Los Angeles Athletic Club, Jacobs applied himself just as diligently to handball. In 1953 he competed in his first nationals and finished fifth. In 1954 he was third, and in 1955, playing on his home court in Los Angeles, he won the singles, defeating Vic Hershkowitz. Up until this victory, handball had largely been a power game of kills, but Jacobs, having mastered the soft game with ceiling shots, forced Hershkowitz to the rear of the court where he could not make his slambang kills. In handball circles Jacobs' plays in this match were as revolutionary to the sport as Dorais' passes to Rockne were to football. Jacobs is the first to admit that Hershkowitz was no longer at his peak when they met—using a boxing analogy, Jacobs likens the match to the Marciano-Louis fight—but most handballers now agree that Jacobs had such a complete mastery of the game, from soft stuff to kills, that he would have beaten Hershkowitz at his best.

In 1956 Jacobs again won the national singles, defeating Johnny Sloan of Chicago in the semis and Hershkowitz again in the finals. In 1957, Jacobs beat Sloan again in the semis and Hershkowitz for the third time in the finals. In 1958 he had to forfeit the finals when he was injured in a collision in a doubles match. The next year Jacobs did not play because of a baffling heart condition. Examination finally revealed that he was breathing too deeply and taking too much oxygen into the blood stream, causing his heart to flutter. Now whenever the trouble arises he breathes into a paper bag for a few minutes. In this way he inhales his own carbon dioxide, thus burning up the excess oxygen. In 1960 Jacobs returned to the national singles and beat defending champion Sloan. He withdrew in 1961 because of a torn tendon, and in 1962 and 1963 he passed up the singles to win in the doubles with Decatur. But in 1964, when Decatur got married on the first day of the tournament, Jacobs returned to the singles. He wanted to vanquish Oscar Obert, who had won the championship the previous two years from Johnny Sloan.

Jacobs has a sharp rivalry with Oscar and his brothers, Rudy and Carl, who were the kings of the four-wall courts in New York until Jacobs began working there in 1960. When one of the Oberts plays, his other two brothers and mother and father are usually in the gallery to shout support, and Jacobs loves nothing more than to crush an Obert before the rest of the family.

As per custom, Jacobs trained for the singles by playing practice matches against two opponents simultaneously. He met Oscar in the finals and won easily. "I didn't want people to think I gave up singles because of Oscar Obert," he says with some finality.

In 1965 Jacobs again entered the singles, and this time he defeated

Dave Graybill, who had a sensational rise in handball after winning a record eleven letters in football, basketball and baseball at Arizona State. What happened in this match was best described by *Ace*, the official magazine of the U.S. Handball Association, which features Jacobs about as often as *Osservatore Romano* quotes the Pope.

"Dave is an all-out, aggressive, offensive-minded player and through his sheer determination, quickness and power he has been able to become one of the nation's ranking players," *Ace* reported in an article entitled "What We Learn from Watching Champions." "But the things he [Graybill] could get away with in competition against some top-drawer performers were his downfall against the complete game . . . of Jim Jacobs." There followed the usual paeans to Jacobs that readers of *Ace* have come to expect.

From time to time, Jacobs travels the country holding clinics for the U.S. Handball Association, which Kendler formed in 1950 after breaking away from the AAU. To the surprise of most players who hear him for the first time, Jacobs does not dote on techniques, such as how to serve, but on what he calls handball concepts.

"Every player is different physically," Jacobs says, "so what is good for one man may be bad for another. Instead of trying to change their swings or serves, I tell them when to go on offense and when to go on defense. There are certain basic rules, and if you violate them and your opponent does not you simply cannot win. For example, never return the ball to the front wall unless you intend to end the volley on that particular shot, because the ball gets back to the server too quickly. Also, whenever possible, take the ball out of the air to keep your opponent in the backcourt. The man closest to the front wall is the man on the offense. I believe I'm effective because my opponents can't get me out of the front of the court.

"Another concept in handball is to make your opponent hit every ball with his weak arm. If your right hand is your strong arm, it's your right hand that wins games and the left that loses them. Unfortunately, many young players have developed their weak arm to the point where it looks as good as their stronger arm, and if the ball is just a fraction to the left of the middle of the court, they'll hit it with their left arm. In the beginning they might do all right but, after playing an hour or two, the basic weakness of the arm begins to show. But there are players who will continue to play with both hands just to get the oohs and ahs.

"I'm supposed to have arms of equal strength, but I really look upon my right hand, my strong hand, as the sword and the left as the shield. I tell players that when they have a comfortable, convenient choice to use their stronger arm."

Jacobs has no qualms about giving pointers to anyone. "The more powerful I make my competition, the better I'm going to get," he says. "I've always believed that if anyone were physically better than I was in a sport I could make up for it by giving more mental effort. This is where contests are won or lost. To me, mental effort is it. When something happens in an athletic contest that you don't understand, when there are tremendous upsets with no justification, the answer is always, *always*, in the mental attitudes of the winning and losing teams or individuals.

"Sports fans always measure everything by what they can see with their eyes, but countless times winning is the result of proper mental application. In practice, for instance, I can make the back-wall kill ten out of ten times with either hand. There is no pressure. Now put 500 people in the gallery and a TV camera there, too, and say, 'Do it again, Jim, only this time it's for the world championship.' What is it that changes? I've already demonstrated that I can do it. So once I've convinced myself that I can do what has to be done physically, I then have to control my emotions.

"When I go to play in a championship match I meet an old friend I call Mr. Emotion. He is very predictable. When I want to win very badly he comes right into my body. But so that he doesn't interfere with what I'm trying to accomplish, I have to take more time in the service box, I have to make more conscious efforts to give my arms clear instructions. The way I react to Mr. Emotion is not to get apprehensive. He is nothing but a feeling, and he is there to let me know how important this match is to me. He acts as a reminder to me that the application of the physical talent that I have is under the complete dominance of what I call my control system, my brain, and that the orders that come out of this control system have to be very clear and explicit, just as if I were addressing some small child.

"All handball players look upon themselves as one identity trying to beat an opponent, but this couldn't be farther from the truth. I have a doubles team right here in my two hands. Each member of this team has assets and liabilities. The control system knows where the strengths and weaknesses of these two hands, Mr. Right and Mr. Left, lie. I expect each one of these hands to show a consideration to the other just like members of a real doubles team do. The only difference between a doubles team and these two gentlemen is that these two hands have one control system, and a doubles team has two control systems. My right hand expects Mr. Left to protect him and never allow any setups. If Mr. Left makes an error and sets up a shot that loses the volley, the control systems up here in my brain will always make the necessary corrections so Mr. Left doesn't lose the game before Mr. Right can win it. If Mr. Left does his part and shields Mr. Right, then Mr. Left expects Mr. Right to win the match for him.

"In a game the personalities of the two hands are completely different. Mr. Left is disturbed very easily because he's mechanical, and if he makes a good shot during play, in my mind, I'll compliment him. I'll say, 'That's it! Beauty!' Never out loud, of course. I never permit anyone to know what's going on inside my control system."

Jacobs' control over his control system is so complete that he likes, in his words, "to plan an important match as though I were a Hollywood writer, and then have it come out that way. When I plan, I don't worry whether I am going to win or not, but I plan *how* I'm going to win, meaning the type of play I'm going to employ in order to get the desired result."

If a match is not going the way Jacobs scripted it—and this does not necessarily mean he is losing—he will ask for a time-out so he can summon up the appropriate mental image to get his game going. Instead of becoming Robin, the Boy Wonder, Jacobs now concentrates on the images of athletes under stress who persevered. This may be Archie Moore, Sandy Koufax or anyone else who has withstood tremendous pressure.

Ordinarily, Jacobs does not discuss his mental processes at length with other athletes—"They'd think I was a little berserk," he says—but he talks about them for hours on end with D'Amato. D'Amato has long been intrigued by the workings of the mind under stress in sports, and he says of Jacobs, "Jimmy is one of the few people who have a good grasp of fear. Like me, he feels that fear is necessary for the success of an athlete. This pressure that all athletes are subjected to prior to competition is a necessary and natural part of competing, and Jimmy understands it as nature's way of preparing him for that which he must do. Jimmy doesn't allow fear to intimidate him. He *uses* it. It makes him aware. Jimmy makes a complete analysis of what needs to be done in a game, and then he fits himself into the requirements, and his ability to do this reflects tremendous determination on his part. The more I studied this guy, the more impressed I became. He is extraordinary. He not only has an excellent mind, but a tremendous physique and stamina. I have never met an athlete like him."

As a youngster in Los Angeles, Jacobs was always fascinated by boxing, and when he was fourteen he bought his first film of a fight—the controversial first Louis-Walcott bout—to find out who really won. After giving the decision to Walcott, Jacobs began acquiring films of other fights. He bought and traded films with collectors and museums around the world. Many films had never been seen before; they had lain in pictorial limbo for years because federal law from 1912 to 1940 prohibited the interstate shipment of fight films. The law had been passed as a result of the race riots that took place all over the country after Jack Johnson beat Jim Jeffries.

In addition to obtaining films, Jacobs also began acquiring the legal rights to show them for exhibition purposes. Whenever he traveled to give clinics for the USHA, he prefaced his remarks by telling the gallery of his interest in fight films and asking for leads. After one clinic at the Multnomah Athletic Club in Portland, Oregon, an elderly man told Jacobs that he had a copy of a very old film. Jacobs agreed to see it, and the man brought out a shoe box containing the sixty-five millimeter nitrate print of the Corbett-Fitzsimmons heavyweight championship at Carson City in 1897. This was the first heavyweight-title bout ever photographed by motion-picture cameras (it was also the fight in which Fitzsimmons introduced his solar-plexus punch) and all copies supposedly had vanished. In fact, the print Jacobs saw was so fragile and brittle it threatened to crumble to the touch. Jacobs bought it and sent the print to a lab where it was softened and a thirty-five millimeter negative made.

In 1959 a collector in Australia wrote Jacobs that he had a copy of the Johnson-Willard fight film. No other copy was known, and the price was $5,000. Jacobs got in touch with Bill Cayton in New York, who was the producer of a TV series, *Greatest Fights of the Century*, and Cayton agreed to advance the money. Jacobs flew to Australia, inspected the film and bought it. He took it to New York where he agreed to pool his collection with Cayton's and go into business with him.

Cayton and Jacobs now have three production companies: Greatest Fights of the Century, Inc., which is preparing a brand-new series with ninety fights never before shown on TV, including the Johnson-Burns bout; Big Fights, Inc., which produces mostly TV previews of heavyweight championship fights; and Knockout, Inc., which produced *Knockout*. Jacobs is also working on another motion-picture feature, a history of the heavyweight championship from Corbett to Clay. As Jacobs sees it, the film will include not only clips from championship fights themselves but human-interest footage showing fighters away from the ring, such as Max Baer clowning on the beach and Jack Dempsey getting beat up by Charlie Chaplin.

"This will be the greatest thing I've ever done," says Jacobs with a Hollywood flair. "It will be sensational, and the thing that will make it unique is not the fights, but the pictures away from the ring. By the time the challenger and champion walk into the ring, you'll know what kind of people they are." Jacobs is halfway through the picture, which will take him two years to complete.

"Jimmy's supremacy over the rest of the world in fight films is greater than his supremacy in handball," says Cayton. "In handball there are players half as good, but in fight films there is no one a tenth as good."

D'Amato and Jacobs first met in 1960 because of their mutual interest in boxing. D'Amato had long contended that most fighters of the pre–World War I era were bums, and Jacobs agreed. Nowadays, the two of them often spend hours shaking their heads over the likes of Stanley Ketchel and Philadelphia Jack O'Brien, and Jacobs occasionally irritates old-time fans by noting the inadequacies of their heroes in articles he writes for *The Ring Magazine*.

"I have seen every fighter from Corbett to Clay under the Marquis of Queensberry rules," he says, "and when some guy ninety-three years old tells me he has also seen Corbett and Clay, the difference is that I don't have to use my memory to go back sixty-nine years. I'm talking about fighters I saw on the screen last night."

While Jacobs' selection of Louis as the best heavyweight champion ever is not particularly surprising, his choice of the most underrated fighter of all time is, however. He is Jimmy Bivins, a heavyweight campaigner of the '40s. As for Cassius Clay, Jacobs says, "He's not the greatest, but he's a wonderful fighter, and it would take the greatest to handle him. His strong point is his tremendous hand and leg speed, tremendous especially for a man who is six feet three and weighs 215 pounds. His confidence is intimidating to the people he fights. But the thing that eventually will hurt him is that he is overconfident. And this, when everything else is equal, is the deciding factor in a contest. When he does lose, it will be a startling loss to someone he and everyone else underestimated."

In Jacobs' opinion, the best fighter, regardless of weight division, was Sugar Ray Robinson. Jacobs has a film of Robinson boxing a six-feet-tall featherweight in the 1939 Golden Gloves. With the eye of an unrivaled connoisseur, Jacobs proclaims the sixth Robinson-LaMotta fight as the finest match he has ever seen, and, in his opinion, the first Marciano-Walcott fight was the most thrilling heavyweight bout. As might be expected of a man of Jacobs' acumen, he knows fighting styles thoroughly, and he is able to spot flaws in the styles of fighters working these days. On occasion, he will tell a fighter what he is doing wrong. The fighter generally pays no attention.

*　*　*

Jimmy Jacobs no longer thinks of himself as Robin, the Boy Wonder, and he now plays handball only once a week. "All my physical and mental energies go into Big Fights, Inc., my fight film business with Bill Cayton," he says. Two films they produced were nominated for Academy Awards as best feature-length documentaries. Big Fights also does all the pocket-billiards matches on network television, and, according to Jacobs, the company is worth $15 million.

Jacobs and Cayton co-manage two boxers, Edward Rosario, challenger for the world junior-lightweight title, and Wilfred Benitez, who at 22 is the youngest fighter in history to have won three world championships (junior welterweight, welterweight and junior middleweight). Cus D'Amato runs the training camp that Jacobs and Cayton maintain in Catskill, New York.

Jacobs continues to collect comic books, and his holdings now amount to 880,000 copies. "Stupid, isn't it?" he asks with a laugh, then adds, "I've never been happier in my life. Making a great deal of money is a lot of fun."

A CHAMP FOR ALL TIME!!!

JOE PALOOKA

April 19, 1965

I N RECENT years the heavyweight champions of the world have been, from an overall point of view, unsatisfactory. Fortunately, however, for boxing buffs (especially those who live in dream worlds), there is one heavyweight champion whose reign is unsullied and unbesmirched by questionable tactics. That champion is Joe Palooka of the comic strips.

Joe Palooka is the most popular sporting hero in the history of the funnies. When he appeared on Coast Guard recruiting posters, enlistments were said to have doubled. The city of Wilkes-Barre, Pennsylvania, his hometown, named a mountain after him, and the state of Indiana erected a thirty-foot limestone statue of Joe on Highway 37 between Indianapolis and Bedford. In the eyes of citizens everywhere Joe Palooka is the American dream come true. He is strong but modest, manly but virtuous, tolerant but principled. He would never think of wrestling cops, much less of drinking. He never mouths off. There is some swearing in the strip—usually expressed by $!$%#—but the worst expletive Joe himself ever utters is a mild "tch-tch," and his cry of triumph is almost always a subdued "tee hee."

Joe Palooka is only twenty-nine years old, but he has been champion for the last thirty-five years. He was sixteen when he won the title in 1930 by knocking out the villainous Jack McSwatt, yet, for a champ who has aged as little as he has, he has changed in a number of subtle ways. His black hair has, without benefit of dye, become blond. His eyes have shrunk from big round circles to two black dots. When he started his career he was just a dumb Polish boy—"Polack" was the word in that unreconstructed period—from the hard-coal country, and his mother tongue was broken English punctuated only by "gulp, gulp." Now Joe lives in Old Greenwich, Connecticut, and speaks almost as crisply as Gene Tunney. He is married to Ann Howe, "lovely socialite," who was his fiancée for eighteen years. Nothing is more demonstrative of Palooka's rise in status than his marriage. To David Manning White and Robert H. Abel, a couple of highbrow commentators on mass culture who edited *The Funnies, An American Idiom*, Palooka's marriage to the daughter of a cheese tycoon is a "dramatic" example of "social mobility."

As a matter of fact, Joe has risen so high in social status that he has not fought in more than ten years. The McNaught Syndicate, which edits and distributes the strip, fears that boxing is in such disrepute that Palooka's image would suffer if he stepped into the ring again. As a result of this thinking, Joe now passes the time collecting antiques with Ann in nearby Norwalk, and Knobby Walsh is reduced to managing a folk singer.

Joe Palooka is the brainchild of the late Hammond Edward (Ham) Fisher, a controversial sort who was as complex as Joe was simple. "Fisher's trouble was that he hated people," says Al Capp, who worked as an assistant to Fisher before branching out on his own with *Li'l Abner*. "His day was ruined if he saw somebody eating." Fisher was a pudgy little man who was obsessed by Joe Palooka. He lived and died for Joe, whom he treated as a real human being. He commonly used the pronouns "we" and "us" when speaking about Joe, and Harold Conrad, the fight publicist, says that Fisher used to get so carried away "that you'd expect Joe to walk into the room."

Like Palooka, Fisher came from Wilkes-Barre. He was born in 1900, and as far back as he could remember he was always drawing, much to the disgust of his father, a businessman. After finishing high school,

Fisher put in a two-week stint at college, knocked around at odd jobs and then at the age of twenty, he got a job with a local newspaper as a reporter, cartoonist and part-time advertising salesman. Wilkes-Barre was then a thriving fight town, and one day in 1921, while hanging around a pool hall, Fisher ran into an acquaintance, a big, burly Polish boxer named Joe. "Hiya, Ham," Joe said. "Why don't I and youse go up to the munysippal goluff course and have a game of goluff?" At once a light bulb marked "idea" lit up in Fisher's brain, and he hurried back to the paper, where he dashed off a comic panel about a boxer named Joe Dumbelletski, envisioned as "a dumb, good-natured fighter, a tenderhearted guy that doesn't want to hurt anybody." Fisher looked upon Dumbelletski as "the perfect strip character," but almost ten years passed before Fisher could persuade any paper to buy Joe. During the course of trying to peddle the strip, Fisher changed Joe's last name to Palooka, a term he picked up from Leo P. Flynn, who managed Jack Dempsey. As Flynn defined the word, a palooka meant a fighter who was a set-up, a pushover, and since the initial episodes had Joe acting as a pushover for McSwatt, the new name seemed appropriate. Fisher later said that, to his horror, he discovered that palooka was a corruption of a Greek slang word meaning bull thrower. (In *The American Language: Supplement I*, H. L. Mencken notes that Jack Conway, a baseball player who became a writer for *Variety*, originated the word as slang for a third-rater. Conway is also credited with introducing baloney, high-hat, pushover, payoff, belly laugh and scram.)

In the late 1920s Fisher moved to New York and went to work as a salesman for the McNaught Syndicate. In a whirlwind thirty-nine-day trip, Fisher sold Striebel and McEvoy's *Dixie Dugan* to forty-one papers. Awed, Charles McAdam, president of the syndicate, succumbed to the Fisher sales line and gave Fisher permission to sell Palooka. He could have saved himself the trouble. Fisher had already told editors that on his next swing he would be back with the most terrific comic strip ever. With the editors practically panting to see it, the brash Fisher had no difficulty selling Palooka to thirty papers in just three and a half weeks.

The first appearance of Joe Palooka occurred on April 19, 1930, and Fisher was so proud of the beginning story line that he redrew it in 1943 as Joe reminisced to Army buddies on how he won the title. The first sequence opened with Joe as a strong, dumb kid, trying to help his family make ends meet. His family consists of Mom ("She's nice an' fat an' kin she cook. Golly!"), Pop, a spindly coal miner, little brother

Steve, who later becomes world middleweight champ, and kid sister Rosie. Joe answers a newspaper ad for a boy to work at a haberdashery run by Knobby Walsh, who was modeled on Knob Levison, a Wilkes-Barre cigar-store proprietor. "An' is the celery rilly a whole three dollars—honist?—Oh boy!" asks Joe. "Uh—that's a typographical error," says Knobby. "It shoulda read two dollars—Ya'll git a raise—uh next year."

Joe gets the job, and one afternoon when Knobby goes off to play pinochle Joe innocently allows a gang of thieves to loot the store because he thinks they have charge accounts. Knobby is ruined, and he fires Joe, who, sob, slinks home. While Knobby is drowning his sorrows in a saloon, he overhears Jack Mulfie, manager of Jack McSwatt, the champion, telling the bartender that he is looking for a pushover opponent for a five-round exhibition in Wilkes-Barre. For $200 Knobby gets Joe, who knows nothing about the money, or, for that matter, boxing, but who is eager to help dear Mr. Walsh. Joe shows up for the fight wearing polka-dotted swimming trunks, and for the first four rounds he takes a dreadful drubbing from McSwatt, who laughs as he counts the punches he bounces off Joe's chin. But Joe won't give up despite Knobby's guilt-stricken pleas to quit. Just as the bell rings for the start of the fifth, Knobby gets an idea: he tells Joe that McSwatt is the head of the gang that looted his haberdashery. "W-What?" exclaims Joe. "WHY DINT YOUSE TELL ME!!!" He rushes at McSwatt shouting, "YOUSE UN-HONIST CROOK!" He belts McSwatt to the canvas with a mighty right and, as the referee tolls the knockout, Joe yells, "GET UP AND I'LL GIVE YOUSE MORE—" Inasmuch as a five-round exhibition was then considered an official fight in Pennsylvania, Joe is declared the champ, and he is carried on the shoulders of the cheering crowd to his dressing room, blushing furiously and mumbling, "Tch tch." He tells Knobby that since he hates fighting he will defend the title "only against crooks an' bullies."

Joe is true to his pledge. He takes on a series of villainous contenders, usually symbolized—as western badmen are by black hats—by gigantic unshaven jaws, slant eyes and agitated beads of sweat popping off their foreheads. They invariably curse, &!$%!, but no matter what they do Joe always triumphs. With Joe, right is might, and since he is the essence of goodness he never loses. Oddly enough, he never fought a black man. Occasionally Joe Louis, Sugar Ray Robinson or some other black fighter would ask Fisher about this, and his standard reply was, "But how would you feel when Joe beat him?"

Fisher considered himself an ultraliberal when it came to politics, and the strip had one of the few black characters in the funnies, Smokey, the valet. In the early days Smokey was a black-faced, pancake-toting bundle of "yowsuhs" and laughs, but throughout the 1930s he began to lose some of his Uncle Tom characteristics and reached the point where he was not only valet and cook but "sparring partner and revered companion," as well. Smokey also began to grow lighter and lighter in color, until one day, in the early 1940s, he suddenly disappeared altogether from the strip and has not been seen since. At the time of his disappearance Smokey, so Al Capp says, was sounding like John Gielgud.

Besides boxing, romance was one of the main themes of the strip. Shortly after winning the title, Joe meets the socially prominent Ann Howe, who happens to visit his training camp on a lark. She is immediately struck by his modest and simple manner, and she invites him to her home. Mr. Howe is the head of the cheese industry in the United States, and Mrs. Howe is a complete snob. Like Ann's friends, she disapproves of Palooka, but Ann stands up for him: "He's just the most lovable innocent baby ever lived! Can you show me one man in our set who's as clean or fine? Ooh how I love him! I want to love him to death! I want to snuggle him—mother him—I—I—." Knobby tries to break up the romance—"You gotta cut her out! It ain't good for yer racket. . . . Ya know she's too high sassiety fer youse, and ya'd only make it tough fer her!"—but Joe, gulp, gulp, gulp, is in love. Joe and Ann commence their rocky, eighteen-year-long engagement, which is sporadically threatened by plane crashes, title fights, wars and amnesia. In a 1933 strip Joe tells Ann why they cannot marry at once. "I certny wunt have youse marry me until I kin give youse ever'thing in the world," he says, overlooking the fact that as champ he must certainly be in the big money. Ann replies, "I wish you didn't feel you have to have money for me, precious. I'd gladly live in poverty with you. It would be paradise."

By the mid-1930s the strip had become fantastically successful. It was appearing in more than 600 newspapers and had more than 50 million readers. When, after one fight, Joe announced that he had eaten nothing but cheese during training, the sales of cheese shot up so spectacularly that the National Cheese Institute gratefully crowned Fisher "Cheese King of 1937." Fisher himself was well on the way to making $250,000 a year just from the strip alone, and he added to this with royalties from radio, movies, comic books and a slew of enterprises using the Palooka image. He hobnobbed with the rich and famous, and he drew them into his strip. Joe boxed with Dempsey and Tunney, and the strip was peopled with such celebrities as Clark Gable, Bing Crosby, Fiorello LaGuardia, Jimmy Walker, Claudette Colbert and Jim Farley. Occasionally a regular character in the strip would be modeled on someone in real life such as Ruffy Balonki, the crude hairy challenger, obviously patterned after Tony Galento, and the rotund Humphrey Pennyworth, for whom Toots Shor is supposed to have served as inspiration. All in all, Palooka was so prosperous that Fisher was able to hire assistants to do most of the work for him. After receiving the story line, they would draw and color the strip, except for blank ovals indicating Palooka's face. When an installment was ready for McNaught, Fisher would arrive at the studio groaning mightily, roll up his sleeves and draw the faces. No assistant was allowed to touch Joe's face. "It was like some sacred relic," Capp recalls. "Nothing profane could go into that place."

For all his success, Fisher remained a tight man with a dollar. In a bitter memoir entitled "I Remember Monster," which appeared in the *Atlantic Monthly*, Capp wrote of Fisher, without naming him, "It was my privilege, as a boy, to be associated with a certain treasure-trove of lousiness, who, in the normal course of each day of his life, managed to be, in dazzling succession, every conceivable kind of a heel. . . . From my study of this one l'il man, I have been able to create an entire gallery of horrors. For instance, when I must create a character who is the ultimate in cheapness, I don't, like less fortunate cartoonists, have to rack my brain wondering what real bottom-of-the-barrel cheapness is like. I saw the classic of 'em all. Better than that, I was the victim of it."

Capp modeled Soft-Hearted John, a paragon of penuriousness, on Fisher. In turn, Fisher accused Capp of having stolen the idea of Li'l Abner from Big Leviticus, a repugnant hillbilly character who fought Palooka in the early '30s. Capp retorted by lampooning Fisher as Happy Vermin, a cheap cartoonist who kept L'il Abner locked in a dimly lit closet drawing a comic strip about hillbillies for which Vermin grabbed all the credit. "I'm proud of having created these characters!!" Vermin exults to L'il Abner. "They'll make millions for me!! And if they do—I'll get you a new light bulb!!"

Fisher's feuds aside, Palooka plodded onward and upward in public esteem. Perhaps his best-remembered adventure of the 1930s was his enlistment in the Foreign Legion. It seems that after a particularly grueling fight Joe is accused of carrying his opponent the distance so gamblers can make a betting coup. At about the same time, Joe has a minor tiff with Knobby and, out of desperation, he and Smokey join the Legion. But to Fisher's loudly announced public anguish, it appears that anyone who then joined the Legion could never get out, and to resolve the situation Fisher got permission from the White House to have President Franklin Delano Roosevelt intercede. F.D.R. was shown in the strip two days running, telling Knobby that he had persuaded the President of France to discharge Joe. After that Fisher was a somewhat familiar figure in Washington, and he took to referring to the President as "Frank" when he was back in New York.

The greatest change in Joe occurred when he enlisted in the Army in 1940. His language started to improve. He began saying "shouldn't" instead of "shunt," because Fisher wanted him to serve as a model soldier. Despite his newly acquired polish, Joe himself realized he couldn't become commissioned—"I don't diserve t'be an' don't know enuff t'be"—and he served as a private for six years. Fisher later claimed that the expression "GI Joe" originated with Palooka.

The outbreak of war gave Fisher the chance to preach, using the strip as his soapbox, and he became a moralist second only to Walter Winchell. The crooks and bullies of the prize ring became the fascist rats of Nazi Germany. "THE WORLD'S GOTTA BE RID OF FAS-CISTS EV'RYWHERE!!" Joe exclaims to Jerry Leemy, his Army buddy from Greenpernt, while both are on duty with the French underground. Villainous Germans seem to surround Joe. While giving a boxing exhibition with Biff Williams aboard a troopship, Joe is washed overboard. A German sub surfaces, Joe clambers aboard, kayoes the captain with a left hook and captures the vessel. Aboard another troopship, a German spy inadvertently bunks with Joe. Joe clobbers the fellow, who has the rather odd habit of opening a porthole in the blacked-out ship and signaling with lighted kitchen matches. There was a bit of a furor when Joe shot a German soldier in the back during the North African campaign, but Joe didn't pay any mind. While serving with Yugoslav Partisans he helps ambush a German patrol. "Nize shooding, Choe," says Big Mike, a Partisan, but Joe answers, "Only got two, tch tch!"

Back on the home front, an escaped German prisoner of war with a gigantic unshaven jaw is captured by Knobby and a friend. When he boasts that the Nazis are going to murder everyone in the United States—"Ya! Like Rotterdam and Varsaw—Ha ha"—Knobby holds a gun while his friend beats up the German. He belts the German with a left hook to the jaw ("Fer the women an' kids you rats killed in London—"), a right smash to the nose ("Fer th' French an' th' Dutch an' th' Cath'lics an' th' Poles an' th' Protestants an' Czechs an' Jews—") and a savage wallop to the belly ("An' that was fer the soldier that fed ya an' ya killed at th' prison camp—"). The Nazi sags to the ground mumbling, "Kamerad Kamerad," while in the background a curvy blonde in a bathing suit, armed with a club, says, "Please—Please let me smash him."

From time to time, Joe returns from overseas to lend a hand on the home front. He and Knobby attend a party given by a blackmarket profiteer. The guests are only interested in a good time, and when Joe starts telling them about the war instead of his title fight with Red Rodney, one says, "Oh, don't be gloomy," while another pouts, "Give him a drink." But Joe tells them all off: "I've just come back from where the fightin's goin' on—there's kids dyin' out there an' I can't wait t'get back alongside of 'em."

Joe took so many cracks at the Nazis that Fisher liked to boast he was number one on Hermann Göring's liquidation list for the United States. While Göring was under arrest awaiting the Nürnberg Trials, an American correspondent asked him about Joe Palooka and Ham Fisher. Göring said he had never heard of either. When Fisher learned of this he was heartbroken.

The war over, Joe returned to the ring. He had a tough fight with Humphrey Pennyworth, the blacksmith from West Wokkington Falls, Ohio, and only managed to win when Pennyworth, knocked to the canvas, was unable to rise because his behind was stuck fast in the crushed ring floor.

By the late 1940s, public pressure was mounting for Joe's marriage to Ann. The wedding finally took place at the Palooka homestead in Wilkes-Barre on June 24, 1949, and in keeping with his notion that Joe was a living, breathing human being Fisher mailed out engraved invitations. Among those who accepted were Chief Justice Fred Vinson, Attorney General Tom Clark and General Omar Bradley. "I want to make the Joe Palooka marriage the realest and loveliest kind of marriage," Fisher said. "They're going to be the ideally happy and adjusted couple."

Unfortunately for Fisher, he himself was not happy in the years that followed. He suffered from diabetes and complained of failing eyesight. He would rage endlessly about Capp. In February 1955 the board of governors of the National Cartoonists Society suspended Fisher for "conduct unbecoming a member." The society charged that he had used altered drawings of *L'il Abner* to prove Capp's work was pornographic. A few days after Christmas that same year Fisher ended his life by taking an overdose of pills.

Moe Leff, an assistant, carried on the strip before leaving in 1959. The McNaught Syndicate engaged another artist, Tony DiPreta, who had worked as an assistant on *Mickey Finn* with Lank Leonard. Nowadays DiPreta draws the strip from scripts submitted to the syndicate by several free-lance writers. Any number of the old characters are still hanging around. Some have aged, some haven't. Little Max, the mute shoeshine boy, is still about nine. On the other hand, Joe's little sister, Rosie, has grown up. Humphrey Pennyworth still lives in West Wokkington Falls, and every once in a while he makes a trip to New York on his tricycle. Jerry Leemy, who made a fortune with Pennyworth setting up a chain of Humphreyburger restaurants across the country, has retired from business and passes the time playing the horses. It is a sign of the times that Leemy never mentions the Dodgers anymore.

Joe and Knobby own a restaurant in Manhattan, but Joe's life is centered, at least in the Sunday strips, on his home life in Old Greenwich with Ann and their two children, Joannie, who has been eight for the last several years, and Buddy, who seems to have stopped growing at four. Joe is still heavyweight champ, but he hasn't put on the gloves in years. He leads a nice suburban life, but it is a dull one to many readers. Instead of boxing, he goes skiing with Knobby or bluefishing with Leemy. Sometimes he takes the kids sledding. Joe still looks as fit as he did in the past—if anything, his shoulders have broadened—but he lacks the zip. Gone are the plots of the prize ring. The villains of yesteryear are no more. Life seems drab for Joe and even for Ann. The strip is stale. Happily, there is some talk that Joe may soon return to the ring. His old fans certainly hope so. Joe owes it to them. If he doesn't fight, its a $!%# shame.

*   *   *

About 150 newspapers carry Joe Palooka as a daily strip, but it is no longer a Sunday feature. Joe has returned to the ring a number of times, and he has now been the heavyweight champion of the world for fifty-one years even though he still is only twenty-nine years old.

HE BEATS THE DRUMS
FOR CHAMPS AND BUMS

HAROLD CONRAD

July 8, 1963

H AROLD CONRAD, the drumbeater, publicity man or flack, for the Liston-Patterson fight in Las Vegas, is in creative ecstasy. He is so excited about dreaming up stunts, or what he calls "gimmicks," to captivate the public that he is unable to sleep at night. Conrad lives for gimmicks. When he thinks of a particularly bright one, he is overjoyed. He figures he needs at least a dozen good gimmicks for a heavyweight title fight. He doles them out over a four-week period, beginning with the more basic gimmicks that set the mood (grimly determined underdog, blithely confident champ) and ending up, a few days before the fight, with the superdupers (secret sparring, hushed-up injury, the visiting hypnotist). Each week Conrad dispenses a ration of gimmicks according to a planned schedule of hoopla. On a Sunday, a slow news day, he might plan to have the underdog flatten a sparring partner. On a Thursday, when the TV people are in town, he will arrange to have one of the managers chased from the opponent's training camp.

What makes these gimmicks distinctive is that: a) they are plausible, and b) they are artfully based, somewhere, somehow, on the truth. When, for instance, a manager is tossed out of the rival camp, it is not because the ouster was faked but because Conrad knew that the manager would be thrown out if he dared to appear. Of course, it was Conrad who not only suggested that the manager show up but also who tipped off the other side that the "bum" was in the crowd. Indeed, Conrad treads the delicate line of truth with such mingled brass and aplomb that Ben Hecht hailed him as a "press wizard," and Budd Schulberg modeled the character of Eddie Lewis, the sportswriter turned fight publicity man, in *The Harder They Fall* on him. In his last movie Humprey Bogart played Eddie Lewis, and Schulberg says, "Close your eyes, and the legendary Bogie sounds like our very own Harold Conrad."

Conrad is unlike any other drumbeater in recent years. Instead of being short, squat, rumpled and cigar-smoking, he is tall, slender, well-tailored and addicted to a cigarette holder. Elegant is the word that Conrad's friends use to describe him. On the most routine working day, he can be found dispensing hokum in a $250 suit, an ascot and dark glasses. His ensemble is so sartorially striking that Sonny Liston and his manager, Jack Nilon, are often slack jawed in awe. Once when Nilon managed to pull himself together for a contemptuous snort, Conrad dismissed him with a flick of a manicured hand. "I'm around to give you bums some class," he said.

Conrad is the thinking man's press agent. In his spare hours he reads omnivorously, paints abstracts and finishes furniture culled from the Salvation Army. He is married to Mara Lynn, an actress-dancer who has appeared in films *(Let's Make Love)*, on the stage *(This Was Burlesque)* and in numerous television shows. With their nine-year-old son, Casey, they live in a cavernous old-fashioned Manhattan apartment that Conrad has done up in burnt ocher and black. "Who else but Harold would have dared to have done that?" asks Dr. Carl Fulton Sulzberger, a psychiatrist friend and old Broadway buddy. "Harold has superb taste."

Conrad has, among other things, been a Broadway columnist; shot pool with Leo Durocher; done publicity for a Florida gambling house run by Frank Costello and Joe Adonis (his job was to keep the joint's name *out* of the papers); "won" a gold medal for the United States in the 1948 Olympics (while working for J. Arthur Rank, he forced a

British producer to show a film of the 400-meter relay race that proved the United States was not guilty of a technical violation); written Joe Palooka radio scripts (Ham Fisher, the Palooka cartoonist and a slow payer, used to mollify Conrad by inserting his name in the strip); and maintained fervent friendships with Serge Rubenstein and Ed Leven, two of the most gifted swindlers of the time.

Milton Berle, an old Hollywood acquaintance, esteems Conrad as a first-rate raconteur, and, for a while, the Duke of Windsor found him to be a charming drinking companion on the Riviera. Conrad met the duke one summer while trying to buy Monte Carlo for an American syndicate. The deal fell through, but Conrad passed the evenings buying rounds for the duke and talking about boxing, while the duchess played chemin de fer with Louis Jourdan. The relationship came to an end one night after the duke toddled off to bed. "How come the duke never springs for a drink?" Conrad happened to inquire of the bartender, an Englishman. As Conrad recalls it, "The bartender drew himself up like a fusilier and said, 'Sir, the King never buys!' "

Sophisticate that he is, Conrad has been stunned but once in his life, and that after Robert Harrison, the publisher of *Confidential*, asked him to do a film script based on the magazine. Given the key to the magazine's secret files, Conrad spent a couple of entranced days going through them, emerging with a pair of sprained eyeballs. He never wrote the script (the idea of putting pen to paper apparently caused his hand to become unsteady) and even today, when asked about the experience, his face glazes over and he is only able to muster a dazed, "Wow, gee, golly."

Much of Conrad's deep interest in boxing stems from his fascination with the rogues populating the sport. He looks upon them as works of art that should be esteemed in an all too pedestrian time, and when he encounters an old character such as Evil Eye Finkel, of Slobodka Stare and Double Whammy notoriety, he will spend an hour chatting at close quarters, even if the Eye has not been bathing of late.

Conrad first became involved with boxing in his late teens when he went to work for his hometown *Brooklyn Eagle*. At the time there was at least one club fight going every night, and Conrad covered them all, including the Broadway Arena, where the boys from Murder, Inc. hung out, giving one another hotfoots and forcing spiced candy on fans in the lobby.

Around the *Eagle*, Conrad was a dapper figure who dazzled the staff.

He took to wearing a chesterfield and derby and squiring Manhattan show girls. He became friendly with Damon Runyon and, from the late 1930s until the outbreak of World War II, he wrote a thrice-a-week Broadway column for the *Eagle*. Once a year he talked the paper into sending him to Hollywood for two weeks, where he furthered his taste for high living.

During the war Conrad served in the Army Air Corps, first in Intelligence, then as a publicity man for the show, *Winged Victory*. He never rose higher than private first class, but at a distance he was often taken for a general since he wore a gorgeous uniform tailored for him by a theatrical costumer. After the service he returned briefly to the *Eagle*, worked as nightclub and movie editor on the *Mirror* and ghosted a novel, *The Curtain Never Falls*, an amusing tale about a comic who is a heel, for Joey Adams, the comedian. According to friends, Conrad dashed it off in six weeks, and at the end of every week he would dispatch a finished chapter to Adams, who was out on the road with a nightclub act. Adams would toss the manuscript on the breakfast table the next morning and say to his cronies, "Gee, I'm bushed. My fingers are sore again from typing all night." When the novel appeared it received excellent reviews, and Adams went around saying he had written it about Milton Berle. Actually, Conrad had based the character on Adams. (Conrad himself will not admit that he wrote the novel for Adams. He does, however, proudly own up to authorship of another novel, *Battle of Apache Pass*, which he wrote under his own name. "This Cochise was a hell of a character," he says.)

In the late 1940s, Conrad moved to the Coast, where one of his first jobs was acting as press agent for something known as the American Rollerskating Championships, then held in Oakland. While there he looked up Casey Stengel, an old friend from Brooklyn who was managing the Oakland team in the Pacific Coast League. "We had a couple of drinks," Conrad recalls, "and I asked Casey if he would do me a favor. 'What is it?' he asked. I tell him all I want him to do is put on a pair of skates and pose for photographers. He says, 'Sure, just as long as I don't have to skate. I don't know how.' So he's game. I get the photographers and put the skates on Casey. Just as he stands up, I give him a good shove from behind, and he goes sailing! We got a lot of space with that."

Conrad spent the early 1950s in Hollywood writing movie scripts. He never made a big score financially, but he had an active social life palling around with the late Serge Rubenstein. "I met him when he first got out of the can," Conrad says. "You had to admire his ingenuity. Here was a guy who could control the market, steal the Bank of Japan, shake the Bank of France. That's really moving! What a background! Why, his father was Rasputin's accountant." Rubenstein had a Napoleon complex, and everywhere he went he carried a Napoleon uniform with him. "He could hardly wait for a costume party," Conrad says, "even if he had to throw it himself." Few persons cared to attend Rubenstein's soirees because of his notoriety, but Conrad was always on hand. "I had to be *there*," he says. "You can imagine the characters who went."

Conrad introduced Rubenstein to Ed Leven, a young Hollywood con man. Leven looked up to Rubenstein as a god. Rubenstein so admired Leven that he refused to become involved with him legally. The closest they ever came to a deal was when Rubenstein okayed Leven's credit, which was nonexistent, with Harry Winston, the New York jeweler. As a result, Leven, who was hoping to marry Dolly Fritz, a San Francisco heiress, obtained a $6,000 engagement ring on approval. Alas, private detectives hired by Miss Fritz's guardians broke up the romance. Knowing observers speculated that if Leven had succeeded in marrying Miss Fritz he would have split the swag with Rubenstein. Conrad denies this. "All Rubenstein wanted," he says, "was a chance to sell Leven some stock."

In show-business circles, Leven is celebrated for his gall, and there are any number of people who try to top one another with "Leven stories." As Leven's closest friend—if friend is the word—Conrad figures in most of the stories and is held as the supreme arbiter of their authenticity. For several years Leven was a producer in Hollywood. His greatest epic was a film with the appropriate title of *Run for the Hills*. It starred Sonny Tufts and Barbara Payton. Just as Leven was about to start production on the picture, he was tossed into jail for traffic violations. But his luck held: he met an agent locked up on a drunk charge, and by the time the agent's bail had been posted, he and Leven had finished casting the minor roles.

"Leven was always looking to hustle money," Conrad says. "He always had a script of some sort. I suspected him immediately, but I didn't want to believe it. When a guy's talking millions, that's big numbers. You're hoping against hope, and you bulldoze yourself. He was always dropping big names, and he seemed to be some sort of a financial genius. He came up with something new all the time, and his deals always missed just by a hairline, so you couldn't write him off."

Once Conrad lent Leven $4 for gas so he could drive to Palm Springs to buy RKO from Howard Hughes for $18 million. "Leven had it all planned," Conrad says. "He was going to be head of the studio, and I was head writer. He had the whole deal wrapped up. But then it turned out that the two guys backing Leven were really only looking to establish a bigger credit rating of their own, and the minute it was mentioned in the press that they were offering $18 million for RKO, they had made their point. They withdrew and told Leven to get lost. But by this time Leven's hanging around my joint and doing all his business on my phone. He owed $450, and the phone company shut the service off. Out there they don't fool around. He was looking for money to produce *Run for the Hills*. After the picture, he said he had to go east, but we could have his car, a big Cadillac. We have it two weeks and a cop on Sunset Boulevard stops my wife and says it's a stolen car." The Conrads became fed up with Leven, especially after he spread the word that he was tired of having Conrad sponge off him, and so on his birthday Mara baked a cake and wrote on the icing, "To Leven, a complete rat." "Mara was serious," Conrad says, "but that didn't bother Leven. He cried and said, 'No one ever baked a cake for me before.' "

When Rubenstein was murdered in New York and Leven went to San Francisco county jail for grand theft and thence to San Quentin twice (the first time for violation of the labor code and the second for violation of parole), this broke up what Conrad calls his "great quinella." He moved back East and spent several years writing scripts, mostly for pilot films that never got off the ground. Before the second Patterson-Johansson fight in 1963, Conrad returned to his first love, boxing, this time as a publicist. After his experience in Hollywood, he had a head start on anyone else.

Conrad likens his role in building up a fight to that of a producer casting a spectacular. "Once the sportswriters rely upon you, you can get away with a lot of things," he says. "Not lies, but you can broaden things. Tongue in cheek. Fun things. Cus D'Amato is one of the real characters. Of course, maybe D'Amato is for real. He's a method actor. He can register any emotion, and you believe it. Anger! He's angry. Amazement! He's amazed. He's better than Brando. Up in Toronto for the Patterson-McNeeley fight, we staged an argument about $1 million that was supposed to be put up. So Cus and I have this argument in front of two local reporters. D'Amato's yelling he's calling the fight off, and of course, we want the local guys to print that. I say to the two guys, 'Now, fellows, don't print that.' And they say, 'We won't. We don't want to hurt you.' I'm going crazy. The writers start to leave, because they don't want to intrude while D'Amato's yelling he's taking the fight out. Cus and I had to follow them out of the room. 'Don't print this story,' D'Amato's telling them. They keep saying they won't. What can we do? Finally D'Amato offers to give one of them a lift in his car. Then I knew that writer was had. Ten minutes alone with D'Amato, and D'Amato could sell him anything. I take the other writer, and I say to him, 'Gee, I'll bet that guy's going to write the story about Cus canceling the fight and your paper's going to get stuck.' And the windup, of course, is that both guys print the story.

"Then I decide to build up McNeeley," Conrad continues. "I find out there's an old boxer training at night in McNeeley's gym in Toronto. So I told the gym man not to say who's training, and I let the word out that something's going on in the gym at night. It was great. The newspapers started writing about McNeeley holding secret practice. And then when McNeeley denied it—which was the truth—that made it a better story. If the writers had come to me, I would have said I didn't say McNeeley was training. I only said I understood some guy was training secretly. You lie to writers once, and you're dead. But you have to leave a lot of loopholes."

Sometimes a gimmick will just happen. "Before the Liston-Patterson fight in Chicago," Conrad says, "Jimmy Grippo, the hypnotist, writes a letter to each fighter offering to hypnotize him so he can't feel the punches. Grippo is trying to work it so neither fighter knows about his offer to the other fighter. But he scrambles the letters in the envelopes, so Liston gets the letter to Patterson, and Patterson gets the letter to Liston.

"This is a natural! I put D'Amato on the Jack Eigen radio show, and he really shouts about how Liston is trying to pull something with a hypnotist. The next morning Cus is with the reporters, and I say to him, like I'm disgusted, 'These guys need copy and you drop a story like that on radio.' Immediately all the writers get excited and yell, 'What? What?' They're hooked. This is great psychology. Now they're begging Cus to tell them. If he had told them straight out, they would have said, 'What are you trying to sell us?' Now they're asking for the story. So D'Amato announces he's going to the commission with a hypnotist. Everyone was all primed. Newsreels, television, everyone! Cus gets a hypnotist, and this hypnotist hypnotized a dame, touched her with a torch, belted her, and Cus says that this conclusively proves his argument that a hypnotized boxer does not feel pain. Boy, we got a lot of space on that. This is what hooks people who are not fight fans alone. You have to get the public aroused."

To Conrad, the timing is just as important as the gimmicks. "You have to plan it so you'll reach your peak a week before the fight," he says. "Then all the writers come in and take over, and you no longer have to sweat, because they're there. Everything is ready. You've created the hysteria. And the writers are excited by all the space you've gotten before they arrived. One reason I made the most out of having all the longhair guys—Norman Mailer, James Baldwin, Budd Schulberg, Gerald Kersh—in Chicago is that you don't see these guys at a World Series, a pro football playoff or the Stanley Cup. But at a big fight you do, and I think the sportswriters are impressed. Guys are still talking about the scene."

Although Conrad eschews the sensational, a gimmick has occasionally threatened to backfire. Before the third Patterson-Johansson fight, Conrad gave Oscar Fraley, the UPI columnist, an inside tip about Johansson's alleged doping in the second fight. "I never said Johansson was poisoned," Conrad says, throwing up his hands in honest-Injun fashion. "But Whitey Bimstein, who was training Johansson, said, 'Gee, I think he was doped.' So that makes it a story for Fraley. The *Journal-American* picks it up and runs a headline: JOHANSSON DOPED. So three days later two guys from the [United States Senate] Kefauver Committee come in to see Johansson and Bimstein. I speak to these guys and I say, 'You mean this is the way you two guys operate? You want to come in on the tail end of my publicity? You believe everything you read in the papers?' The fight was going great, and so they want to get on the bandwagon. Oh. I really let 'em have it."

The second Liston-Patterson fight should present Conrad with the severest challenge of his career. On form, the fight looks like a flop. The last time the fighters met, Liston knocked out Patterson in the first two minutes and six seconds of the first round. It was no contest. Before that, Liston also knocked out his previous opponent in one round. But Conrad, who will be trying to build up the Vegas fight as an even battle, has already figured his angle.

"Why, Liston's fought less than five minutes in two years," he says. "He's probably rusty."

Liston's complaint of an injured left knee has also been duly noted by Conrad, and should Sonny catch an act at a local hotel, Conrad will spread word of his nightclubbing. By the time the bell rings, Liston will have been billed as a creaking overweight cripple. At the same time Conrad is deflating Liston, he will be building up Patterson, who can be counted on to make only one public appearance (at a Boy Scout encampment where he will talk about the merits of clean living), hold hush-hush drills and impress visiting experts like Al Weill who will exclaim over his fitness and determination. In the meanwhile, Conrad will see to it that pictures of Patterson regaining the title from Johansson are shown at every Elks smoker in Nevada, the moral being it can happen again.

And, of course, there will be other gimmicks galore, some of them superdupers now taking form in Conrad's feverish mind. "This is the creative part of the business," he says, all aglow. "It's the Hollywood bit. It's show business. The writers love it. The younger writers eat it up. This is a new thing to them. They're around baseball, pro football—they don't get this kind of action there. The fight racket has got characters and hoopla. What would the scoffers do without the fight racket? What would they do without fighters to belt? There's all the scheming and intrigue leading up to the fight, then the fight itself. There's no moment like that moment before a heavyweight championship fight. It reaches you. It has to. It's the biggest thing in American sports. Now if all this hoopla had been built up for a phony wrestling match, this would be anticlimactic. But it isn't. It's for a big event, the biggest. The intrigue all leads up to it, and the more hung up you get with the hoopla, the bigger the moment is."

* * *

Harold Conrad keeps busy writing and promoting. He was the promotion coordinator of the "Thrilla in Manila" between Muhammad Ali and Joe Frazier. "No hard sell there," he says. "The government said, 'Go or else.' The joint was packed." With an introduction by Budd Schulberg and a foreword by Norman Mailer, Conrad's Dear Muffo, *a collection of his letters to UPI correspondent Bub Musel about friends and acquaintances, such as Muhammad Ali, Joe Adonis, Lucky Luciano, Ernest Hemingway, Erich Remarque, A. J. Liebling, and Meyer Lansky, is scheduled to be published in 1982.*

AN ABSENCE
OF WOOD NYMPHS

VLADIMIR NABOKOV

September 14, 1959

T O AN army of admirers, Vladimir Nabokov, a bald-
ing Russian émigré of sixty, is best known as the author of the spectacular bestseller *Lolita*. To a comparative handful, however, he is V.
Nabokov, lepidopterist. Respectful colleagues have named four species
of butterflies after him. He is the discoverer of at least two subspecies of
butterflies, one of which, it should be noted, is called (accidentally, but
prophetically) Nabokov's wood nymph.

Nabokov has described his findings, usually signed V. Nabokov, in a
number of scientific periodicals ranging from *Psyche*—"A Third Species
of *Echinargus* Nabokov (Lycaenidae, Lepidoptera)"—to the *Bulletin* of
the Museum of Comparative Zoology at Harvard College—"The
Nearctic Members of the Genus *Lycaeides* Hübner (Lycaenidae,
Lepidoptera)." Rarely can the reader deduce that V. Nabokov, the
lepidopterist, is Vladimir Nabokov, the novelist. Only when writing for
the *Lepidopterists' News*, a rather chatty journal, is V. likely to peep

124   AN ABSENCE OF WOOD NYMPHS

through as Vladimir: "Every morning the sky would be an impeccable blue at 6 A.M. when I set out. The first innocent cloudlet would scud across at 7:30 A.M. Bigger fellows with darker bellies would start tampering with the sun around 9 A.M., just as I emerged from the shadow of the cliffs and onto good hunting grounds." Conversely, Vladimir sometimes artfully assumes V.'s vocabulary, as in describing Humbert Humbert's first wife in *Lolita*: "The bleached curl revealed its melanic root." Melanic is an entomological term meaning "with a blackish suffusion."

Nabokov has had a passionate interest in butterflies since he was a boy of six in Russia. By the time he was ten, he had made such a nuisance of himself with the net that solemn Muromtsev, the president of the first Russian Duma, intoned, "Come with us by all means, but do not chase butterflies, child. It mars the rhythm of the promenade." In 1919 in the Crimea, a bowlegged Bolshevik sentry, patrolling "among shrubs in waxy bloom," attempted to arrest him for allegedly signaling with the net to a British warship in the Black Sea. Later, in France, a fat policeman wriggled on his belly through parting grass to observe whether or not Nabokov was netting birds. Shortly after Nabokov arrived in the United States in 1940, he became a Research Fellow at the Museum of Comparative Zoology at Harvard, one place, presumably, where his passion was better appreciated. In 1948 he became a member of the Department of Literature at Cornell, but he has kept his summers free for his beloved butterflies. Net in hand, he roams the West, unmindful of hooting motorists, chiding cowpokes or snarling dogs that, he says, "ordinarily wouldn't bark at the worst bum."

In late May of 1959 Nabokov and his wife, Véra, were staying in a cabin at Forest Houses in Oak Creek Canyon, a sort of watchpocket Grand Canyon, eighteen serpentine miles south of Flagstaff, Arizona. There, tucked away in the woods, Nabokov devoted himself to literature (working on translations of the *Song of Igor's Campaign*, the twelfth-century Russian epic, and *Invitation to a Beheading*, a novel he wrote in Paris during the 1930s) and lepidoptera. For a couple of days, lepidoptera won out.

On a Monday morning, for instance, Nabokov, dressed in dungarees, sport shirt and sweater, emerged from his pine cabin to sniff the air and see the morning sun. "It is now nine o'clock," he said, lying. It was really only eight-thirty, but Nabokov keeps moving all of his clocks and watches ahead to make his wife move faster so he can get to his butterflies all the sooner. "The butterflies won't be up for another hour," he admitted, however. "This is a deep canyon, and the sun has to go some way up the rim of the mountain to cast its light. The grass is damp, and the butterflies generally come out when it's dry. They are late risers. Of course, in the plains they are up earlier at eight o'clock and flying merrily."

He moved inside, sat down on a sofa and picked up a thick brown volume entitled *Colorado Butterflies*. He opened to Nabokov's Wood Nymph on page eleven. "This butterfly which I discovered has nothing to do with nymphets," he said, smiling. "I discovered it in the Grand Canyon in 1941. I know it occurs here, but it is difficult to find. I hope to find it today. I'll be looking for it. It flies in the speckled shade early in June, though there's another brood at the end of the summer, so you came at the right time." He turned to page 161 showing Nabokov's Blue. "Another group of butterflies I'm interested in are called Blues. This I discovered in Telluride in southwest Colorado." He picked up another book, Alexander Klots's *A Field Guide to the Butterflies*, and opened to the page on the Orange-Margined Blues. Proudly, he pointed to a sentence which read, "The recent work of Nabokov has entirely rearranged the classification of this genus." A look of bliss spread across his face. "The thrill of gaining information about certain structural mysteries in these butterflies is perhaps more pleasurable than any literary achievement," he said. Two pages later he pointed to the entry on *Lycaeides melissa samuelis*, a subspecies known as the Karner Blue, and said, "I discovered it and named it *samuelis* after Samuel Scudder, probably one of the greatest lepidopterists who ever lived. Karner is a little railway station between Schenectady and Albany. People go there on Sundays to picnic, shedding papers and beer cans. Among this, the butterfly."

Mrs. Nabokov called him to breakfast—soft-boiled eggs, toast and coffee. "The Southwest is a wonderful place to collect," he said over his soft-boiled eggs. "There's a mixture of arctic and subtropical fauna. A wonderful place to collect."

At 9:35, (Nabokov standard time) he got up to get his net and a blue cloth cap. The thrill of the chase was upon him as he left the cabin and headed south down a foot trail paralleling Oak Creek. "Good luck, Professor!" the motel manager shouted. Nabokov chuckled. His eyes sweeping the brush on either side of the trail, Nabokov said, "This Nabokov's Wood Nymph is represented by several subspecies, and there's one here. It is in this kind of country that my nymph occurs."

He stopped and pointed with the handle of his net to a butterfly clinging to the underside of a leaf. "Disruptive coloration," he said, noting the white spots on the wings. "A bird comes and wonders for a second. Is it two bugs? Where is the head? Which side is which? In that split second the butterfly is gone. That second saves that individual and that species. You may call it a large Skipper."

Nabokov walked on. At 9:45, he gave a quick flick with the net. "This is a checkered butterfly," he said, looking at his catch. "There are countless subspecies. The way I kill is the European, or Continental, way. I press the thorax at a certain point like this. If you press the abdomen, it just oozes out." He took the butterfly from the net and held it in the palm of his hand. "This," he exclaimed, "is a beauty! Such a beautiful fresh specimen. *Melitaea anicia*." He took a Band-Aid box from his pocket, shook loose a Glassene envelope and slid *Melitaea anicia* home to rest. "It's safe in the envelope until I can get to a laboratory and spread it."

In good spirits, he pushed on. Something fluttered across the trail. "A common species," he said, walking on, maneuvering the net before him. "The thing is," he said, "when you hit the butterfly, turn the net at the same time to form a bag in which the butterfly is imprisoned." No sooner had he spoken than he darted forward. "A large male!" he cried as he deftly made a backhand volley. He held the net up for examination. "I'm not going to kill it," he said. "A common species." He released the butterfly which flew off.

Nearby, another butterfly was feeding on a flower, but Nabokov ignored it. "A dusky-wing Skipper. Common." At 10:03, he passed a *clarus* sitting on a bare twig. "I've seen that same individual on the same twig since I've been here," he said. "There are lots of butterflies around, but this individual will chase the others from its perch."

Further down the trail, Nabokov swung but missed a Blue. "Thirty-fifteen," he said. He walked off the trail into an apple orchard where he detected a Hairstreak feeding on a flower. He caught it, then released it. "Forty-fifteen," he said.

Nabokov started walking back toward the cabin. He noted a day-flying Peacock moth. "In quest of a female. It only quiets down at certain hours of the day. I have found them asleep on flowers. Oh, this is wretched work. Where is my Wood Nymph? It's heartbreaking work. Wretched work. I've traveled thousands of miles to get a species I never got. We went to Fort Davis, Texas, but there was no Wood Nymph. Toad-like sheep with their razor-sharp teeth had eaten everything. Horrible!"

At 10:45, Nabokov lunged wildly off the trail and raced up a rocky incline. Whatever it was had escaped in the underbrush. As he picked his way down, he sighed, "There I did something I shouldn't have done. I went up there without looking for rattlesnakes, but I suppose God looks after entomologists as He does after drunkards." At 11:00, he stopped short. "Ah," he said, a tremor of delight rocking him ever so slightly. "Ah. Oh, that's an interesting thing! Oh, gosh, there it goes. A white Skipper mimicking a Cabbage butterfly belonging to a different family. Things are picking up. Still, they're not quite right. Where is my Wood Nymph? It is heartbreaking work," he complained. "Wretched work."

Back at the cabin, Mrs. Nabokov, fresh from writing letters, greeted her husband in Russian. "Let us hurry, darling," he said. Mrs. Nabokov smiled indulgently and followed him down the porch steps to their car, a black 1956 Buick, where she got behind the wheel. Nabokov, who does not drive, did not want to go fast, and to be sure that his wife did not exceed forty miles an hour a warning klaxon was attached to the speedometer. But just as he moves clocks forward a half-hour, his wife moves the klaxon up to sixty. "I always put it a little higher so he doesn't know," she said as he listened intently. "Now I'll put it at forty."

The car would not start. "The car is nervous," Nabokov said. "The car?" asked Véra. "The car," said Vladimir. At last it started. Mrs. Nabokov drove onto Highway 89A and headed to a butterfly hunting ground several miles north. The klaxon went off, and Mrs. Nabokov slowed down. A motorcyclist whizzed by in the opposite direction, and Nabokov shuddered discreetly. The Nabokovs wheeled past the Chipmunk Apartments. The name delighted him. "They have considerably improved all the motels across the country," he said. "No comparison with what they were in the early '40s. I shall never forget the motel-keeperess who said, when I complained that they didn't have hot water, 'Was there any hot water on your grandmother's farm?' " A gale of laughter swept over him.

At 11:26 (Nabokov standard time), Mrs. Nabokov swung over to the left side of the road and parked by Oak Creek. Nabokov leaped out. "Now we'll see something spectacular, I hope!" He hopped across the rocks in the creek, slipped and soaked his right leg. He ignored it. His eyes were on a swarm of butterflies flitting around a puddle. "These are all males and this is their pub," he said. "They suck moisture in the ground. In mountains, European mountains, where the mules have passed and pissed, it's like a flowery carpet. And it's always the males. Always the males."

He waved farewell to his wife who had stayed on the other side of the creek, and he jogged down a rough trail. He stopped. A butterfly was sipping nectar from yellow asters. "Here's a butterfly that's quite rare. You find it here and there in Arizona. *Lemonias zela*. I've collected quite a few. It will sit there all day. We could come back at four, and it would still be here. The form of its wings and its general manner are very mothlike. Quite interesting. But it is a real butterfly. It belongs to a tremendous family of South American butterflies, and they mimic all kinds of butterflies belonging to other families. Keeping up with the Smiths, you know."

He walked on, then stopped. He said softly, "Now here is something I really want." He swung his net. " 'One flick, one dart, and it was in his net.' I'm not suggesting anything." He pressed the thorax of the prey and displayed the butterfly in his hand. "A Checker," he said, "but it seems to be another form of the butterfly we took earlier. Quite interesting. I would like to take some more."

He pushed off the trail into a stand of bushes. From behind one, he exclaimed, *"Chort!"* Reappearing he explained, "I have been doing this since I was five or six, and I find myself using the same Russian swear words. *Chort* means the devil. It's a word I never use otherwise." Back on the trail he swung his net in forehand fashion and missed a butterfly. "Fifteen all," he said.

Nabokov clambered up a pile of rocks. "Haha! Haha!" he shouted, backhanding a butterfly. "A prize! One of the best things I've taken so far. That's a darling. Wonderful! Ha, so unexpectedly. Haha, look at it on this fern. What protective coloration. *Callophrys*. I'm not sure of the species." He turned it over in his hand. "Isn't it lovely? You could travel hundreds of miles and not see one. Ha, what luck! That was so unexpected, and just as I was about to say there was nothing interesting here today. A female that has hibernated. That was very nice, very nice indeed. Quite exciting. That was one of those things that make coming here worthwhile. This will go to Cornell, this little green thing. The best way to put it is, 'A green Hairstreak not readily identified in the field.' " Beaming, Nabokov boxed it.

Woosh! Nabokov had suddenly struck again. He grinned savagely. "I took two in one diabolical stroke of my net. A female Blue. A Lygdamus female Blue, one of the many species of Blues in which I am especially interested. This other, by freakish chance, is a male Blue of another species that was flying with it. That's adultery. Or a step toward adultery." He let the offending male fly free unpunished.

Nabokov worked over a dry stream bed. "Quite a number of little things have appeared today which I haven't seen before. It's picking up. The next week will probably go much faster. I give the Wood Nymph a week to be out. I may go to Jerome for my Wood Nymph. It's a ghost town on the side of a mountain. I know of several collectors who were there and brought back my butterfly a few years ago."

He returned down the trail. Just before crossing Oak Creek to join his wife, he swung his net. "Three with one sweep of the net. This one is an Angle Wing. It has a curiously formed letter C. It mimics a chink of light through a dead leaf. Isn't that wonderful? Isn't that humorous?" He discarded the other two butterflies and danced across the creek to Véra where he carefully boxed the Angle Wing. "They won't lose any color," he said. "I saw an Indian moth, probably taken in the middle of the eighteenth century, that had been presented to Catharine the Great, and the color was still fresh. Some of the butterflies of Linnaeus, the first great naturalist, a Swede, are quite fresh. They are less fragile, I suppose, than pickled human beings."

Mrs. Nabokov headed the Buick south to Sedona for lunch. "I lost two butterfly collections," Nabokov recalled as the car sped along (someone had tampered with the klaxon). "One to the Bolsheviks, one to the Germans. I have another I gave to Cornell. I dream of stealing it back."

At 12:15, the Nabokovs drove into Sedona, which a sign proclaimed as the Flying Saucer Capital of the Universe. "It's a kind of quest, but they are going the wrong way," Nabokov said. After gathering their mail and lunching in a local restaurant, the Nabokovs drove south. "We would like to see if I can get a Blue butterfly." His eyes wallowed in the gorgeous wind-swept buttes. "It looks like a giant chess game is being played around us." At 2:20, Mrs. Nabokov parked the car by the side of the road. Net at the ready, Nabokov was off like an eager boy. "Mind the snakes," his wife called. "I'm going to inspect the grove," he said, "It interests me." Mrs. Nabokov took a net from the back seat and joined him. "You should see my wife catch butterflies," he said. "One little movement and they're in the net."

The grove was disappointing. "*Rien*," Nabokov muttered. He probed some bushes. "There is nothing," he said. "A hopeless place." He cautiously inspected a rocky area. " 'Suddenly we heard an ominous rattle, and Mr. Nabokov fell like a log.' " He went back to the car. "I'm sorry this was not a very great show," he said. "Sad." Still, he couldn't leave quite yet. He moved down the edge of the highway peering into bushes. "In Alberta you have to watch for bear." At 2:35, he got in the car, and Mrs. Nabokov drove back to Sedona to shop. There he followed her into the supermarket. "When I was younger I ate some butterflies in Vermont to see if they were poisonous," he said as his wife hovered over the cold-cuts counter. "I didn't see any difference between a Monarch butterfly and a Viceroy. The taste of both was vile, but I had no ill effects. They tasted like almonds and perhaps a green cheese combination. I ate them raw. I held one in one hot little hand and one in the other. Will you eat some with me tomorrow for breakfast?"

Back in their cabin, the Nabokovs set up drinks and hors d'oeuvres for the owners of Forest Houses, Robert Kittredge and his wife. The Kittredges arrived promptly at four (4:30 NST) and Nabokov excused them for being late. He and Kittredge, a fledgling novelist, have the same publisher in England. The conversation hopped from subject to subject. Nabokov expressed an enthusiasm for Dinah Shore and Jayne Meadows ("I like her big teeth"), his fascination for Lawrence Welk ("the most antiartistic man"), and an interest in birthdays ("William Shakespeare, Shirley Temple, and I have the same birthday, April 23rd."). Occasionally the talk would alight upon butterflies. In delight, Nabokov recalled a pregnant White butterfly that came all the way from Ireland by ship ("She laid her eggs immediately in a kitchen garden in Quebec in 1860"), a marvelous day in Alberta when he found a "treasure, a nitra Swallowtail, sitting there on bear dung."

When the Kittredges left at 6:30, Nabokov burrowed into a pile of scientific papers and pulled out the thickest one, his article on the Nearctic members of the Genus *Lycaeides* Hübner. "The most interesting part here," he said, settling himself on the sofa, "was to find the structural differences between them in terms of the male organ. These are magnified thirty-four times. These are hooks which the male has to attach to the female. Because of the differences in the size of the hooks, all males cannot copulate with all females. Suddenly in Jackson Hole, I found a hook intermediate between the two. It has the form of the short-hooked species, but the length of the long-hooked species. It is almost impossible to classify. I named it *longinus*. This work took me several years and undermined my health for quite a while. Before, I never wore glasses. This is my favorite work. I think I really did well there." Yes, the Soviets were aware of his work on butterflies. Only in November of last year, one Lubimov had attacked him in the *Literary Gazette*. "He said that I was starving in America, compelled to earn a precarious existence selling butterflies." Nabokov laughed merrily and picked up another paper, this one dealing with an elaborate count of wing scales. "It's impossible to understand," he said, beaming. "But I proved my point, and it will stand forever."

The next morning, Nabokov was as chipper and as restless as ever. "Come on, darling," he called to his wife during breakfast. "The sun is wasting away! It's a quarter to ten." Mrs. Nabokov took her time. "He doesn't know that everyone is wise to him," she said. At 10:10, Nabokov at last succeeded in luring her behind the wheel. "We are going to Jerome, a ghost town," he said happily as the car moved south on 89A. "We are looking for my butterfly, the Wood Nymph, which should be out, I hope, on Mount Mingus." While the car sped through a veritable Lolitaland ("See Tuzigoot Ruins," "See Historic Fort Verde"), Nabokov said, "Butterflies help me in my writing. Very often when I go and there are no butterflies, I am thinking. I wrote most of *Lolita* this way. I wrote it in motels or parked cars. The funny thing is in Russian the word 'motil' means moth. The English word motel spelled backwards is 'letom.' That means 'in summer' in Russian. T. S. Eliot spelled backwards is toilets. You have to transpose the t and the s. Powder backwards is red wop! Red wop! Isn't that wonderful!"

Nabokov reached Jerome ("Welcome to Ghost City. 3 Places to Eat") at 11:10. "Shall we catch my butterfly today?" Nabokov asked. While Mrs. Nabokov stopped to let the car radiator cool, Vladimir nipped into a store to ask directions. "Are you from merry old England?" the proprietor asked him. Nabokov came back to the car, and his wife drove up Mount Mingus. "We're getting into oaks and pines," he said, joyfully. "The greatest enemy of the lepidopterist is the juniper tree. Charming! Charming! Charming butterfly road!" Mrs. Nabokov swung off the road and parked by a marker announcing the elevation to be 7,023 feet. Both took nets from the back seat and walked up a dirt road bordered by pines. A yellow butterfly danced crazily by. Nabokov swung and missed. "Common," he said. "I'm just getting warmed up." A fifteen-minute search of the terrain revealed nothing.

At 12:20, Mrs. Nabokov drove to the Potato Patch Picnic Ground, a quarter of a mile back down the mountain. Nabokov headed toward an iris-covered meadow. "I can't believe there won't be butterflies here," he said. He was mistaken. "I'm very much disappointed," Nabokov said after searching the meadow. "*Rien. Rien.* Iris is not very attractive to butterflies anyway. It's rather ornamental, and that's it." On the way back to the car, Mrs. Nabokov called excitedly. "Here's a yellow! Here's a yellow!" "I saw it, darling," Nabokov replied calmly. "It is very common. Just an orange Sulphur."

Nabokov got in the car. "It was very sad. 'And then I saw that strong man put his head on his forearms and sob like a woman.' " At 12:40, Mrs. Nabokov stopped again. "This will be our last stop today," Nabokov said. Véra took a net, and they walked up a dirt road. "It is this kind of place that my nymph should be flying, but with the exception of three cows and a calf, there is nothing." "Do we have to mix with cows?" asked Mrs. Nabokov.

They got back in the car and drove back to Jerome. "Sad," said Nabokov. " 'His face was now a tear-stained mask.' " Five minutes later, he had Véra stop at Mescal Canyon. "We may be in for a surprise here," he said. Nabokov walked up a dirt road alone. Mrs. Nabokov lent her net to their visitor. With a whoop of joy, the visitor snared a white-winged beauty. Cupping it in his hands, he showed it to Nabokov who dismissed it. "A winged cliché," he said. It had been a poor day for hunting. There would be other days to come, but the visitor wouldn't be there. As the car swung out for the journey home, Nabokov spread his arms and said sadly, "What can I say? What is there to say? I am ashamed for the butterflies. I apologize for the butterflies."

* * *

Vladimir Nabokov died in Switzerland in 1977. Shortly before his death I went to Los Angeles to do a story on the El Segundo Blue butterfly that lives in the El Segundo Sand Dunes. Originally the dunes covered an area of about thirty-six square miles, but housing and other development had reduced the surviving habitat to a mere 245 acres. Almost all this acreage had been bought for $44 million by the adjacent Los Angeles International Airport for possible expansion, but inasmuch as the El Segundo Blue had recently been officially declared an endangered species by the U.S. Department of the Interior, expansion was being contested. The scientific name of the El Segundo Blue, actually a subspecies, is Shijimiaeoides battoides allyni. The subspecies name was bestowed in honor of Arthur C. Allyn, a former owner of the Chicago White Sox, a butterfly enthusiast and founder of The Allyn Museum of Entomology in Sarasota, Florida. Given Nabokov's interest in the Blues, he undoubtedly would have been amused.

ABSOLUTELY STUCK ON STAMPS

HERMAN HERST JR.

August 23, 1971

N OT LONG ago, Herman Herst, Jr., who may be the world's leading enthusiast of philately, discovered that Dr. Irving Keiser, an entomologist who specializes in stamps with pictures of insects on them, had the 1939 United States baseball issue in his collection.

"What does this stamp have to do with insects?" asked Herst.

"Look at it," said Dr. Keiser.

Herst peered at the stamp through a magnifying glass and said, "All I see is a guy ready to catch a fly."

"You've got it!" exclaimed the doctor.

At this point a less understanding and dedicated man might have turned to collecting entomologists, but Herst, the author of *Stories to Collect Stamps By* and other works, was enthralled. Plunging ahead in search of further funnies, he found in the doctor's collection a copy of the 1945 Turkish stamp depicting the battleship *Missouri*. When Herst asked (hopefully) what relation that stamp had to insects, the doctor replied, "She's in the mothball fleet."

It takes no more than this to put Herst in heaven. Seven days a week, every day of the year, Herst looks at stamps, writes about stamps, talks about stamps and even dreams about stamps "in color." To Herst, no hobby, sport or pastime can compare with philately. There is, he says, the thrill of the chase after an elusive stamp, to say nothing of the absolute joy of unexpected discovery. Just looking at stamps can give Herst a sense of pure esthetic bliss. Furthermore, there are the friendships to be found in philately, "friendships that transcend race, religion and nationality," says Herst, a gregarious sort who has been to Europe forty times in search of stamps.

Then there is the knowledge to be acquired from stamps. Herst's mind is stuffed full of information, ninety-nine percent of it gleaned from studying stamps. He can talk at length about the membership of the Confederate cabinet (the Confederate post office made such a profit that after the Civil War the North tried to get the postmaster general to take the job in Washington), dwell on the history of whaling or the settlement of South Africa. Mention sports, and Herst is off at a galloping pace about Ira Seebacher's collection of sports depicted on stamps, pausing to throw out the fact that the former British colony of St. Kitts-Nevis in the West Indies once issued a set of stamps to raise money for a cricket field, or that the Bahama Islands not only issued stamps with game fish pictured on them but used a hooked sailfish as a postmark. He will tell how Fred Mandell sold the Detroit Lions so he could go into the stamp business in Honolulu, or recount how a bunch of kids once made hockey pucks out of bundled sheets of the very rare Providence postmaster's provisional of 1846.

Continuing in the sporting vein, Herst is fond of relating a racetrack incident that took place in Havana in 1940 when the American Air Mail Society held its convention there. The collectors just wanted to stand around the hotel lobby talking about stamps, and they were dismayed to learn that their Cuban hosts had scheduled an afternoon at the track. When a couple of collectors suggested no one would be interested in going to the races the Cubans said, "They'll be interested in this." Out of politeness the collectors went to the track and picked up a list of entries. To their astonishment, there was a horse named Stanley Gibbons running in the first race and Stanley Gibbons was the name of a well-known British stamp dealer. The horse was an improbable long shot, but the collectors bet him on the hunch. Stanley

Gibbons won. The collectors looked at the second race entries. There was another long shot named Perforation. They bet. Perforation won. So it went through the rest of the card. In every race there was a long shot with a philatelic name that paid off handsomely.

"No one in the stands except the philatelists realized what was happening," Herst says. "The American Air Mail Society convention was one of the few stamp meetings from which attendants were privileged to go home with more money than they had come with." The Cuban government, which apparently had arranged the whole deal to make the Americans happy, was so pleased that it surcharged a stamp commemorating the convention.

Now sixty-two years old, Herst has been a stamp dealer and auctioneer since 1936. His slogan is, "If it's U.S.A., see Herst first." His home and office are in Shrub Oak, New York, and alongside the driveway is an enormous painting of a postage stamp. The stamp is Barbados, *Scott's Catalog* No. 109, the so-called "olive blossom" because it was issued in three colors. The stamp intrigued Herst as a boy, and he has adopted it as his trademark, painting out Barbados and substituting Herst.

Herst ordinarily arises at eight and puts in a full day exuberantly examining stamps, cataloging lots for sale at auction (he has sold more than $10 million in stamps at auction since 1936) and trotting to a bank vault in Peekskill to examine his philatelic treasures. The workday ends at midnight, but around four in the afternoon Herst takes a break. He pours himself a small nip and relaxes by talking about stamps or writing letters about stamps to friends and acquaintances at home or abroad. Every day Herst dispatches fifty to one hundred letters to philatelic pen pals, and it does not bother him that many of his correspondents haven't bought a stamp from him in years. "I just love it," Herst says. Indeed, one need not write a letter to Herst to get a letter. A recent visitor was astounded to get four letters in one week. "Thought you'd be interested," Herst explained.

Herst has such a compulsion to write that when he goes off on a trip with his wife, Ida, he pecks away at a typewriter on his lap in the front seat of the car while she drives. Besides *Stories to Collect Stamps By*, he has written a couple of other books, *Nassau Street* and *Fun and Profit in Stamp Collecting*, and coauthored the scholarly *Nineteenth Century U.S. Fancy Cancellations* and *The A.M.G. Stamps of Germany*. Several times a year he writes and publishes his own periodical, *Herst's Outbursts*, copies of which are sent gratis to anyone sending in six stamped self-addressed envelopes. So far, more than 6,000 people have written in to subscribe, and recent issues include a photograph of Herst kissing the Blarney Stone on a trip to Ireland and a long piece on the infamous Jean Sperati of Paris, "one of the most dangerous stamp counterfeiters ever to wield stamp tongs." Sperati, Herst told his readers, was a genius who even made his own paper, duplicating that of original stamps. Fortunately, Sperati's American counterfeits were few, limited mostly to Confederate stamps, and, although the counterfeits were superbly done, Sperati tripped himself up by using the faked postmark of Middlebury, Vermont.

Above and beyond writing his own magazine and books, Herst serves as an untiring correspondent for any number of philatelic publications. Last February he and Ida took a two-week vacation in the Bahamas and, as Herst reported to readers of the 1971 spring issue of *Herst's Outbursts*, "Aside from the fishing, swimming and just relaxing, we spent the time producing this issue of *Outbursts*; fourteen of our weekly columns for *Mekeel's Weekly* Stamp News; sixteen of our monthly columns on 'Stamps' for *Hobbies*; feature articles for *Western Stamp Collector*; a series of articles for *First Days*; two articles for *Philatelic Magazine* of London and one for *Stamp News* of Australia, for each of which we are American correspondent."

As a philatelist, Herst has received honor after honor. He is one of only five persons to receive the gold medal of the New Haven Philatelic Society, the most coveted philatelic award in the country, for his exceptional contributions to stamp collecting. Herst himself is not only a member of the American Philatelic Society, but one of its five accredited experts qualified to pass on United States stamps submitted for authenticity. He was the stamp consultant for the old radio program *The Answer Man*. He is a member of the American Stamp Dealers Association, the Oklahoma Philatelic Society, the Royal Philatelic Society of Canada, the British Philatelic Association, the Texas Philatelic Association and five dozen other stamp organizations. He is a founder-member of the Cardinal Spellman Philatelic Museum, and he was once pleased to hear the late prelate remark that it was easy to be a cardinal but difficult to be a philatelist.

Stamps aside, Herst is a rabid joiner and do-gooder. "I'm everything!" he exults. "I'm a Kiwanian, a thirty-second degree Mason, a Shriner! I'm in the Baker Street Irregulars where I've been invested as Colonel Emsworth, V.C." Herst is also a member of the American Civil Liberties Union, the Manuscript Society, the American Feline Society (he feeds stray cats), the Bancroft Library of the University of

California and various other organizations, including the Boy Scouts, for whom he is a merit-badge examiner in stamp collecting. "I just can't say no," Herst says of his multitudinous memberships.

When it comes to memberships or honors, he is rivaled only by his dog Alfie, a gigantic German shepherd. Alfie is mascot of the destroyer *Alfred*, an honorary citizen of West Germany, an honorary postman of the Italian post office and recipient of a commendation promulgated by the German Shepherd Squad of Scotland Yard. Alfie's honors have come about through the efforts of his energetic master. Back in the 1950s Herst discovered that federal law permits private carriers to issue "local" stamps in delivering mail to and from post offices that do not offer home delivery or pickup. Herst issued his own Shrub Oak local stamp, and in 1967 he put a picture of Alfie on a second issue. The stamp shows Alfie carrying a letter in his mouth.

Herst's discovery of the "local" loophole in federal law prompted several persons elsewhere to print their own stamps. A narrow-gauge railroad buff on Long Island issued a triangular stamp for local mail on his midget line, but the Federal Government confiscated his stamps and suppressed the mini-service because he had put the prohibited words "United States" on the stamp. Similarly, federal authorities seized the local stamps used for delivery to Rattlesnake Island in Lake Erie because they were "in similtude" to government issue. In Walpole, Massachusetts the members of the "906 Stamp Club," all inmates of the Massachusetts Correctional Institution, operate a local post office carrying letters from cells to the prison post office. Requests to have the route extended have been denied, says Herst, who is a patron of the prisoners and goes there once a year to speak and judge the inmate stamp show.

In the course of a year Herst gives thirty to forty speeches before all sorts of groups. "I am the most in-demand speaker in philately," Herst says. "That's because I don't charge."

Before a staid audience of stamp collectors, Herst is fond of posing as a collector of tea tags. With a straight face, he solemnly talks about the pleasures of collecting tea tags from unusual varieties of tea bags. Using philatelic jargon, Herst will hold up a tea bag and say, "This is the double-string variety. Note the misprint, 'Tooo-Long.' " If the audience is receptive he will go on about tea bags all night. Several years ago Herst was paying a hotel bill in Portland, Oregon when a woman in front of him dropped her purse and the contents spilled all over the floor. "I'm terribly embarrassed," she said to Herst. "You must think

I'm crazy, but I collect tea bags." Herst shouted, "So do I!"

A self-confessed screwball, Herst comes by his quirks naturally. His father was a somber lawyer who died when Herst was four, but his mother was an individualist. A concert violinist, she played in an all-girl band that John Philip Sousa once organized and served as Lillian Russell's accompanist. During World War II she was founder, president and sole member of IRCFD, otherwise known as the Issue Ration Cards For Dogs society, and as such was the author of innumerable letters to the editor of *The New York Times*. Whenever Mrs. Herst was accosted by a panhandler, she would not give him a dime but would invite him home for chicken-noodle soup.

Herst, who has been known from childhood as Pat because he was born on March 17, began collecting stamps when he was eight and early on developed affinities for certain stamps and countries. He started collecting the Barbados "olive blossom"; the very name Straits Settlement smacked of romance to him; and he developed a deep love for Nepal. "Nepal is one of *my* countries," he will confide to a fellow collector.

When he was not engrossed in stamps, Herst was an unruly youngster. Once a policeman collared him for stealing apples from a grocery store and Mrs. Herst exclaimed, "Really! And I can't even get him to eat fruit." At the age of twelve Herst was shipped off to Portland, Oregon, to live with an aunt. He attended high school in Portland and then went to Reed College, where he was graduated in 1931. He got a job as a reporter on the *Morning Oregonian*, but, as he wrote in *Nassau Street*, his autobiography, "the increasing shadows of Depression fell across the lumber capital of the nation, and unfortunately I found my services dispensed with. I was given a letter to *The New York Times* calling attention to my abilities." Bumming east on freights, Herst duly presented himself to the editors of the *Times*. He worked there briefly selling classified advertising and then moved to the *Newark Star Ledger*. But a couple of days in Newark introduced Herst to two facts of life he had not previously encountered: first, commuting from New York to Newark was "a somewhat reverse form of existence," and second, "people in Newark in 1932 did not believe in classified advertising."

Taking another job, Herst labored for two weeks like a busy elf, cutting imitation leather into fancy letters for theater marquees. Unfortunately, his rate of production slowed noticeably after using a razor-sharp knife to cut the letters "G" and "S," and he left joyfully with bandaged fingers for a position in a Wall Street firm, Lebenthal and Company, dealers in municipal bonds.

Paid only twelve dollars a week, Herst was not long in supplementing his income (and that of his fellow workers at Lebenthal's) by forming a syndicate to buy up stamps and sell them at a profit to dealers on nearby Nassau Street. Talk around the office dealt less with bonds and more with stamps, and the head of the firm decreed that there was to be no more mention of stamps. Falling back on what sociologists call collective representation, Herst said, "Let's call them worms," and the Worm Syndicate at Lebenthal's continued to do business. Given an hour for lunch, Herst spent four minutes wolfing down orange juice, coffee and a doughnut and the remaining fifty-six minutes discussing the finer points of philately with dealers and collectors. At Lebenthal's Herst worked furiously because he believed in giving value for money received ("When Pat works," says Ida, "things fly in all directions"), and he was promoted to cashier. Despite an assured future on the Street, Herst quit in 1935 to become a stamp dealer.

From the start, he loved being in stamps full time, and the saddest part of each day came when he had to lock the door to his office at 116 Nassau Street, an ancient, narrow thoroughfare as rich in characters as a Moroccan *souk*. To begin with, there were the "satcheleers," little men, mostly East European Jews, who, with no overhead and no capital except their wits, made the rounds of dealers and collectors, toting stamps in voluminous satchels, on speculation and consignment. Adhering to their cultural milieu, they spoke a rich patois that has surcharged stamp collecting with soul-felt Yiddish expressions. For Herst, who was deskbound serving collectors during the day, the satcheleers were as necessary as bees to a flower, since they pollinated philatelically all over town.

Satcheleers still exist in the stamp world, and although Herst now lives forty-five miles outside of New York City he lets them know in advance when he is about to visit the metropolis so they may open their satchels and spread their wares before his eyes. For several years, Herst has been making notes on the satcheleer subculture, and he is particularly taken by the exploits of one known as Morris ("I wouldn't kill a fly") Coca-Cola, a diminutive Russian who wore oversized secondhand coats that cascaded off his birdlike shoulders and gathered in rich drapery around his ankles.

In Herst's first heady days on Nassau Street satcheleers were not the only characters. At 90 Nassau Street lurked the Burger brothers, Gus and Arthur, elderly Germans who moved into the building in 1886 and hadn't dusted a thing since. Their premises were awash with all sorts of papers and stamps, many of them rarities, including discoveries made by the brothers themselves when they bicycled through the South in the 1890s looking up Confederate veterans with "old letters." The building that housed the Burgers was equally ancient. Five stories high, it had no elevator, and the rest rooms were marked "For Males" and "For Females."

Despite the Victorian clutter around them, the Burgers knew the exact location of every stamp, and when they had finally fetched forth, amid clouds of dust and cobwebs, a superb sheet-corner margin copy of, say, the United States three-cents 1851 (*Scott* No. 11), their price was outrageous. Arthur would say to Gus, "What should we ask for this?" Gus would answer, "Twenty dollars." Arthur would then tell the collector, in earshot all the while, "Just what I was thinking. Forty dollars."

In Herst's time, outfoxing the brothers, dubbed the Burglars, became a sport for experts. Anyone who outwitted them was elected to the Fox Club, which made its headquarters in the office of Percy Doane, an auctioneer. "The rules were simple," Herst says. "One had to visit the offices of the Burger brothers, buy a stamp from them at retail and then put it in one of Doane's auctions. If the buyer netted a profit on the deal after paying Doane the commission, he was in. But simple as the rules were, the attainment of membership was fraught with certain difficulties. In the first place, the stamp would have to be bought sufficiently below its value to permit a profit at auction. Since the Burgers were usually anticipatory in their prices, asking a figure at which an item might be expected to sell ten years hence, this made a profitable sale more than unlikely. The only way would be by finding the Burgers uninformed on the true value of something—and these Joves hardly ever nodded."

One character Herst knew well, Y. Souren, was like someone out of a Peter Lorre-Sydney Greenstreet movie. Souren, whose real name was Souren Yohannasiants, was a Georgian who had fled Russia during the revolution with a $100,000 collection of clocks hidden under the hay in a donkey cart. In the late 1930s Souren occupied a fancy office on Park Avenue, and visitors were admitted only after scrutiny, as though suspected to be members of a spy ring. He kept a private dossier on stamp dealers, collectors and those stamps that had passed through his hands. He had X-ray machines, ultra-violet apparatus and cameras at hand, and he was fond of bringing forth, with appreciative Near Eastern chuckles, photographs of what Herst describes as "unquestionably the same item, perhaps with a straight edge [of a stamp] reperforated [to make it more valuable], a fancy cancel added or other stamps added to the cover." Souren also had photographs of ads by stamp dealers offering items that were misleading. "Comes in handy whenever I want something from someone who doesn't want to cooperate," Souren told Herst.

Years ahead of the FBI, Souren had a camera hidden in the ceiling of his front door. "He was always afraid of being robbed," Herst recalls in *Nassau Street,* "and with good reason, for in his heyday it is doubtful whether any premises short of the Bureau of Printing and Engraving and the stamp vaults in Washington held a more valuable accumulation of stamps. He showed me photographs of every person who had passed through that door in recent days. I saw my photograph several times."

With Herst, Souren unveiled his treasures, including his gem of gems, a block of the United States twenty-four-cents 1869 inverted center, which went with him everywhere. Souren had the block mounted between glass panels in a small holder that he secreted in a special coat pocket. "Several times over a sandwich or a meal he would take it out and admire it," Herst says.

Always a keen student of stamps, as well as a collector, Herst was not long in putting his knowledge to profit. While examining some minor purchases one day, he happened to notice that a copy of the United States thirty-cents 1869 looked a bit odd. The flags were on top of the stamp instead of the bottom. It was a rare error, *Scott* No. 121b, which then catalogued at $4,500. Herst had paid three dollars for it, and he sold it for $3,300. He bought a car and steamship tickets for himself and his mother for a trip to Europe, where he made several coups. In London, Herst learned the Coronation issue of Southern Rhodesia had suddenly become scarce because it was withdrawn from sale. The set had a face value of about thirty cents, but a British dealer offered Herst four dollars and three cents for a set. Herst called New York, where the set was selling for only forty cents, and asked a dealer to ship as many sets as possible. Herst wound up selling some sets for five dollars each. In Paris, Herst made a find at one of the bookstalls along the Seine, an old album containing at least 500 copies of the United States fifty-cents

Omaha, *Scott* No. 291. He bought the collection for twenty dollars and within six weeks had disposed of all the stamps for almost $1,000.

Back home on Nassau Street, Herst reacted with philatelic foresight on Pearl Harbor Day. The minute he heard news of the attack, he addressed five envelopes to fictitious addresses in Tokyo. When Germany declared war on the United States, Herst sent five envelopes to fictitious addresses in Berlin. Eighteen months later all the envelopes came back to Herst with a series of unusual postmarks and censor stamps, and they have been in his World War II collection ever since.

Too old for the service, Herst talked about stamps to wounded veterans in hospitals. He believes stamps are excellent therapy. He also asked every serviceman he knew to remember him wherever they went. Most did, and Herst now has the first letter mailed by the Marines from Guadalcanal, a collection of stamps used for espionage purposes, copies of Hitler's personal mail and the only propaganda leaflets dropped on the Japanese on Kiska and Attu in the Aleutians.

"I don't collect the conventional things," says Herst. "Philately has no limits. There's nothing in life that philately doesn't cross." To prove his point, Herst once made a bet with a collector that he (Herst) could start a specialist collection that would win a prize at a major stamp show, and that he would assemble the collection at a total cost of less than five dollars. Herst won the bet with a collection of wanted notices sent out on postcards by sheriffs in the 1870s and 1880s. "In those days, mail service was faster than criminals," says Herst, who has scant regard for the present United States postal system.

In 1946 Herst moved from Nassau Street to Shrub Oak. "I had to get away," he says. "I couldn't get any work done. My office had become a lounge. There were all sorts of people there. One guy and his wife wanted to spend their honeymoon there."

In Shrub Oak the bane of Herst's existence is getting common stamps from people who send in a "rarity." Herst will run to his stock, pick out a copy and send both back with the reply, "Now you can have two of them!" He is often called in to appraise estate stamp collections, and, from time to time, genuine rarities do come his way. A ten-year-old boy in New Brunswick, New Jersey discovered a copy of the five-cent Kenya stamp showing Owen Falls Dam with Queen Elizabeth upside down. Herst acted as agent for the youngster and sold the stamp, the only copy known, to the Maharajah of Bahawalpur for $10,000. The money was set aside for the boy's education.

When Herst pays a bill he often mails out a mimeographed sheet headed, "My hobby is philately" in which he notes that stamp collecting can not only be fun but a profitable hobby if one collects intelligently. In Herst's opinion, too many neophytes and collectors buy foolishly. "Age does not make value" is one of Herst's favorite sayings. Other Herst commandments are, "Cheap stamps never become rare," "Condition is a factor only in relation to value," "Demand is a more important factor than supply," "Beware of pitfalls that trap the unwary" and "There is no substitute for knowledge."

Herst is the first to admit he doesn't know absolutely everything about everything philatelic. Several years ago in one of his auctions he offered a cover (the collecting term used for an envelope) postmarked Harrisburgh, Alaska. A collector in Chicago called up and told Herst that he wanted to bid $400 for it. Flabbergasted, Herst asked why, and the collector said, "Harrisburgh is the original name for Juneau. When Alaskans chose the name Harrisburgh, post-office officials in Washington said they already had enough Harrisburghs and to change the name. This is the only cover I know postmarked Harrisburgh." Herst says, "The collector got the cover for $40 and he was overjoyed. You treat collectors fairly, and you'll never lose."

Recently Herst was in Albany, New York to judge the show put on by the Fort Orange Stamp Club. As he walked by the exhibit panels his enthusiasm appeared to flag. Was Herman Herst, Jr. beginning to falter? Then he came upon a display of the intricate and seemingly boring regular United States issues of 1908 and 1921. "Ah," said an acquaintance, "don't bother with those." Herst stopped short. "Don't say that," he said. "They're exciting." Peering closely at them, he scribbled a high mark on his scorecard and said, "I can talk to these stamps—and they answer."

* * *

Herman Herst, Jr. has moved to Boca Raton, Florida, and instead of selling stamps he appraises them and writes about them, he says, "for every weekly in the United States, one in Canada, three in the United Kingdom, one in India, one in Australia and one in South Africa. I do about 20 stories a week, all different." He also continues to write books. The Compleat Philatelist was published in 1980, and his More Stories to Collect Stamps By is scheduled to be published in 1982.

WITH A QUACK, QUACK HERE

DONAL O'BRIEN

September 27, 1971

T HE FLAGPOLE sways, and the wind rips the small-craft warning into shreds. The sea is an insane lather of whitecaps. Far to the east of Long Island Sound, the red edge of the sun slides over the horizon, flashing bolts of fire on the windowpanes of houses along the coast. Four miles out lies the granite-block seawall, slick with onionskin ice. The temperature is below thirty degrees, and the forecast calls for continuing northwest winds. It is a time and place for normal persons to avoid, but Donal O'Brien, Jr. arrives at the launching ramp with his boat, peers at the distant seawall and exclaims, "Gee, I can hardly wait to get out there!"

O'Brien is a duck hunter, a fanatic duck hunter. He loves ducks with such passion that a nephew calls him Uncle Duck. His decoy collection is one of the best in the country, and he himself is a superb amateur decoy maker whose carvings have won a number of best-in-shows at national and world championships. He is an excellent shot, and he

trains tough, willing retrievers. A black Labrador that he raised and
sold, Whygin's Cork's Coot, has twice won the National Open
Retriever Championship. For O'Brien, ducks have a magic that other
creatures lack. When he shoots one, he does not toss it aside but
smooths the feathers in admiration. When his wife and four children
are asleep in their house in New Canaan, Connecticut and the snow lies
thick on the ground, O'Brien likes to slip out of the house to look at the
birds in the moonlight.

By profession, O'Brien is a lawyer, a partner in a Wall Street law
firm. "It's great to be able to come home from the office on a Friday
night and know that at 4:30 Saturday morning I'm going to be getting
up to shoot on the Sound," he says. "Duck hunting is very physical and
very basic to me. I like the whole thing, feeling the cold, picking up the
decoys, and when I am home on Sunday and think about what I did on
Saturday, I'm revitalized and prepared to go back to the office to be
civilized for five days." For a good part of the season, O'Brien risks his
life getting revitalized for the office.

Shooting from the seawalls in the Sound ranks among the most
dangerous pastimes known to American sportsmen. Some hunters get
badly frostbitten, and others just disappear. Shooting off the coast of
Maine can be risky, but usually there is a lobsterman or fisherman
around. In November, December and January, the Sound is a vast,
blank piece of water exposed to the wind and waves with only ducks—
and duck shooters—on the move; the sailors and fishermen have retired
to the fireside. It is a hard trip out to the icy rocks, and one misstep into
the chilling water can mean death, but for O'Brien the seawalls hold an
unmatchable spell, although he admits, "I have a ball of fear in my
stomach every time I go out."

A couple of years ago O'Brien and a friend, Bob Johnson, embarked
at dawn for the four-mile run to one of the walls. The weather was
rough, but they made the trip safely. With O'Brien bouncing up and
down in the sixteen-foot outboard, Johnson clambered onto the rocks.
He reached for an oar held by O'Brien to pull the boat in close, but a
swell rocked the boat and Johnson slipped into water sixty feet deep.
When he sputtered to the surface, O'Brien grabbed him by the scruff of
his parka and pulled him into the boat. "It was freezing cold, about ten
degrees," O'Brien recalls, "and I think Bob went into shock. He
couldn't function. He was lying on the bottom of the boat. I told him to
put his boots up in the air to drain the water. But he didn't have the
strength."

O'Brien gunned the boat back to the ramp. He threw the anchor overboard, jumped out, ran ashore, got into his car and drove the trailer into the water. He climbed back into the boat, pulled in the anchor, started the engine and ran the boat straight up onto the trailer. He then got into the car and pulled the boat ashore. He got Johnson out of the boat and stripped him of his cold, wet clothing. "I took my clothes off and gave them to him," O'Brien says. "I was left with long johns and hip boots."

O'Brien took Johnson to a diner where he made him down four or five cups of coffee. "He was absolutely gray and shaking," says O'Brien. "At nine o'clock we went into a package store, me in my long johns and hip boots, and Bob all dressed up and walking like Frankenstein. The guy in the liquor store literally thought something was going to happen to him. He was scuttling along the walls, and I remember saying, 'Don't worry, we're not going to harm you, we're not going to rob your store, we're duck hunters, and this guy fell in.' We got a bottle of brandy, Bob drank it, and at twelve o'clock we were back on the wall, shooting."

Now thirty-seven, O'Brien was born in New York City. He became interested in ducks when he was five, and by the time he was ten and he began shooting with his father, he could identify every duck he saw. He even picked his prep school—Hotchkiss—and his colleges—Williams and the University of Virginia—for the hunting and fishing to be found around them. While in law school, O'Brien, who has a fondness for painting but no time, seriously started carving decoys because he could whittle away at a head between classes.

"The first thing I do in making a decoy is to draw the duck I have in mind," O'Brien says. "I'm working on a black duck now, and I decided I wanted a low head. I sketch to scale, and I may make twenty or thirty sketches, all free-hand, and usually without a model in front of me. When I get something that appeals to me, I'll cut it out for my pattern." When all goes well, it takes O'Brien about half a day to make a shooting decoy and two days for a contest bird.

In 1966 O'Brien entered his first contest, the U.S. National on Long Island. He won best-in-show in the amateur decorative miniature class, an award he has won on two subsequent occasions. He prefers, however, to concentrate on the working-decoy division, the division in which there is the most competition. He was the U.S. National amateur champion in working decoys in 1969 and regained the title this year. In addition, he has won best-in-shows in 1969 and 1970 in the Maine contest and, this past June, in the first world championship, he won best-in-show in the working-decoy class and in the class for working-decoy pairs. Decoy contests are like dog shows in which classes are judged and the winners compete for best-in-show, and along the line O'Brien has dozens of bests-in-class.

O'Brien also brings a most practiced eye to decoy collecting. The art of decoy making is uniquely American, which is one of the attractions to O'Brien. "I get hooked on the things that are purely American," he says.

The classic period of decoy making began in the mid-nineteenth century with the advent of the breech-loading shotgun. In those days there was a seemingly inexhaustible supply of waterfowl and an expanding and hungry populace. The period ended, says Historian William J. Mackey, Jr., a friend of O'Brien's and author of *American Bird Decoys*, with the passage in 1918 of the Migratory Bird Treaty, which put a stop to market hunting. Perhaps the finest decoys were carved by Albert Laing and his followers of the Stratford, Connecticut school. To O'Brien, Laing, who died in 1886, was "a Michelangelo," and O'Brien's collection includes a number of gems by Laing, among them a black, a canvasback, a sleeping broadbill and a drake whistler in a tuck-head position.

O'Brien also has a number of decoys by Benjamin Holmes, Shang Wheeler, who died in 1949, and other members of the Stratford school. "The Stratford decoy tends to be a little bit oversized," says O'Brien, "always hollow, except for the cork bird, with the head its finest feature. The head is very realistic, tends to be quite puffy in the cheek and always has considerable detail in the bill. It's a sleek bird, not cluttered up. There is no wing carving, no feather carving. There is usually a crease down the back separating the wings, and in the cork bird the tail is frequently inlaid. Stratford decoys catch the overall impression of ducks. They're full-bodied, tapering to a flat bottom. They're not round like Jersey decoys. The Stratford birds had to take rough weather and big seas, and a dewdrop weight was normally used instead of a keel. I consider myself in the Stratford school, though a lot of my decoys are made with keels."

A friend, Tom Marshall, a former fieldman for Ducks Unlimited, admires O'Brien's carvings but deplores the keels as unnecessary. In turn, O'Brien is dismayed at Marshall's continued use of a number of original Shang Wheeler decoys in his working rig. In a voice somewhat reminiscent of Titus Moody's, Marshall says, "Shang made 'em to hunt over, not look at."

O'Brien's collection is very strong on New England shorebirds, especially decoys from Nantucket. "From a collecting standpoint, I enjoy the shorebirds more than the ducks," he says. The gem of the shorebird collection is a set of six Eskimo curlews that O'Brien acquired several years ago from a friend who is a seventh-generation Nantucketer. Now believed to be extinct, the Eskimo curlew was avidly hunted on Nantucket during the nineteenth century. All told, O'Brien's decoy collection, displayed in a special room built as an extension to his house, numbers about 600 birds. It includes decoys from Connecticut, Chesapeake Bay (some of these are by Lee Dudley—"one of the greats"), Cape Cod, Maine and Long Island. The collection is genuinely staggering to see. O'Brien first met Kenny Gleason, one of his hunting companions, when Gleason happened to come to the house to fix the phone. "When Gleason saw the decoys," O'Brien says, "we couldn't get him out of the house."

"There's a tremendous excitement in decoy collecting," O'Brien says. "There's a whole mystique to it. I never forget where good decoys are. Once I was on a trip up to Maine, and I stopped for gas. There was a sporting-goods dealer across the street, and in the window were a number of Maine decoys, including a couple of mergansers. They were just like Tiffany jewels. I went in to talk—I use a soft approach, and this may cost me at times—but the owner wouldn't sell. Last fall I put sixty decoys in my car, good decoys, and drove up to Maine. It took me twenty minutes to put all sixty on the floor, and after I finished I said to the owner, 'Now you suggest a trade.' He stepped back, looked and finally said, 'Oh, you win.' We made a trade. I got the mergansers, and he got three very good birds in return."

O'Brien's year begins the first week in October when he goes to New Brunswick, to shoot black duck and teal. In mid-October the season opens in Connecticut, and he begins shooting surface feeders—blacks, mallards, teal and widgeon—in marshes and on the Sound. His working rig generally consists of thirty-seven absolutely stunning black ducks that he carved himself. Hunting inland marshes, he will use as few as two or three decoys because the clever blacks would be wary of a large rig in a small area. "I try to simulate the wild-duck situation," O'Brien says. "Also, more things can go wrong with a big set in the marshes."

"When the inland water freezes over," O'Brien continues, "the ducks start to use the open water. Then I work with a fairly large rig of two to three dozen. You're trying to attract the birds from a long distance. When we shoot from the seawalls where the birds feed on the rocks, I try to have a few decoys right close in. Some of these will be feeding decoys with the bills in the water. There will be other decoys twenty or thirty yards out, in a dew-drop shape. I try to leave something open in the middle, though that's not important for the black duck, which can land on a dime. Finally, I'll have some stringers or liners out of range. Three or four of my black ducks have high necks. They're watch birds. Few of the commercial decoys have high necks, but you watch blacks. There will always be a few with high necks. That's an alert bird, and I'll usually have a couple out in the middle of the rig, and the last high-neck bird will have a comfortable low-neck bird in front of him."

To O'Brien, the black duck is a marvelous bird. "They're the wariest," he says, "and you have to be happier with fewer. They're very coordinated in the air and seem much more in control of what they're doing than the broadbill or canvasback."

When the first half of the split season closes in Connecticut in late October, O'Brien hunts for grouse and woodcock. In early December he begins duck hunting again. By now weather conditions have made the Sound perilous, and the best shooting is when the water is at its icy worst.

Late in January, O'Brien and his friends do most of their shooting from lieout boats anchored a few hundred yards from the lee shore where they try to hold steady in the calmer sea. "We'll put out a lot of broadbill decoys," he says. "The last day of last season, we put out about one hundred. Broadbill are very sociable birds—they like a lot of company. A very good setup is shaped like a fishhook. You follow the shank of the hook, come around to the barb and extenuate the barb.

"One of the great sights is the broadbill coming in. They'll come in quite high, and they'll see the rig. They'll spill the wind right out of their wings. They come down incredibly fast, and the next thing you know they're boring right in at you and landing right there in the hollow of the hook. All you see is black. The black head and the black chest. We let them come until they're not going to want to come anymore. Then we sit up and these birds go into a flare, and they really are moving. All of a sudden they turn from black into a tremendous pattern of black and white, and if the sun's out, they're really beautiful."

When the broadbill season ends on January 31, O'Brien is depressed, though his wife Katie, he admits, "really has had her fill of it." But February and March are not lost time. In those months O'Brien does most of his serious contest carving for the U.S. National, which is held in mid-March. He spends hours studying his heads, going so far as to put them on the dashboard of his car so that he can study details on the drive to and from his office. "Another reason I drive to New York is so I can look out the window and watch the ducks," he says. "Even along the Harlem River by the Columbia boathouse, I see canvasback, broadbill and black duck."

In April, O'Brien forgets about ducks momentarily when he starts trout fishing. He has his own trout stream on his property and for a number of years he was entranced with the idea of breaking the world record for brook trout. But come summer, when O'Brien and his family vacation on Nantucket, he gets back to his carving, making decoy heads on the beach when the stripers and blues aren't hitting.

In September, O'Brien is busy getting ready for duck hunting. As befits a hunter of his ardor, he usually has several retrievers about the house. He trains them himself, but during the summer he may ship a dog off to a professional trainer for polishing. In the 1960s O'Brien competed in retriever field trials, and although he did well, it simply took too much time from real shooting.

O'Brien's passion for ducks has not gone unnoticed at his law firm. In a skit at the last Christmas office party, a young associate played the part of O'Brien dressed up in hunting clothes. O'Brien didn't complain. In fact, he wasn't around at the time—he was off on a duck hunt in Texas.

*   *   *

In the fall of 1981, O'Brien lent some of his best decoys for an exhibit at the Museum of American Folk Art in New York. I went to see the exhibit, but O'Brien wasn't there. He was hunting in Spain.

THE OBSESSIONS OF
A LATE-BLOOMER

DICK WOLTERS

August 18, 1969

Amerian males, slumped in front of the tube, putting on a pot and approaching forty, arise! Take as your example in life Richard A. Wolters, the illustrations editor at *Business Week*. To middle-aged millions reared on the unrequited dreams of Walter Mitty or diverted by the brilliant ineptitudes of George Plimpton, the positive achievements of Dick Wolters offer direction, inspiration and thrust.

Thirteen years ago Wolters was just another weary commuter, slogging home to a loving family, a relaxing drink and an hour in an easy chair. Then he discovered sports, and now, at the age of forty-nine, he is a distinguished (and sometimes controversial) fly-fisherman, skeet shooter, retriever trainer, sailplane enthusiast and author of five books, *Beau*, a sporting memoir, *Gun Dog*, *Water Dog*, *Family Dog* and *Instant Dog*. The owner of multitudes of equipment, some of it ingeniously self-devised, he has a customized camper that draws wows on the back roads of Maine and Montana. In Manhattan he is a pillar of the

155

Midtown Turf, Yachting and Polo Association, where he lunches with the likes of Lee Wulff, Ed Zern, Ernie Schwiebert and other big shots of the outdoors. Wolters is generous with advice, even among his peers, and comparative strangers often phone him to inquire about hatches on the Battenkill, the proper discipline for a listless Labrador or the name of a good little parachute rigger. Wolters is pleased to serve as a guru; as a matter of fact, he resembles one. He has a bushy mustache and an extraordinarily thick head of hair that grows almost to his shoulders, with the result that he looks rather like Mark Twain. Dressed in a vintage Abercrombie suit, his hatband studded with field trial pins, he is a sight to remember.

Wolters did not become interested in sports until he was thirty-six. Like many other American males approaching middle age, he was too busy with a career and building a home to get involved. He played tennis as a youngster in Philadelphia, but he gave it up when he entered Penn State to study chemistry. Upon graduation in 1942 he went into rocket and then atomic research for the government. He took part in A-bomb tests in Nevada and in the Pacific, but bored with research, he gambled on turning his hobby of photography into a living. He succeeded and became a magazine photographer.

In 1954 he became the first picture editor of *Sports Illustrated* and soon thereafter, more or less in the line of duty, was persuaded to go fishing. He returned to the office proudly bearing a four-and-one-half-inch trout—a catch that should have got him arrested but instead set him on fire. "Given the way I've always embarked on projects, I'm sure that had I been on a construction magazine I would have learned to operate a crane," he says. "But suppose I'd been on a woman's magazine?"

Fly-fishing helped establish two basic rules that Wolters has since followed in choosing a sport.

1. The sport must be readily available. Fly-fishing was only minutes away on the Amawalk, an excellent stream in northern Westchester.

2. The sport must be within reach financially so that he can afford the best in equipment and accomodations. "I must go first-cabin," he says.

Wolters is very methodical, and when he began fishing the Amawalk he kept a log noting stream conditions, water temperatures, fly hatches and the number of trout caught. In 1956 he fished a total of forty-five times and caught eleven trout, much to the merriment of his friends.

After the season ended he practiced casting on his lawn and started tying flies.

He built a rotary tying vise from sundry spare parts, including a shaft stripped from a motor his son Roger found on the street, and he constructed his own tying table. He also designed a fishing jacket with all sorts of special pockets. "Anything I go into I go completely whole hog," he says. "I go *all the way out*. I don't fiddle around watching television."

In his second year on the Amawalk, Wolters improved. He fished fifty times and caught 166 fish. Having learned his basics, he began fishing elsewhere in the East, and he even made a special trip to England to fish the Test. He set new goals for himself, to fish with the tiniest of flies and to catch and release the limit of trout every time he fished the Amawalk. He was very fond of fishing and the men he met in the sport. One of his best friends was the late Jack Randolph, the outdoor columnist for *The New York Times*, who, on occasion, made Wolters the subject of jokes or misadventures. Wolters did not mind, because, as he says, "I enjoy humor, especially the give-and-take between friends." Randolph sometimes got as good as he gave. Once he spent a baffling afternoon on a stream casting some flies Wolters had tied, and every time a fly hit the water, the feathers would disappear. Wolters, who was hiding nearby and chuckling to himself, had used sugared water instead of head cement on the tying thread.

It was Randolph who, perhaps in an attempt to get even, suggested that Wolters go bird shooting. Wolters accepted the challenge, figuring he might be able to get some feathers for fly tying. On the trip Wolters fired three shots and hit three grouse, the only one in the party of six to get a bird. Randolph was stunned. Wolters was elated, and to improve his shooting he took up skeet, setting the private goal of winning the Outdoor Editors Shoot the next spring, a competition that he figured was within his class. He won it, all right, and gave a little bow toward Randolph.

Wolters enjoyed bird shooting, but what really intrigued him was watching a dog work in the field. He just had to have a dog, and he bought an English setter pup. It died of distemper, and he bought another, which he named Beau. He began training Beau when the dog was only seven weeks old. Gun dogs, so tradition has it, are not to be trained until they are at least six months to a year old, and they are then supposed to be approached with a spiked collar and a whip. Old-time handlers also have maintained that training a dog when he's a pup is supposed to take something out of the dog. But, as Wolters later wrote in *Beau*, he was able to take a fresh tack, because "I came to dog training late in life. I didn't have the advantage, or what I might now call the disadvantage, of having a father or grandfather to teach me how to raise a hunting dog. Traditional dog training is an art that's based on too many old wives' tales. Like the one about never keeping a hunting dog in the house, it will ruin his nose for game. That was written by an old woman who hated dogs and her husband."

By the age of three months Beau sat, stayed and came on command. Wolters took daily walks with the setter, and whenever the pup would start to walk behind, Wolters would turn around so that the dog was in front. Beau quickly learned his place was out front, but when he got too far out, beyond what would be shotgun range, Wolters whistled to bring him in closer. At five months Beau could quarter a field following hand signals. The dog learned to hold point on a bird in the front yard through an unusual trick. Wolters rigged a grouse wing on the end of a line on a fly rod. As he swung the rod, Beau would get excited seeing the "bird" in flight. Suddenly Wolters would lower the rod and drop the wing on the ground. Beau instantly would freeze on point. In the field Beau proved to have a good nose to go with his eyes.

When Beau was eight months old Wolters received an invitation to lecture at North Carolina State College, where Dr. Frederick Barkalow, Jr. of the zoology department was teaching an adult education course in hunting. Dr. Barkalow had read Randolph's columns in the *Times* about Wolters's training of Beau, and he offered Wolters some fine quail shooting if he would come down with Beau and lecture. Wolters went, and Beau did very well indeed, earning glory in the field on the final day when, as a substitute for older dogs that failed, he stood on point twenty-eight times for the excited class.

Wolters had no idea that he had been doing anything revolutionary in dog training, but after returning from North Carolina he happened to hear about a study on dogs being done at the Animal Behavior Laboratory at Hamilton Station, a division of the Roscoe B. Jackson Memorial Laboratory in Maine. Wolters, his wife and Beau drove to Bar Harbor, where they met Dr. J. Paul Scott, a former Rhodes scholar, who was heading a scientific investigation of the behavior of dogs in the hope that it might shed light on the behavior of humans. Olive Wolters, then doing graduate work in psychology, was able to put the research findings into layman's terms for her husband. It was immediately apparent to Wolters that he not only had been right in starting Beau so young, but that Dr. Scott and his colleagues had made some truly important findings for dog owners everywhere.

These discoveries were fodder for Wolters, and he immediately began work on a training book, *Gun Dog*, which was published in 1961. "I had never written, I was a poor speller, but I told myself I was going to do the book," Wolters says. "There is no use making excuses for yourself." The book got rave reviews and it is now in its twelfth printing.

By now Wolters was hooked on dogs. Unfortunately, the training fields he had used for Beau were giving way to shopping centers and housing developments, and there was a dearth of grouse and pheasant next to the Wolters' home. He decided to switch to Labrador retrievers, a breed he very much admired and which did not necessarily need a ready supply of live birds. Using Labs and what Dutton, his publisher, calls the Revolutionary Rapid Training Method, Wolters wrote two books, *Family Dog*, which deals with the dog as a house pet, and *Water Dog*, for the amateur retriever owner-handler. Both books have done well. His latest book, *Instant Dog*, is a humorous work done in collaboration with Cartoonist Roy Doty. There is some sound advice in the book, but most of it is broad satire, such as how to teach a dog to sit by stepping on his tail or how to feed a dog from the dinner table. There is even an elaborately long recipe, "Instant Supper," for dogs that calls for a dressed three-pound pheasant, green pepper, fresh asparagus, heavy cream and rice. To Wolters's delight, some reviewers have taken *Instant Dog* as a serious work.

By the early 1960s Wolters was moving in pretty doggy circles, and doggy people can be bitchy. "He had the gall to own one setter and to write a book about training gun dogs," says one doggy critic. "Just who the hell is he?" Another doggy acquaintance says, "When Dick moved into Labs he irritated some people, especially in the rich Long Island crowd. Dick is not the most self-effacing guy in the world, and a lot of people resented him." Wolters says, "Part of the resentment may have been caused by my books. New ideas go down hard, and there are people who just didn't agree with my theories, so they didn't like me. I wasn't in Labs for more than a few months when I saw they didn't have adequate training equipment. I went to a field trial when I first had my young Tar, and a woman said her dog couldn't compete because he didn't know how to work far enough. She said, 'I can't throw the dummy that far in training.' She was like most of us. She couldn't afford bird boys or raise live birds or hire a trainer. So that night I got to thinking, and some people couldn't take the results of my thinking."

What Wolters thought up was a sort of Rube Goldberg rocket device that could propel a dummy farther than any human being could fling it. He worked out a rough idea and then got in touch with Arthur Johnson, a ballistics expert in Washington. Together they codesigned the finished product, the Retriev-R-Trainer, a hand-held device that can shoot a dummy one hundred yards. Twenty-two blank cartridges serve as the propellant, and the charges can be changed to vary the distance. For some time Wolters took delight in visiting field trials to hear gasps of amazement from some of his critics. The Retriev-R-Trainer is sold nationally, and Wolters collects a small, but ego-pleasing, annual royalty. The Retriev-R-Trainer has since proved to have a number of other uses. It can be adapted to hurl a fishing lure 250 yards, throw a line one hundred yards and fire a flare, among other things. Once Wolters loaded up with a magnum charge and shot a golf ball out of sight. "This business of trying to come up with new things, with new ideas, innovations, this is really a lot of sport to me," he says. "To me, the sport of a sport is going in and giving it everything you can and coming up with something new."

In 1962 Wolters became president of the Westchester Retriever Club, and he approached the job with characteristic zest. Until then the club had been somewhat loosely organized, holding only "fun" or "picnic" trials. Wolters set out to make the club more attractive and more effective by getting American Kennel Club recognition and permission to hold sanctioned trials.

Meanwhile, Wolters was active on other fronts. Fishing and dogs were his passion, and if some Eastern field-trialers were snippy, Midwesterners and Westerners were friendly and open. Wolters bought a camper truck, and he and Olive, the two children, Roger and Gretchen, and a pair of Labs would drive west on vacation, stopping to fish, visit kennels or attend field trials. Wolters spent hundreds of hours remodeling the camper. For instance, he built a special kennel compartment for the Labs above the right rear wall, installed extra lights, put in a shower, made fitted dish racks, rigged up a canopy for an outside patio and built an observation deck on the roof. He bought a climbing bike, which fitted on the back, and when the family stopped to camp he would tootle off on the bike to fish. Should Olive need him, she only had to call on a walkie-talkie. The camper, named Lablubber's Land-lubber II, is so self-sufficient that when they visit friends the Wolterses stay in the camper instead of the home. When the Wolterses visit a camper rally people line up at the door for a tour. To many persons, unfamiliar with Wolters's other sporting activities, he is reverentially referred to as "the guy with that camper." Wolters says, "The camper falls in with my idea of having things that are compact. I enjoy small things that are well designed."

Wolters stayed active in Labs until 1965. But by then he felt there was little more he could do with dogs, and some of the people were unpleasant. One day while walking down the street with a royalty check in his pocket, he saw a car he liked. It was an MGB GT, and he bought it at once. Why not race cars? He took driving lessons. But he was not long in finding that sports-car racing was not for him. He didn't care for too many of the people ("somewhat flashy," he says), and then he really did not understand engines. He would have to rely on someone else to do the tinkering. Moreover, racing looked as if it might be expensive. One day while racing at Lime Rock in Connecticut, Wolters saw a youngster cartwheel a car. "It didn't bother me to see the accident," Wolters says. "The boy walked away without a scratch. But he totally wrecked his car. I realized one thing then. He had a wealthy father, I didn't, and next week he'd be back in a new car. I wouldn't. I saw myself getting into something that was going to be over my head financially."

A year and a half ago a friend, Phil Gilbert, president of Rolls-Royce Inc. in America, suggested that Wolters try soaring. Wolters went aloft with another friend, Arthur Hurst, and he was enthralled. Soaring was convenient at the Wurtsboro, New York airport, only an hour's drive from home. "It cost me $450 for lessons to get my license," he says. "And after you get your license you can rent, and the cost will come to about what it costs you to ski." In his first year of soaring Wolters set a personal goal of one hundred hours in the air. "I made it," he says. "I held my wheel off from landing until the sweephand came around to the minute, and then I touched down. That's a lot of flying for a sailplane, especially since my early flights were only twenty minutes long. But I find this to be one of the most challenging sports I ever set my mind to."

After getting his license Wolters bought a German-made sailplane, a

Ka-8B, and then a Libelle, a compact fiberglass ship also made in Germany. He recently sold it and got back what he had invested, because the demand for sailplanes exceeds the supply. He now owns a new model Standard Libelle. "The people in soaring are tremendous," Wolters says. "They're hot competitors, but they help one another, and they are out to help you. Some dog people wouldn't talk to you if your life depended on it. They keep their little tricks to themselves. But the people in soaring, the top people I've met, George Moffat [the 1969 national soaring champion], Gordie Lamb, Gleb Derujinsky, are out to help others. George will come up to me and say, 'That landing wasn't quite right,' and then he'll tell me what to do. When I bought my first Libelle I got a phone call from Ben Greene down in North Carolina, the 1968 champion. I had met him briefly at the Nationals and had flown with him in Pennsylvania. And he warned me I was getting into a slippery little ship and told me what to watch for. This is the camaraderie in this field and I really enjoy it."

Last year Wolters qualified for the silver badge, becoming only the 1,494th American to meet the standards set by the *Fédération Aéronautique Internationale*. To do this, he had to climb 3,280 feet above release by the tow plane, make a flight of five hours' duration and make a thirty-two-mile cross-country flight. Olive crewed for him on the last, keeping in touch by radio (Wolters's call sign is "Old Dog") as she sped along roads in the camper truck with the twenty-eight-foot-long trailer for the glider hooked up behind. Wolters completed the flight by landing in the field of a startled farmer. Having gotten his silver badge, he qualified for the Eastern regional cross-country competition and won the standard class. During the flight he got extremely low and feared that he would have to land in an apple orchard. Inasmuch as the trees were only twenty-five feet apart and the wingspan of the Ka-8B is fifty feet, he thought he might have what he called "a real problem of geometry." Fortunately, he hit a good lift and shot up to 6,000 feet. Upon landing, he asked about the apple orchard and was told, "That's no apple orchard—them's cherries."

"I think I can get pretty good at soaring," Wolters says, "but I'm not too sure I want to become a really hotshot competitor. My ambition is to qualify for the gold badge in 1969 and then go for diamond. There are only 109 diamonds in the history of American soaring. In diamond you have to make a 300-mile flight and climb 16,000 feet above your low point. I'll probably go out to California to do that. I hear that the lee wave off the Sierra Nevada is sensational."

With fishing still available in season on the Amawalk, the Labs at home ready to retrieve and a book on soaring in the works, it would seem that Wolters's time is filled. Yet he has noticed a small chink in the calendar in January and February when the Wurtsboro airport is closed by snow. That happens to be the time of the year when the nearby Hudson is frozen over and iceboaters from a hundred miles around take to the river. "Iceboating sounds very attractive," Wolters says. "I am sure I will want to delve into it. Some of the principles I've learned in soaring apply. Iceboating might be just the sport to fill in the entire year very nicely."

* * *

Wolters never did get involved with iceboating, but he did go on to get two diamonds in soaring, one for goal, the other for altitude. He got the diamond for altitude by ascending 25,000 feet over Mount Washington in New Hampshire. (On the same day a friend in another sailplane was killed.) In 1971, Wolters left Business Week *to free-lance as a writer and photographer, and although he had to give up soaring because of the demands on his time, he ballooned across Switzerland, and when he was fifty-five he took up mountain climbing in the Alps. His toughest ascent was the climb up the Breithorn, 14,000 feet high. At fifty-seven, he gave up parachuting after suffering a heart attack. After recovering, he did the Cresta Run in St. Moritz (which he photographed on the way down) and resumed hang gliding in the United States and Lichtenstein. He crashed a couple of times before he gave it up. "I figured it was a stupid sport," he says, "but I had to try it." In the last two years, Wolters traveled 20,000 miles, which included two trips to England and one to a remote fishing village in Newfoundland, to do research on his latest book,* The Labrador Retriever, The History . . . The People. *He was able to devote two years to this book on the Lab because of the continuing sales of* Gun Dog, Water Dog *and* Family Dog *which have sold, exclusive of book club sales, more than 300,000 copies to date.*

SHHH! IT'S THE BLACK GHOST

ART BROADIE

December 8, 1980

WHEN THE Black Ghost can't get off a shot at a squirrel hiding on the opposite side of a tree, he takes off his jacket, drapes it over a bush, ties a piece of string to the branches and walks to the other side of the tree as the squirrel scampers to the jacket side. The Black Ghost sits still for five minutes, then jerks the string, moving the jacket. Bang! Another squirrel for the pot when it runs to the Black Ghost's side of the tree.

Sometimes when the trout are not hitting, the Black Ghost will wade down a stream, sending waves into both banks. Then he gets out, walks back upstream to where he entered, has a leisurely smoke, picks up his rod and starts catching trout. "Got to wake 'em up," he says.

To those who know him, the Black Ghost is the best hunter and trout fisherman around. Doubtless there are other outdoorsmen as good as he is living in small towns throughout the country, but the Black Ghost, who can stand for all of them, certainly is an original.

The Black Ghost is Arthur T. Broadie, a cadaverous, sixty-year-old boiler-plant operator at the Franklin D. Roosevelt Veteran's Administration Hospital in Montrose, New York. Tufts of hair spring out of both ears, and he usually wears a grin that gives the impression that he knows something no one else does. That is often the case. He is called the Black Ghost because he drives a pickup truck with a homemade camper on the back that has Black Ghost streamer flies painted front and rear.

"The idea of the Black Ghost came to me suddenly one night down on the job," Broadie says. "I was looking at the doggone truck, and I thought I ought to decorate the thing. Pretty near every day I fish for trout, I'll use the Black Ghost sometime or other, and then I wanted a CB handle that no one else had. I checked the paint locker, and I had all the colors I needed. I made a template, drew the streamers on in pencil and painted them. Everything seemed to fit together."

The Black Ghost's old camper, which he stripped down this year for parts for a new camper, had the words "Black Ghost" spelled out beneath the painted flies, but he left off the lettering on the new camper because the old one used to inspire all kinds of exclamations when he drove past Bunch's Place, a favorite black hangout in Peekskill, New York, Broadie's hometown.

It may seem odd that the Black Ghost—a sort of contemporary Daniel Boone on wheels—would choose to live barely thirty-five miles north of New York City, but then Broadie spent most of his life practicing his hunting and fishing skills on estates in the area, wherever and whenever he pleased, regardless of the no-trespassing signs and the fish and game laws. Indeed, poaching—hunting and fishing on posted property—was, is and probably always will be a Broadie family custom. "I've never been a game hog," Broadie says, "but I do believe that if there is a chunk of ground out there and some guy says it's his, that doesn't mean those critters on it are his."

For the Black Ghost the thrill of the chase is not just pursuing game but being pursued by an angry landowner after he has bagged his quarry. "Got to find me a little hidey-hole," he will say when scouting some fresh territory that might offer sport. The hidey-hole is usually a brier patch into which the Black Ghost will hurl himself like Peter Rabbit with Mr. McGregor in hot pursuit. "People don't like to mess with brier patches," says Broadie, who has poached some land so often that he knows each and every hidey-hole by heart.

Years ago, the whole Broadie clan—Grandpa, Pop, Uncle Will, Art and his two younger brothers—used to fish Forbes Pond in the small town of Croton. "I loved Forbesie's," says Broadie, and his love only increased when a stern gentleman bought the pond and the surrounding acreage for his estate. Broadie came to know the new landowner's habits well, and although the landowner had no such knowledge of Broadie or even his name, he became determined to catch the poacher. It was a game in which Broadie took great delight. "One day I'm up there fishing the pond, and here comes the new owner with a state trooper," Broadie recalls. "That turkey yells, 'There he is!' like he was sure he was going to catch me. I took off through the woods with the two of them after me. There was no way I was going to beat them out of there, but I knew this hidey-hole, a big rock with a slope underneath it that was covered by blackberry bushes. I headed right for it. I was no sooner in my hidey-hole than I heard the trooper jump on the rock. Then the owner got there. 'What happened?' he asks the trooper. The trooper says, 'He must be to the road by now.' I was tempted to grab his ankle and say, 'Nope, I'm right down here in my hidey-hole.' After they left, I skeedaddled out of there, and I didn't go back . . . for a week."

The Black Ghost was seven years old when he first went poaching. Dusk was falling as Grandpa and Pop led him quietly through the woods to the edge of a lake. There Pop stripped down, waded out into the water and began lifting what seemed like rock after rock off the bottom. Suddenly a rowboat bobbed up, Pop and Grandpa bailed it out, and all three got in and went fishing. "Ain't nobody to mess with you at this time of night," Grandpa said.

Knowledge of the best hunting and fishing on estates—such as that of Dr. Edward L. Thorndike of Columbia University, "that fellow who wrote the dictionary"—was "handed down in the family," Broadie says. "I figured those estates were all my territory. Don't forget that this was the Depression. Pop was a railroad man, and he was only working two or three days a week. Everything was a meal. Even the game warden didn't pay attention to the season most of the time."

Broadie attended Hendrick Hudson High School and, although he played hooky to fish or hunt, he graduated in three years with an 89.6 average. "Latin knocked the hell out of it," he says, "but I've always been glad I took it because I can break down words to figure out what they mean." Most of the time, Broadie talks like a rustic, but when he gets serious he will start using words and phrases such as "indigenous," "cogitating" and "my poaching proclivities." "Sometimes you got to go along with the crowd," he says.

College was out of the question, so Broadie worked for an auto mechanic and then in the New York Central Railroad repair shops at Harmon—when he wasn't loose in the field. Deer were then protected by a closed season, and Broadie learned that the warden was out to nail whoever was hunting at DeRahm's Brook where it flowed into Constitution Marsh across the Hudson from West Point. "One morning the warden shows up at the brook at four o'clock," Broadie recalls. "He looks around, no one else is there, and so he hides in some bushes. He waits and waits. Five o'clock goes by, and no one has shown up. Six o'clock. Still no one. Then this nice big fat buck comes down to the brook. The warden looks around. He doesn't see anyone. He pulls out his .38 caliber revolver, shoots the buck and packs it out of there. A couple of days later I met the warden in a place where he hung out, and I just casually said to him, 'How does the venison taste?' That was the end of the conversation, and after that he never did run me into the woods."

When he's out hunting, Broadie chews on black birch twigs to keep himself from getting thirsty, and he habitually moves with stealth, even when entering a room. "People who grew up in the city can't be quiet in the woods," he says. "They walk with their feet out because they grew up on pavement." The only man Broadie ever knew who was quieter than he is in the woods was the late Nelse Kingsley. "I'd be stock-still waiting for a squirrel," Broadie says, "and all of a sudden I'd hear Kingsley's voice right behind me, asking, 'Seen anything, Art?' "

The New York Central found Broadie to be a quick learner. With the skills he acquired in the Central's shops, he is able to do all his own truck and car maintenance and repairs, plumbing and electrical work and carpentry. "I can put in the footings, lay up the foundation and completely build a house and put every damn thing in it," he says. He also ties his own Black Ghosts and other flies and jigs, does decorative leatherwork, makes knives, carves decoys and designs and builds his own duck boats. In the days when he hunted Constitution Marsh in winter, he built an air boat that could hit sixty miles an hour skimming across the ice. When he cuts down a Christmas tree, he always cuts two, the extra one for spare branches which he inserts into holes drilled in the trunk of the first tree to make it absolutely symmetrical. "I'm learnin' all the time," he says. "How many guys would look at a picture of something in a book and say, 'I'm going to make me one of those,' and then make it? I do."

In 1943, Broadie married his wife, Alice, and then spent, by his own recollection, "exactly three years, one month and nineteen days" in the Army. When he returned home, he worked as a welder and pipe fitter until he landed a job with the Veterans Administration in 1963. Of course, he also returned to poaching. What else could a man like Broadie do with the 2,000-acre Camp Smith Military Reservation at his disposal? Broadie's activities so incensed the colonel in charge, whose children had a pet deer with a red ribbon around its neck, that he took to patrolling the roads himself at night in a Jeep. As Broadie learned, after one narrow escape, the colonel would park the Jeep at the crest of a steep hill with the lights out. When he heard a noise on the road below, he would release the brake and zoom downhill, aiming for the intruder. Broadie was after ducks, not deer—he hasn't hunted deer in twenty-five years because that season conflicts with the bird season—and to avoid the colonel he clambered up the back side of a mountain, Anthony's Nose, before sunrise one morning. By eight o'clock he had worked his way down the other side into some prime duck country. Suddenly he heard an explosion, the whine of a shell overhead and another explosion behind him as the shell landed. He had arrived just in time for artillery practice. He ducked into a hidey-hole behind some rocks and waited out the bombardment for three hours. The next time Broadie hunted ducks at Camp Smith was between six and seven-thirty in the morning. "Nobody gets up at six to start firing artillery in the peacetime Army," is the way Broadie figured it.

Art and Alice raised four sons. The oldest is thirty-five, the youngest twenty-six, and Broadie took them all hunting and fishing. "Set them down anywhere, and they can make a dent," he says. "All fishermen and hunters and all law-abidin' citizens."

The Black Ghost has used a fly rod ever since his sixteenth birthday. His father gave it to him shortly after his mother died. "It was a three-piece, nine-foot el cheapo club," he says. "No one had any money. It had an old skeleton reel that cost twenty-nine cents, and I used to buy fly lines, mill ends twenty-five- to thirty-feet long, in a stationery store for twenty-five cents. I didn't even know anyone who owned a fly rod. In those days the only thing I knew about fly-fishing was what I read in magazines. I had the whole month of June to practice with cork-bodied bass bugs. Everybody used big plugs for bass, and they all laughed at me when I showed up with little bugs—until I started taking four to five fish for every one they were taking.

"Then I started to use the fly rod to fish for trout. First I used bait, worms and shiners, and it wasn't too long before I'd get my limit. Then I'd switch to flies. Eventually I started going without bait. I went to flies because I realized I could turn fish loose without injuring them. After I started releasing more fish, I started catching more fish. Maybe it's because I was more relaxed. This was the '30s, and guys used to climb up and down my back for releasing fish. Some guys still feel that they have to prove themselves by bringing home a fish."

Broadie remembers the days on which he caught certain fish the way other people remember where they were when Pearl Harbor was bombed or when Bobby Thomson hit the shot heard 'round the world. "The memory bank up there in my head tells me what to do when I want to go fishing," he says. "Different streams have different rhythms, and you have to know what the trout want. For instance, on some water the fish like a fairly long retrieve of a streamer, and on others they like short twitches. Even the same stream changes from spring to late spring, with water temperature and water flow. When the water's high and the temperature's low, you can't rip a streamer in front of a trout's snoot. You have to tease him out. When the water gets real low and warm, that's high-speed fishing. You got to startle them into grabbing aholt.

"It all depends on the stream. Up on the Ausable, you want to use several flies at once, tied on about thirty inches apart. The flies should be a brown, a gray and a black. The idea behind it is this: if I get a fish right away, I know what color I caught him on. If it's on the brown fly, I put on another brown fly but with a little different pattern. Then I may take a fish a little faster. My theory is that I'm coming closer to whatever natural insect they're feeding on, what's indigenous to the stream. You can take two streams just six or seven miles apart, both with the same species of insects, yet those insects will differ slightly from one another in color or markings.

"Now if you want your heart to jump right out of your mouth, get on a stretch of the Beaverkill, tie on a size-four streamer, then six feet up the leader tie on a six-inch dropper and a dry fly. Overall, the leader is eighteen feet long. Flip that streamer twenty or twenty-five feet downstream, and hold the rod up so that the dry fly is hanging up in the air.

You make the dry fly dance up and down. Then you just dap the water with it. I mean a trout will *smash* it. But where your heart jumps out of your mouth is when a twenty-inch brown decides to eat the streamer that you've forgotten all about. That jars your turnips!''

Nearly every spring the Black Ghost manages to dredge up at least one brown trout of three to four pounds from the turbulent lower Croton River when water thunders downstream from a reservoir that serves New York City. "I can tell you about this because I know no one is going to go down there to catch these fish," he says. "Conditions have to be just right, and there were just five days last spring when I had proper conditions. I need a rising water level on a dark, dismal, rainy day when herring are being washed downriver. They got nitrogenosis *[sic]* and their eyes are blowed out. Last spring, in all those five days, I got just one hit, and I took a twenty-two-inch fish. How many guys will fish five days to get one fish? But then I know I'm going to get a good fish or not get anything."

Last summer, before driving to Montana to fish during his vacation, Broadie was invited to fish Cedar Pond Brook, across the Hudson from Peekskill. Little known to the public, it is an historic stream that was fished in the late nineteenth century by Theodore Gordon, the father of dry-fly fishing in the United States, and later by Ray Bergman, whose book, *Trout*, first put Broadie on to the Black Ghost streamer. Unknown to Broadie, an expert for a local water company seeking to dam the stream had testified at a state hearing, shortly before, that no trout existed in the lower reaches of Cedar Pond Brook. However, in only two hours of fishing, Broadie, who had never been on this water before, landed and released seven brook and brown trout. Using a Black Ghost, he did not so much fish the brook as attack it. Standing ankle-deep in fast water, he would whip the streamer upstream and retrieve it quickly in and around the rocks. He ignored the pools and seemingly defied every other convention as he sloshed around the brook, which was only twenty feet wide. One would have thought that the trout would have fled in panic, but on several occasions Broadie took fish almost right at his feet. "Got you, turkey!" he would exult.

As he explained later, "During the bright part of the day, few trout are in the pools, but that's where most of your fishermen will spend their time. The few fish in the pools are only six to seven inches, and they have no brains, anyway. The good trout are behind the rocks where the water is broken. And they're there for several reasons: they have a better chance of picking up food, the white water gives them more cover, they get more oxygen and there's always a backwash so they can just hold there without wearing themselves out. A lot of people don't think that fish can hang out in that water, but they're the easiest to catch because they've got to make a snap decision when they spot something that might be lunch floating by. Yet when it gets dark, a pool might contain fifteen to twenty fish. Where do they come from? They drop down from the fast water."

Broadie prefers to fish alone—"Why should I waste fishing time telling some turkey what I'm doing and why I'm doing it?" he says— but his reputation is such that other fishermen, including those who consider themselves truly expert, will try to see what he's up to when they spot his camper near a stream. Bill Elliott, the wildlife artist who illustrated the new edition of Joe Bates's *Streamers & Bucktails: The Big Fish Flies*, all but swaggers when he talks of his own fishing exploits, but the mere mention of Broadie's name causes him to fall on the ground like Dracula before a cross. "You've never seen anyone fish until you've seen Art fish," Elliott says. "I had heard about him, and whenever I saw that camper with the big Black Ghosts painted on it, I would park and try to sneak up on him and watch to see if I could learn something. The first time I watched him, he was fishing a run with a big Black Ghost streamer, and I've never seen a man cover as much water as he did. I saw him make six casts and take six fish. He can put life into a fly better than any man I've seen. After I sneaked up on him the third and fourth time, he finally turned around and said, 'For God's sake, if you want to see what I'm doing, c'mon over here.' "

"He's extremely opinionated," Elliott continues, "but I like that because he knows what he's talking about. He's a guy who watches a lot and notices things that other people let pass by. He's very unorthodox. One time on the East Branch of the Croton River, there was a pouring rainstorm. The water was getting roiled and cloudy. Wanting something that the fish could see, I was using big nymphs, and I took six fish over fifteen inches. I was very proud of myself. When I got about 150 feet above the Phoebe Hole, I noticed a guy in a yellow slicker and a cowboy hat. It turned out to be Art, and he was doing quite well, but the crazy thing was that he was using a big Royal Coachman, a dry fly, and he was catching two fish for my one. No fish were rising for a hatch, and most guys wouldn't consider dry flies at all, but Art was bringing them up. He's capable of making fish show themselves."

Asked about the incident, Broadie figures he wasn't at all unorthodox. He was doing what his memory bank told him to do. "First of all," he says, "the fly was a *fanwing* Royal Coachman, and that's important. Second, it was September, we'd had our first cold weather, it was raining and everything correlated just so. You see, these fish know they're not going to get any succulent dry flies anymore, the good fly hatches are over. They think these fanwings are the last, and they want them. They're a delicacy. That morning on the East Branch, that memory bank just clicked up there, and I said to myself, 'Hey, this is the last day they'll be suckers for dry flies.' And that fanwing is a devastating fly, though I've never seen anything on a stream that looks like it. But the fanwing has to be tied just right with the wings spread quite a ways apart so that if you drew a line around the whole fly it would form a perfect circle. Then you want to use a leader that'll twist casting, but be strong enough to unwind so that the fly goes flip-flop, flip-flop, flip-flop, as it rolls on the water. Float that past a rock with twelve to fourteen inches of water and a little hidey-hole underneath, and it looks like that fly is alive, flip-flop, flip-flop."

In the fall, the Black Ghost either goes bird hunting or fishes the Hudson for stripers and carp. A few weeks ago he was fishing from the railroad trestle north of Garrison where Constitution Marsh empties into the river on the ebb tide. Broadie's youngest son, Eugene, was with him. Eugene has a big, bushy mustache, looks like an NFL linebacker and says little. Another man, a local landowner, was also fishing from the trestle. "Pop," said Eugene, "I'm going to see if I can get some ducks, heh, heh, heh." "You do that, Gene," said the Black Ghost.

After Eugene had gone back to the camper, got a shotgun and ambled off down the tracks, the landowner started to chivvy Broadie. "I've heard you've poached in your time," he said.

"Where did you ever hear such talk?" asked Broadie.

"Around," the man said.

"Around?" asked Broadie. "Lots of things are said 'around' "

"You can level with me," the man said.

"Level with you?" said Broadie. "I don't have to level with anyone."

"Level with me," said the landowner.

"Mister," said Broadie, "I like to hunt grouse. So does Gene. Where you live, there are grouse. As Gene says, and you can ask him when he comes back, those are a couple of nice dogs you've got at your place. They don't bark when Gene comes around."

As the landowner's jaw started to go slack, Broadie had a hit. It was

a striper. "Got you, you turkey!" he shouted. Then the Black Ghost
turned to the landowner and said, "One other thing. I've always said
I'm the biggest liar in forty-eight states."

*   *   *

*Such a liar Broadie may well be, but after this piece appeared, various outdoor
writers denounced me, the state police stopped Broadie's camper on sight, and the
local conservation officer announced that he was going to nail the Black Ghost,
come what may. Broadie just chuckled.*

SPARE THE ROD(S) AND SPOIL THE CAST

LEFTY KREH

April 7, 1980

WHEN A STUBBY, bald, fifty-five-year-old man named Bernard (Lefty) Kreh shows up at a fishing-club meeting or sporting-goods show, fishermen gather like sunnies around a worm. Elderly Wall Street brokers, oil tycoons and blue-collar workers alike shout, "Lefty! Remember me? Hey, Lefty!" The reason for all the excitement is, as Kreh immodestly puts it, "There ain't nobody in the country who knows more about fishing than I do."

At home in both fresh- and saltwater, Kreh is one of the best light-tackle fishermen ever and a master caster with fly, plug or spinning rod. Ambidextrous, he can cast a spinning rod and a plug rod, one in each hand, simultaneously, or, dispensing with a rod, he can easily cast the whole length of a ninety-foot fly line with just his bare hands. He can hold a crowd around a fly-tying bench in thrall as he ties everything from a huge saltwater streamer known as Lefty's Deceiver to a *Caenis* mayfly on a teensy-weensy No. 24 hook. He also makes his own jigs,

175

plugs, spoons and "the best carp doughballs anyone ever made." He designs new rods, reels, fly lines, anchors and tackle boxes, and he knows as much about knots as anyone in the world. Professionally, he is the outdoor columnist for the *Sun* in Baltimore, and he is the author of three books, one of which, *Fly Casting with Lefty Kreh*, has been translated into Japanese, German and Swedish. Lefty once held sixteen world saltwater-fishing records, but as he says, "I never deliberately tried to catch a record fish. I think that's the wrong approach. I simply caught sixteen fish that were world records. I don't want to compete with anyone but myself."

A camera bug, Kreh has taught advanced nature photography for the National Wildlife Federation for the past ten years. Perfectionist that he is, he develops his own color film when he has the time, and he keeps 10,000 slides filed so neatly that he can locate any one slide in fifty seconds. "You got to be organized," he says. His luggage and tackle are color coded, and he can take off instantly from his Cockeysville, Maryland home on a trip for smallmouth or tarpon or trout, or to give a lecture on the West Coast. Although Kreh defines an expert as "any SOB more than 150 miles from home with a slide show," he travels extensively each year, showing slides and lecturing on such topics as "Why We Fish," "Fly Casting and Its Problems," and "Light Tackle in Saltwater." On the road, Kreh always makes it a point to get in a day or two of fishing with the best fishermen in each area. "The main reason I lecture is that it allows me to travel on someone else's money to gain the latest information," he says. "That's how I keep on top of everything."

Filled to the gills with fishing expertise, gifted with gab and equipped with a seemingly limitless repertoire of jokes, putdowns and one-liners, Kreh comes across to his audiences like a cross between Jack Nicklaus and Don Rickles. When his slide projector broke down and had to be fixed during a talk at a Trout Unlimited meeting in Linden, New Jersey, Kreh announced he would fill in the time with a few Polish jokes. There was a stir when three men stood up and one said, "We want you to know we're Polish."

"That's all right, fellas," said Kreh. "I'll tell them nice and slow so you can understand."

Everyone, including the three men, laughed, but Poul Jorgensen, a flytier who was on the program with Kreh, says, "Anyone but Lefty would have had his head punched in." Kreh says, "Everybody ought to be able to laugh at himself. When you stop laughing at yourself, you're in trouble. People take things too damn serious."

Kreh himself had a hardscrabble life as a youngster in Frederick, Maryland. The oldest of four children, he was six when his father, a brick mason, died and his mother had to go on relief. "There were no toys," Kreh says, "but I had a good time." The North Bench Street neighborhood was tough, and he responded to the challenge. After Joe Louis won the heavyweight title, Kreh, billed as the White Bomber, fought a kid from the black neighborhood, Jimmy Hill, who was the Brown Bomber. "A white kid stole a beautiful rug from a store and rope from a trucking company, and the kids put up a ring in a neighbor's backyard," Kreh recalls. "They charged kids to see the fight. I hit Jimmy with a lucky punch on the chin and knocked him out. I had beat up a lot of kids before, but I had never knocked anyone out. I thought I had killed him, and we all ran off leaving Jimmy on the stolen rug. The lady who owned the house saw him unconscious, and she called the cops, who identified the rug, and a couple of us almost wound up in jail. The kid who stole the rug was never even questioned, but later he was killed pulling a holdup. I might have wound up in jail or getting killed myself, but when I was eleven I was told that I could go to a Boy Scout camp if I would wash dishes. I did, and I joined the Scouts. The Scouts gave me a moral base, and that really helped save my life."

On his way to becoming an Eagle Scout, Kreh won the first angling merit badge in his part of Maryland. In his spare time he earned money trapping muskrats and mink and catching catfish in the Monocacy River, which he sold to local stores. "The river was only a two- or three-mile walk away," he says, "and I'd go there to bush bob. I'd take strands of mason twine, put hooks on them, bait them with freshwater mussels and tie the twine on branches overhanging the river. In those days there were a lot of freshwater mussels to be found. You could take half a bushel on any sandbar. The catfish would roam the banks at night and grab the bait, and the limb would set the hook and fight the fish. The average catfish was ten to fifteen inches long, and I got ten cents a pound, cleaned. Ten cents was a lot of money, and frequently we'd get catfish up to six pounds."

In high school Kreh was a basketball guard despite his lack of height. He got the nickname Lefty because he would dribble downcourt with his right hand and then suddenly change to dribble, pass or shoot with his left hand. When he graduated in 1942, he joined the Army and served as a forward observer with the 69th Division in France, Belgium and Germany. While in the Army, he became a Roman Catholic. "In Frederick I'd gone to the Baptist church, and as a poor kid I saw that poor people were kind of looked down upon," he says. "I looked at all religions, including Judaism, but Catholicism seemed to answer what I wanted more than any other."

Discharged as a corporal with five battle stars, Kreh returned to Frederick and got a job with the old Army Biological Warfare Laboratories at nearby Fort Detrick. He soon became the night foreman in the main production building, raising bubonic plague, anthrax, tularemia and a host of other deadly infectious cultures.

In 1947 Kreh married Evelyn Mask, whom he met in a bowling alley. They went fishing on their honeymoon, but they no longer fish together because Kreh regards fishing as his work, and "I don't want to bring my wife to the office." The Krehs get along famously—"If he was any sweeter, I couldn't stand it," says Ev. As a cook, Ev finds "no challenge" in Kreh since his tastes run from peanut butter to overcooked meat. Once at a friend's house, Kreh set off the smoke alarm after he went back into the kitchen to rebroil a steak he thought too rare. When he orders steak in a restaurant, he tells the waiter, "Cremate it."

At Fort Detrick, Kreh worked nights so he could hunt and fish all day. An expert shot, he doubled on grouse, tripled on quail and nailed pheasants with a bow and arrow. He kept his eye sharp by shooting crows at an immense roost near his home. During one two-and-a-half-year period he calculated that he had fired 7,000 shells at them. His favorite call for crows in the early summer sounded like that made by a baby crow falling from a nest. "A deadly way to attract crows," he says. He also called ducks, geese, hawks, foxes and bobcats. His call for foxes and bobcats, Kreh says, "sounds like a screaming rabbit."

Kreh's proficiency in calling crows and his ability in taking smallmouth bass on small plugs he had carved brought him to the attention of two outdoor writers, Tom McNally and Joe Brooks, who became his friends. They got him started fly casting with a fifteen-minute lesson. "After that, I was on my own," Kreh says. "I developed my own style. I think I was fortunate that there were so few good flycasters in Maryland because I would have wound up copying them. I fished fourteen hours a day, mostly for smallmouth bass in the Potomac, and even though I could cast with either hand, I got pretty tired if I didn't do things right. So I began breaking down the parts of a fly cast. There was no one to talk to, lucky for me, and I found that if I lowered my rod at the beginning of a cast and raised it quickly, I lifted all the line from the water. Then I could make an effortless back cast and not put shock waves into the line. The average guy spends more energy getting line off the water than he does getting the line behind him for the cast.

"The most important thing in fly casting is that the fly is not going to move until the line is tight, so it becomes very important to remove all slack, shock waves or sag before you make your power stroke in either direction. A lot of the techniques I developed on my own were considered near heresy, but I cast effortlessly. Basically, a good flycaster is a guy who can do it without work, and you don't see many of them around.

"I think I know more about casting and about different kinds of casts than anyone else, and the reason is that I am always fishing under different conditions. Take saltwater fly-fishing. To be a good saltwater fly-fisherman you have to be a better fisherman than a freshwater fly-caster. In freshwater, presentation is the main thing, but in saltwater you have to contend with larger tackle, winds, know more casts and then spot and whip a bigger and tougher fish than you'd find in freshwater. The average saltwater fish can tow a freshwater fish of the same size around by the tail. In saltwater fly-fishing, when you see a fish, you've got five to seven seconds to make the cast. In that time you have to determine the direction in which the fish is traveling, the depth and its speed, and then make your cast. George Harvey, of State College, Pennsylvania, is by far the best trout fisherman I've ever fished with, but George would have trouble with three-pound bonefish."

For all this, saltwater fish are not necessarily the hardest to catch. "There are too many variables to say that," Kreh says. "If I were to list the three most difficult fish to catch, they would be these: First of all, largemouth bass in sandpits or quarries with clear water. They are the toughest of all. Second, taking really big tarpon on a twelve-pound-test fly tippet. Third, big brown trout in spring creeks."

In the early 1950s Kreh began to branch out while continuing to work at Fort Detrick. He began writing an outdoors column for the local *Frederick Post* and the *News*, and then for other papers in the area. He also began going on the road to give fly-, plug- and spin-casting exhibitions at boat shows and state fairs. He would cast flies into a cup, knock a cigarette from a girl's mouth and cast four fly rods at the same time, two in each hand. "But that was just entertainment," he says. "Then I'd start to do things that a fisherman could use in the field, such as changing the direction of a cast in midair."

Except for an occasional casting clinic, Kreh no longer gives exhibitions, but he gives private lessons for one hundred dollars an hour. "I'm the best teacher of fly casting there is," he says. "I can spot what a fisherman's doing wrong and correct it right away, no matter whether he's left-handed or right-handed, because I'm the only casting instructor I know who can make all the bad casts with either hand." The tuition fee of one hundred dollars is obviously worth it to some anglers. Recently, a couple from Texas flew to Baltimore in their private plane for a two-hour lesson.

As Kreh sees it, his biggest break came in 1964, when Joe Brooks suggested he apply for the job of director of the Metropolitan South Florida Fishing Tournament. Now sponsored by the *Miami Herald* and Coca-Cola, the tournament, which runs from mid-December to late April, draws hundreds of thousands of contestants. There are divisions for fly, plug and spin fishing, and entrants are encouraged to release their catches after they have been witnessed. The only awards are trophies.

Kreh got the job and quit Fort Detrick. "The Met tournament is one of the finest training grounds in the world," he says. "It has set the standards for light-tackle fishing. The whole south Florida social system is based on fishing and boats, and the guy who runs the tournament, as Joe said, 'is like being the mayor of south Florida fishing.' You are in contact with all the charter skippers and guides in the Everglades, the Keys and the western Bahamas. A large percentage of the guides know that the Met tournament director recommends people to them. When I got the job, guides and charter skippers immediately invited me to go fishing. I learned the favorite spots of the best guides.

"The finest cadre of light-tackle fishermen live in south Florida, and they're fishing twelve months a year. South Florida is the only place in the country where fishermen are judged by their tackle. Down there it's almost a stigma to catch a fish on bait. Twelve-pound-test is about the heaviest spinning line anyone will use, and anything over a fifteen-pound-test leader isn't regarded as fly-fishing. As a result, the area has the best light-tackle fishermen in the world. A good south Florida light-tackle fisherman can take fish anywhere. Why, he can even take a 300-pound grouper on twelve-pound-test line."

Kreh worked as the Met tournament director for nine years. On his four-month vacation every summer, he would fish for trout in Montana and then for carp, with his doughballs, in Maryland. "Hardly anyone in this country fishes for carp, but I'll tell you this, carp are one of the premier gamefish around," Kreh says. "I go carp fishing eight or ten times a year." On rare occasions he has taken carp on wet flies, but his standby bait is his own doughball concoction. The recipe is as follows:

Doughballs à la Kreh

2 cups cornmeal	1 tbs. vanilla extract
1 cup flour	1 tbs. sugar
½ 3-oz. pkg. strawberry Jell-O	1 quart water

Yield: 30 doughballs.

In a two-quart saucepan, bring the water to a boil and add Jell-O, vanilla and sugar. Stir for a minute and then reduce heat so that mixture barely boils. In a bowl combine cornmeal and flour by mixing well with a wooden spoon. Sprinkle the cornmeal and flour mixture on the surface of the water. The bubbles will make little volcano-like eruptions through the cornmeal-flour mixture. As the eruptions occur, cover them with the mixture until it has all been used, then stir for 20 or 30 seconds. Remove from stove and let cool. Mold the dough into balls one inch in diameter. Use immediately or store in refrigerator for as long as three days. Serve on a No. 2 hook.

"I make my doughballs about two-thirds the size of a golf ball," Kreh says, "and they sink right to the bottom. They are gummy enough to stay around the hook but soft enough so I can easily set the hook."

In 1972 Kreh became the outdoor columnist for the *St. Petersburg Times* and a year later moved to Baltimore when he got a better offer from the *Sun*. In his columns Kreh writes about a variety of subjects besides fishing and hunting: why leaves change color in the fall, wild flowers, bird feeders, conservation, the aerial transport of seeds. He is always giving his readers sound advice. "If you want to be a good fisherman, question everything, especially the absolutes," he says. Freshwater fly-fishermen using wet flies, nymphs and streamers ordinarily employ a five- to ten-foot leader, but Kreh, going against convention, often uses a leader no more than eighteen inches long with a sinking line. "I don't use it in tiny brooks where the impact of the line might spook the fish, but otherwise I use it all the time," he says. "You have more control, and you get down faster. I've taken wild rainbows with a leader so short, maybe two inches at most, that I couldn't tie another knot in it."

According to Kreh, hunting is changing rapidly in this country, and fishing is about to follow. "I pretty much gave up hunting fifteen years ago," he says. "Attitudes about hunting have changed. It used to be that you were proud to know a good hunter. Nowadays a good hunter keeps to himself. Also the land that's left is being closed off. The farmers aren't the old sons of the soil they used to be. They've been off to college, and they have a different view of life. They're sure as hell not going to let you on their land to shoot pretty little birds, rabbits or deer. They aren't even going to let their own children shoot them. They regard animals as part of the family.

"What you're going to see is a lot of hunters turning to fishing, and attitudes in fishing are going to change. Right now offshore fishing is dying. Going out from Ocean City, Maryland for white marlin and making a 180- to 200-mile trip in a day is not only going to be expensive, it's going to be unpopular. The macho guy who likes to go offshore is going to be looked on like some guy who's driving around in a big gas guzzler, and he's going to feel ashamed. The trend in fishing will be back to the 1940s, when people fished close to home. With the pressures on trout streams and bass lakes, we will become like the English, who fish for roach or carp. I personally think carp have a big future.

"Our concepts are going to change, and I think that may be to the good. The one thing wrong with most fishermen in this country now is that they have restricted themselves to several species, or one type of fishing. You meet a guy who fishes only for trout or for bass, or you meet someone who says, 'I only use a fly rod.' That's wrong. I can tell you, they miss out on a lot of fun."

HE'S GOT A VERY
FISHY LOOK

CHARLES E. BROOKS

September 3, 1979

T HE SIGN at the precipitous edge of the Black Canyon on the Yellowstone River warned that this was grizzly-bear country. It was also Friday the thirteenth, but Charles E. Brooks, former secret agent turned angling writer, paid no heed. "Come on," he said. "Those salmonflies are hatching down there." When a companion asked what they would do if they ran into a grizzly, Brooks, a bear of a man himself, said, "I'll sing. They don't like noise."

Five hours and seven miles later, Brooks clambered out of the canyon. There had been no grizzlies, but plenty of plump cutthroat and rainbow trout—all released. Brooks had gone down into the canyon because he was interested in checking on the salmonfly hatch and seeing what his deerhair-and-hackle imitation of the adult would do. It outfished all other ties. Salmonflies, as they are called in Montana, are actually huge stone flies, insects that grow to two inches in length, and Brooks has been studying them for years. Indeed, ever since he retired as an Air Force major in 1964, he has been examining almost everything that creeps, crawls, swims or flies in the trout country of southwestern Montana in an effort to make himself a better fisherman. As a friend once put it, "Charlie's trying to climb into a trout's head."

Brooks's books, notably *Larger Trout for the Western Fly Fisherman, The Trout and the Stream, Nymph Fishing for Larger Trout*, have won him a growing reputation as an angling author and authority, and his latest book, *The Living River*, his intimate account of the Madison River, is destined to secure it. In all likelihood, Brooks is ready to join the ranks of the "holy three," namely George LaBranche, Edward Ringwood Hewitt and Sparse Grey Hackle, as a sainted American angling author. He is an original. His style is clear, direct and without pretense, and his works are packed with telling detail gleaned not only from scientific studies but also from the thousands of hours he has spent creeping, crawling and swimming—often underwater—to get a trout's or salmonfly's view of the world.

Brooks, now sixty, is not a trout fisherman to the fly rod born. He was a hillbilly raised in the Missouri Ozarks during the worst years of the Depression. His father was badly hurt in an industrial accident in 1929, and the family, which included his mother and six brothers and sisters, lived in a succession of shacks. The Brookses kept body and soul together by chopping cotton. When Charlie was nine, he traded a bagful of deer tails to a local flytier for two dollars and fifty cents in cash, a big box of materials, one hundred hooks and an hour-and-a-half lesson in tying—"the greatest bargain I ever made in my life." Fishing the Current River with his own flies, cane pole, chalk line doused with linseed oil and horeshair leaders, Brooks "caught fish like nobody's business, and they were always welcome at home because we ate everything."

After he graduated from grammar school in 1933, Brooks became a migrant farm worker. He sent all his wages home to support his family, except for the five cents a day he kept to buy bread and buttermilk. "I had that for supper," he says. "The farmers usually provided some kind of dinner, and I never did eat breakfast until I was twenty-five or twenty-six."

After his father died in 1936, Brooks joined the Civilian Conservation Corps and worked in the West. Impressed by the mountain streams of Montana and Wyoming, he promised himself he would live there one day and write about fishing. Eager for a high-school education, he left the CCC in 1939 when the football coach of the high-school team in

Milan, Missouri, promised him a job if he would play. Brooks was the outstanding defensive player in the history of the school, led the conference in punting and scoring and also lettered in baseball, basketball and track. He completed high school in three years with a straight-A average. All the while, he held down two jobs, rising at five in the morning and going to bed at eleven each night. The first month he was there, several teachers complained about his whistling and singing in the halls, and when a teacher asked him why he did it, he said, "I'm so happy to be here. But I'll stop. I can be just as happy inside."

In 1942, Brooks joined the Army Air Corps as an aviation cadet. In time he was commissioned as a bombardier. He flew fifty missions over Europe. His pilot, Richard Witkin, now transportation reporter for the *New York Times*, says, "Charlie's the only man I ever met in my life who enjoyed war. I don't mean he liked to kill people, but when I was going through flak and enemy fighters, I was scared witless. To Charlie it was a thrill. To him, flak and enemy fighters were exciting. He's the last of the great adventurers."

Released from active duty in 1945, Brooks got temporary work as a park ranger at Yosemite but was turned down for a regular job because he lacked a college degree. He thought of going to Stanford, but he felt he could not learn any more there than he could from books or life. By now, married and knowing that he wanted to write, Brooks decided that the best thing he could do was to reenlist in the Air Force, put in his twenty years and then retire to explore and write.

Brooks was assigned to counterintelligence. One of his favorite assignments turned out to be scouting possible invasion sites along the Alaskan coast. He quickly discovered that the tide went out too far to allow an amphibious landing, but his superiors were slow in digesting this information, so he spent several months fishing trout and salmon streams under the guise of being a wealthy sportsman. When Brooks left the Air Force for good, in 1964, he and his wife, Grace, set out for West Yellowstone, where they built a house.

Brooks soon began his research in Montana by observing the nymphs and larvae of insects that serve as food for trout in the Firehole, Gibbon and Madison rivers. "My aim is to fish the nymph imitation at the right place with the right motion," he says. "I wanted to find out what nymphs were in the water, and what action I should impart to the imitation." In one hundred-yard stretch of the Madison, he observed Mayfly nymphs of the species *Siphlonurus occidentalis*, the gray drake, as it is known to anglers. "I found that the gray drake has to have a silt bottom around weeds, a current speed of not more than one and three-fourths miles per hour and a depth of about twenty inches," he says. "The nymph is slow-moving and clambers around weeds. It moves about in the early morning or late afternoon. It doesn't like bright sunlight." While Grace fished an imitation gray drake so that it either swam along the bottom or seemed to climb the weeds, Brooks watched the reaction of the trout underwater. As a result of this type of investigation, Brooks ties his nymph imitations without a wing case on the back so that if it should be turned over by the current, a fish won't wonder why it's upside down. "A live nymph never turns upside down in the water," he says. "A nymph imitation has to have color and form and life, and the more signs of life the better." The ultimate in life simulation is Brooks's imitation of any of a number of large dragonfly nymphs. It is basically a one-eighth-inch-wide strip of natural brown seal fur, left on the skin, wrapped around the hook shank. In the water it pumps and breathes enticingly. "It's a rough, scraggly fly, but so is the natural," says Brooks.

To study the nymph of the giant salmonfly, *Pteronarcys californica*, he spent time down in Hole No. 2 of the Madison, breathing through a hose. "I found that the *Pteronarcys* nymphs feed twice every twenty-four hours," Brooks says. "I'd see them come out from under the rocks where they live to feed on algae on top of the rocks. First the smaller nymphs would come out, then the bigger ones and, finally, the biggest. The fish weren't interested until all the rocks were covered with nymphs of all sizes. Then I tried to find out why the nymphs were feeding when they did. I finally pinned it on temperature. In the summer they like to feed at fifty-eight degrees and generally knock off when it reaches sixty-two degrees. In the fall, when the water cools, fifty-two degrees will bring them out to feed."

At times, when a nymph would get washed away from the rocks by the current a trout would glom onto it. To simulate the nymph in the current, Brooks began fishing what is now known as the Brooks Method. Using a short leader and a high-density sink-belly line, he casts way upstream and, holding his arms high, allows the nymph to bounce along the bottom in a dead drift.

One autumn several years ago, when the well-known dry-fly fisherman Art Flick visited Brooks to fish the Madison, a cold snap hit. Brooks took the water temperature. It was forty-six degrees, and he announced that the fishing would not be good until about 11:30 A.M. Meanwhile he would show Flick how to fish the heavy water with the

Brooks Method. Flick got a few strikes, but Brooks explained that these were smaller fish that always began feeding before the bigger fish in much the same way that the small *Petronarcys* nymphs began feeding before the bigger ones did.

At 11:30 Brooks took the temperature, found it was fifty-two degrees and told Flick the trout would start hitting. They did, right on schedule.

Brooks has been active as the permanent secretary of the Southwestern Montana Fly Fishers, a club he helped found in 1969. Though it has never had more than twenty-four members, its accomplishments are noteworthy. Its sole objective is to protect, maintain and improve the trout streams of the region. Among the club's achievements is that of putting an end to the stocking of hatchery trout of catchable size in streams with naturally producing populations. "When you dump thousands of living units into any area not totally a desert or wilderness, you create an immediate shortage of shelter, *and* you create an intolerable sociological pressure on those biological units already there," Brooks says. "It does not matter whether we are talking of fish, rats, monkeys or humans. The result is precisely the same—chaos."

Public support for the Southwestern Montana Fly Fishers' goals has become significant. Indeed, last year's closing of the middle Madison to fishing for an undetermined period so that biologists can study the stream won wide public approval. "The swing is our way," says Brooks. "The people here see that they can prosper because people come from all over the country, even the world, to find what they don't have at home, quality fishing in an unspoiled environment." Then he adds, "My energies in life are expended on a narrow plane. I'm involved in studying, writing about, protecting and improving the ecology of trout streams in southwestern Montana. That's it. I'm not out to save the whole world. People who are out to save the whole world don't save anything. But I can say with certainty that the trout fishing we've got, as good as it is, is going to improve even more."

*   *   *

Shortly after this piece appeared, Charlie Brooks suffered a massive heart attack. He underwent surgery, and is now fishing again, fully recovered.

THE STRANGE FISH AND STRANGER TIMES OF DR. HERBERT R. AXELROD

May 13, 1965

D R. HERBERT R. AXELROD is the great panjandrum
of the tropical-fish world. Dr. Herbert R. Axelrod—the title and the
full name are always run together by admirers as though they were one
word—is without rival in the burgeoning world of tropical fish. Dr.
Axelrod is an intrepid ichthyologist and explorer who has made more
than forty expeditions to South America, Africa, Australia, the Fijis,
Indonesia, Thailand, India and the Malay Archipelago. He can, he
says, recognize more than 7,000 species of fish on sight, and he has
discovered hundreds of species that were lost to science for years or,
better yet, were never seen before by man. More than two dozen species
of fish have been named after him, and one of these, *Cheirodon axelrodi,*
the cardinal tetra, is the biggest-selling tropical fish in the world.

Besides being an incredible discoverer of fish, Dr. Axelrod is a
remarkably prolific writer. He has written more than half a dozen
major books on fish, all bestsellers. His first book, *Tropical Fish as a*

189

Hobby, is in its ninth printing and has sold more than 80,000 copies. Dr. Axelrod has also churned out more than one hundred smaller books and pamphlets on fish, and several hundred articles, as well. His typewriter is always busy. Once on a Friday, Doubleday, the publishers, asked the doctor for a book on fish. On Saturday morning he sat down to write and, by the time he stood up on Sunday evening, the manuscript was completed. On Monday it was accepted and published as *Tropical Aquarium Fishes*. It sold 450,000 copies. As if to show this was no trick, Dr. Axelrod recently turned out a substantial paperback for Fawcett, *Axelrod's Tropical Fish Book*, over another weekend. The book is lavishly illustrated with hundreds of photographs, most of them taken by the doctor, who, with some justification, regards himself as the finest photographer of tropical fish in the world.

When not traveling up some Amazon tributary by dugout canoe or sitting before a typewriter, Dr. Axelrod is kept busy presiding over the seemingly limitless destinies and rapidly multiplying fortunes of T.F.H. Publications, Inc., of which he owns seventy-five percent of the stock. T.F.H. Publications, Inc., or TFH as it is known in the trade, is the General Motors of the pet world, and its offices are in, of all places, Jersey City. Here, in a yellow three-story building of his own design, the doctor publishes *All-Pets* magazine, a monthly given over to such articles as "The Four-Toed Tortoise" and "Peafowl, from a Hobby to a Business." It is here that he also publishes his own very special baby, *Tropical Fish Hobbyist*, which not only has the largest circulation of any aquarium magazine but is, as the cover has proclaimed, THE ONLY AQUARIUM MAGAZINE IN THE WORLD ILLUSTRATED IN-SIDE WITH COLOR PHOTOGRAPHS!!! Invariably, these photographs have been taken by Dr. Axelrod to illustrate one of his own articles about an expedition he headed, net in one hand, rifle in the other, into some obscure backwater in search of a spotted *Corydoras* catfish. Among the subscribers who have thrilled to the doctor's accounts of rare adventure was the late Winston Churchill, who carried on a correspondence with him about fancy goldfish. Churchill, however, was merely one of a number of world figures enthralled by the doctor. He has been on intimate terms with Emperor Hirohito of Japan, a renowned sea-slug specialist; the former King of the Belgians, Leopold III; and the President of Brazil, Humberto Castelo Branco, who asked Dr. Axelrod to draw up a conservation program for the Amazon.

In addition to magazines, Dr. Axelrod also publishes thousands of booklets dealing with all aspects of the pet world. Among those he has published are such bestsellers as *Modern American Mouse, Colorful Egglayers, Trick Training Cats, Your Terrarium, Horned Toads Pets, Monkey Business, Snakes as Pets* and *Rats as Pets.* For some time now Ernest Walker, former assistant director of the Washington Zoo, has been after TFH to publish a companion volume, *Bats as Pets,* but Dr. Axelrod has resisted his friend on the grounds that there are no pet shops selling bats. Walker keeps several free-flying bats in his Washington apartment, and whenever Dr. Axelrod comes to call, Walker, fearful lest his pets escape, opens the door a crack and whispers, "Come in quickly."

At least once a month Dr. Axelrod makes a trip to Florida, where TFH owns five tropical-fish farms near Tampa. TFH is the biggest breeder of tropical fish in the world; at last count there were approximately six million fish down on the farms. All in all, TFH so dominates the field of fish that a couple of cosmetics companies, seeking to diversify, recently offered the doctor $7 million to sell out. He refused, because he was making piles of money, and he has used part of the substantial profits of TFH to further the study of fish. Two years ago he reprinted Jordan and Evermann's four-volume classic on systematic ichthyology, *The Fishes of North and Middle America,* which had long been out of print, and presented 2,000 sets to the Smithsonian Institution free of charge. The Smithsonian has been selling the volumes at twenty-five dollars a set, and all the proceeds go toward tropical-fish research and expeditions. On occasion Dr. Axelrod has dug deep into his own pocket to finance expeditions by others when he has been tied down by affairs in Jersey City. He dispatched Dr. Jacques Gery of the Laboratoire Arago of the University of Paris to Gabon to search for exotic fish, and Dr. Martin Brittan of Sacramento State College has taken a couple of treks into unexplored Brazil in quest of an elusive blood-red tetra, thanks to the doctor's largess.

In his own spare hours, infrequent though they may be, Dr. Axelrod is fond of playing Bach sonatas on the violin and reading extensively about the sciences. He holds degrees in mathematics, chemistry, physics and biology and, since he is fluent in French, Spanish, Portugese, German, Hebrew and Japanese, can get along in Russian and Polish and grasp the essentials in Hungarian and Swedish, his range of reading matter is wide as well as deep. The doctor has been a crack golfer, bowler and swimmer (when only ten he swam fifteen miles, from the American shore to the Canadian shore of Lake Ontario), but his favorite sports nowadays are racing pigeons and fishing. He is one of a handful of anglers who have caught an Atlantic sailfish on a fly rod, and when he made his first million dollars he celebrated by building four of the most luxurious pigeon coops in existence on the roof of his Jersey City emporium. At noontime he often clambers up to the roof and sends the pigeons flying while he munches on a sandwich. When in residence in Jersey City the doctor always lunches on a double liver-wurst on rye sent in from Bauer's Delicatessen, but on the road he is a far more adventurous gourmet. As one might expect, his favorite dish is fish, any kind of fish, but in the jungle he sometimes gluts himself on howler-monkey stew. A good meal counts for a lot with the doctor. In fact, he once broke a trip from an aquarium in Frankfurt am Main to Cairo where he was to inspect fish carvings inside a pyramid, just to stop off in Rome for a highly touted plate of spaghetti.

This man of enormous energies and myriad talents is also a man of mystery. Rumors abound about Axelrod. One rumor, essentially true, has it that he dwells in splendor in an opulent bomb shelter and fortress tucked into the Jersey coast. Another story goes that, though the doctor is well into his seventies, he does not look a day over forty-five. In point of fact, Dr. Herbert R. Axelrod, ichthyologist, explorer, author, lin-guist, tycoon and sportsman, is only thirty-seven years of age. Meeting him for the first time is somewhat like discovering the real identity of the Wizard of Oz.

Dr. Axelrod, a burly six-footer, purposely keeps himself from public view for several reasons. For one, he believes that his private life is his own business. For another, he has no desire to be called at any hour of the night by an aquarist in Oklahoma City whose swordtails have fallen prey, say, to a mild case of *Ichthyopthirius*. For still another reason, Dr. Axelrod finds most people are bores. He once refused to meet Jacques Cousteau; he thought Cousteau was a bore. Indeed, Dr. Axel-rod has been known to interrupt conversations with close friends by yawning in their faces and telling them to leave because he was bored. "I'm not rude for rudeness' sake," says the doctor. "I just don't have time to beat around the bush." When he was younger he worried that he had a personality problem, and he consulted a psychiatrist. The psychiatrist dismissed him at once on the grounds that Dr. Axelrod was the happiest man he had ever met, because he had no inhibitions. Possibly as a result of his complete lack of inhibitions, Dr. Axelrod is tremendously fond of quarrels and litigation. In recent years he has been sued fourteen times, and the filing of each suit gave him as much joy as the discovery of a new species of fish. Several cases arose out of denunciations Dr. Axelrod made of certain fish dealers in *Tropical Fish Hobbyist*, but inasmuch as he considers himself the world's ranking expert on tropical fish, he has no doubt that he will win them all. As a matter of fact, he has so far won thirteen of the lawsuits, with the other one pending. "I like to match wits," says the doctor. "A lawsuit is a chess game. When there's no challenge, I'm not interested."

Dr. Axelrod grew up in Bayonne, New Jersey, just to the south of Jersey City. Bayonne, a grimy oil-refinery town fronting Upper New York Bay, is an unlikely place to spawn a naturalist of Dr. Axelrod's stature, but in the days of his youth it still possessed marshlands and creeks not befouled by refinery wastes. The family had little money— Axelrod's father, Dr. Aaron Axelrod, now vice-president of TFH, taught mathematics in a local high school—but young Herbert earned pocket money by pressing pants, with characteristic gusto, for an overwhelmed tailor and by catching blue crabs, which he sold to Chinese laundrymen. For a dime he purchased a nondescript pair of pigeons from a fellow urchin, and he housed them in a sawed-off orange crate he kept hidden wherever he could down alleys and under stoops. Despite his best efforts, the pigeons made their mark on neighborhood porches and roofs, and protesting landlords forced the family to move several times. "I was crazy about the pigeons!" Dr. Axelrod recalls in a typical burst of enthusiasm. "I took them to school and hid them there. I used to take them into my room at night. I couldn't leave them. I didn't know it, but I actually developed the first mobile pigeon loft. It took the Army years to do that, and I did it as a kid!"

In high school Axelrod's passion for knowledge was such that he asked his father to send him to a Jesuit prep school in Jersey City. But since Dr. Axelrod *père* was teaching in the high school that his son was attending, he refused, because he did not want to denigrate the teaching abilities of his colleagues. Undaunted, Axelrod *fils* took to cutting school two or three times a week to attend Brooklyn Tech on the sly, because the teachers there were stimulating. Whatever Axelrod did, he did to the hilt. He had an IQ of 181, but he was nagged by doubts that spurred him to further efforts. "I guess I always wanted to show off," he says. "I was an ugly kid, with pimples all over my face. I weighed 110 pounds, and no girl would go out with me. I was obsessed with sex."

At sixteen Axelrod was graduated from high school, and at seventeen he enlisted in an Army officer college training program. He was sent to study engineering at the City College of New York and the University of Delaware. When the Germans almost broke through American lines in the Battle of the Bulge in 1944, all the students were rushed overseas, except Axelrod, who was too young for combat. He was apprehended at the gangplank and sent to Fort Lewis, Washington, while his clothes and equipment sailed off to France. At Fort Lewis, Axelrod served out his Army career as a private in an engineering company and whiled away his idle hours as a violinist in the Tacoma Symphony.

Upon discharge from the Army, Axelrod resumed his studies at CCNY, then transfered to New York University when offered a scholarship. His major field was mathematics, and at nineteen, he wrote his first published paper, "The Lattice Theory in Boolean Algebra." He took generous helpings of elective courses in languages and the sciences. "The more you learn, the easier it gets to learn," he says. While working on his master's degree at NYU he taught an extension course in aquatic life that attracted great attention because of its novelty. On Saturdays he took his students out to Long Island, where they explored tidal flats and swamps. He made them eat almost everything they collected. On occasion his enthusiasm for nature became so unbounded that the faculty took alarm. He was once censured by a professor for performing a caesarian on a guppy.

For a time Axelrod worked as a laboratory assistant to Professor Myron Gordon. When Professor Gordon went on sabbatical, he recommended that Axelrod teach his course on experimental laboratory animals, most of which were tropical fish. The head of the department, Professor Charles Pieper, asked Axelrod to write out his lecture notes in advance. Axelrod did, and he left them in a pile on Professor Pieper's desk. Professor Pieper happened to be delayed in returning, and in the interim a McGraw-Hill book salesman entered, read through the notes and was entranced. As a result, McGraw-Hill asked to publish them as a book. Axelrod consented, and the subsequent book, *Tropical Fish as a Hobby*, published in 1952, was to make him the leading authority on the subject at the tender age of twenty-four.

In 1950, however, Axelrod, by then engaged in obtaining his doctorate at NYU, was called back into the Army at the start of the Korean war. This time he went in as an officer—a lieutenant—and was sent to Korea, where he studied epidemic hemorrhagic fever, a blood disease, as a member of a field medical laboratory. His work called for him to take blood samples to Japan for detailed analysis and, inasmuch as the plane returned to Korea with a cargo of empty blood containers, Axelrod began filling them up with whiskey. He traded the whiskey for cigarettes, which he stuffed between the filled blood containers on the flight to Japan. As his import-export business boomed, he also began working on a second manuscript, *Handbook of Tropical Aquarium Fishes*.

On one trip to Japan, Axelrod visited the Tokyo University library, where he pored over the books on fishes. While looking for a misplaced volume, he happened to meet an ichthyologist, Dr. Tokiharu Abe, who showed him a copy of a book, *The Ophistobranchia of Sagami Bay*, that had been written by Hirohito. Axelrod riffled through the pages, then stopped to point out an error in the scientific name of an ophistobranch. Dr. Abe was incredulous, but Axelrod cited the correct reference in an obscure scientific paper he had just finished reading. With that, he bade the doctor adieu, put the incident out of his mind and flew back to Korea with a load of choice six-month-old Scotch.

As Axelrod now recalls it, about a fortnight later he was ordered to appear before General Matthew Ridgway in full-dress uniform. Recalling that a case of whiskey had recently disappeared, Axelrod suspected that military police had seized it as evidence for a court-martial, and by the time he entered General Ridgway's office he was hoping for ten years instead of the death penalty. To his surprise, however, the general had summoned him because Hirohito wanted Axelrod as a house guest. Ridgway wanted to know why, since no American had been asked to see the Emperor since General MacArthur had been relieved of command. Axelrod, forgetting the incident in the library, said he had no idea why he had been invited. Ridgway told Axelrod to accept the invitation and to do his best to get an invitation for himself (General Ridgway), as well. Axelrod said he would see what he could do and went off to Japan, where he spent a week at the summer palace on Sagami Bay, collecting marine invertebrates with the Emperor. Hirohito, who was most grateful for having had the error in his book pointed out to him, listened to Axelrod's plea on behalf of General Ridgway and rejected it, explaining that he and the general really had nothing in common. Axelrod admits that he had to agree. Hirohito then presented him with a jar of preserved eels as a gift for Dr. Leonard Schultz, curator of fishes at the Smithsonian Institution.

Shortly afterward Axelrod was discharged, and he hastened to Washington, where he gave the eels to Dr. Schultz. He also showed Dr.

Schultz a draft of the *Handbook of Tropical Aquarium Fishes*, and Dr. Schultz was so impressed with its potential that he agreed not only to collaborate on the work but to waive his years of seniority as well and appear as junior author. Not long after this Axelrod's first book, *Tropical Fish as a Hobby*, was published, and it was such an instant success that McGraw-Hill asked him to return a dozen complimentary copies in order to meet the demand. The book was successful because no one with a working scientific background had ever before written a book about tropical fish, and moreover, Axelrod, unlike previous authors, revealed breeding secrets. His description of spawning *Hyphessobrycon innessi*, the neon tetra, was of great moment to aquarists everywhere.

Since Axelrod had returned home in the middle of the academic year, he was unable to resume his doctoral studies and teaching position at NYU until the start of the 1952 fall term. As a returning serviceman, he was entitled to receive his salary anyway, and he used the money to finance trips to British Guiana and Malaya, where he bought tropical fish that he sold from a rented store in Manhattan.

By the time the fall term began, Axelrod was well established in business. He gave up selling fish for the nonce and started publishing *Tropical Fish Hobbyist*. Using mostly pseudonyms to protect his scholarly background, he also wrote, published and distributed inexpensive booklets on fish and other pets. Within three years T.F.H. Publications, Inc. owned its own printing plant and bindery, and Axelrod was doing so handsomely that he was able to buy out several Jersey City businessmen who had backed him. Meanwhile, he was also busy on his doctorate in biostatistics. The subject of his dissertation was *The Mathematical Solution of Certain Biometrical Problems*, and in it he demonstrated that the statistical procedures used in twenty-five medical and dental research papers were incorrect. "It was a very startling study," says Dr. Axelrod, who is so fond of figures that he multiplies license plate numbers he sees while driving around in his car.

Dr. Axelrod's main strength in business is his ruthlessness. A couple of years ago he decided to reprint *Stroud's Digest of the Diseases of Birds*, a solid research work by Robert Stroud, the so-called Birdman of Alcatraz, who spent more than forty years in solitary confinement for murder. Stroud's agent had published the book in 1943, but it had been done poorly. Stroud was eager to see a decent edition on the market but, before giving Dr. Axelrod publication rights, he asked the doctor to endorse his appeal for freedom. "You're a murderer!" Dr. Axelrod exclaimed. "If it were up to me, you'd cook!" Stroud angrily gave the rights to another publisher, but the doctor secured the book for TFH by buying out the other publisher. Convicts, incidentally, intrigue the doctor, who has been conducting a pen-palship with prisoners he met when lecturing on tropical fish at the Indiana State Prison. To his amazement, Axelrod found that some lifers had been keeping guppies for more then thirty years despite strict regulations against pets. They had hidden generation after generation of fish in vials strapped to their bodies, and the birth of a new batch was cause for a cell-block celebration. In the interest of science, Dr. Axelrod asked the captive guppy fanciers to keep constant watch on their pets for an intensive around-the-clock study of fish behavior. "After all," says the doctor, "these guys have nothing but time on their hands." To his dismay, however, the prisoners seemed to get sadistic pleasure in keeping prisoners of their own in prison, so to speak, and instead of chronicling fish behavior, they began putting guppies into smaller and smaller containers to see how much confinement they could take before they died. Still, this was not a total loss to Dr. Axelrod, who learned that a guppy can survive in a stoppered inch-long pencil-sized test tube laid on its side.

If there was one turning point in the fortunes of Dr. Axelrod and TFH, it came in 1958, when he took his greatest gamble by publishing the *Encyclopedia of Tropical Fishes*, which he wrote with William Vorderwinkler, editor of *Tropical Fish Hobbyist*. "I did everything that other publishers said I shouldn't do," says the doctor. "We used big pictures. We used big type. They said everything was wrong, that it was a completely lousy book by their standards. They said I was going to ruin myself. I put every cent I had into it, and then I went off to Africa and I said to myself that I'd either come back a millionaire or a bum. The *Encyclopedia* was a success, and we sell 15,000 copies a year. We've been shooting craps in the publishing business for the last ten years, and we've been winning." In point of fact, Dr. Axelrod is a very lucky crap shooter. He remembers a night in Haiti when he rolled seventeen straight passes, then played twenty-one and beat the dealer. Astounded, the owner of the casino and the croupier, who had been following him around, ominously insisted he stay the rest of the night to play twenty-one with them. Dr. Axelrod did, and he cleaned them out, too. "They couldn't believe what I was doing," he says as a matter of course, "so I told them I was cheating."

More than anyone else in the world, Dr. Axelrod is responsible for the changing tastes in the aquarium hobby today. The hobby started in grim seriousness in Germany one hundred years ago, and for years goldfish were the rage. But then, in the 1920s and 1930s, tropicals began to edge in, and in the past few years goldfish have been all but discarded in favor of tropical after tropical, thanks, in good part, to the expeditions, discoveries and writings of Dr. Axelrod. In the last five years alone, TFH imported more species of fish than aquarists had seen in all history. Today Dr. Axelrod, TFH and the United States lead the world in tropical-fish expertise, and Germany, the onetime leader, is a distant second.

A living memorial to the doctor is *Cheirodon axelrodi*, the cardinal tetra, which he discovered lurking in a reach of the Upper Rio Negro, a tributary of the Amazon, in 1954. This discovery is regarded as the greatest ever made in tropical fish, but the doctor himself did not know for an entire year that he had happened upon a species wholly unknown to science. The cardinal tetra, an extremely colorful fish, bears a superficial resemblance to its cousin, *Hyphessobrycon innesi*, the neon tetra, and Dr. Axelrod, thinking he had found a race of giant neons, marketed them as such after bringing back a shipment to the United States. To his astonishment, they spawned differently from the neons, and he at once sent out several specimens to his old friend and collaborator, Dr. Schultz at the Smithsonian, for classification. Upon examination, Dr. Schultz rang up Dr. Axelrod to announce that the fish not only constituted a new species of tetra, but moreover, a close look at their teeth showed that they belonged to a new genus, as well. Dr. Schultz described the new fish in the February 20, 1956 issue of *Tropical Fish Hobbyist* and assigned it the name of *Cheirodon axelrodi* in honor of its discoverer. Then, on the very next day, in an issue of the *Stanford Ichthyological Bulletin*, Professors George Myers and Stanley Weitzman, outstanding taxonomists in their own right, described a specimen they happened to have, and they called it *Hyphessobrycon cardinalis*. The fight started. Debate raged for more than a year and a half until the International Commission on Zoological Nomenclature convened and gave the nod to *axelrodi*. This contretemps is merely one of a number the doctor has figured in with academic ichthyologists, and their asides about his being a pushy upstart rankle him. "I've been hated for years because I've combined science with business. The guys who criticized me initially for selling science for money are now the ones who try to sell me science for money, including some of my so-called best friends," says Dr. Axelrod, happily putting in the zing.

Dr. Axelrod's favorite collecting grounds are the Amazon and its tributaries, which support an extraordinarily large and varied number of fishes. "The Amazon River system, I would judge," says the doctor, "produces enough protein in one month to feed the world for a year." Most of his jaunts into the jungle are done with Harald Schultz, a specialist in Indian ethnology at the São Paulo museum, who is not to be confused with Dr. Leonard Schultz, much less Willie Schwartz, another Brazilian collecting crony. Harald Schultz has been macheted, blowgunned, pummeled, trampled upon and threatened in the course of his field investigations on the tribal rites of hostile Indians, and Dr. Axelrod considers him the bravest man he has ever met. Schultz, in turn, looks upon the doctor as a strong, powerful man, a tremendous genius with a strange personality and a range of accomplishments that can only be likened to those of Charlie Chaplin. He also looks upon the doctor as the most foolhardy man he has ever met. Schultz thinks Dr. Axelrod's penchant for swimming with piranhas is a ghastly business— the doctor believes piranhas are not at all vicious and that their bad reputation has its roots in exaggerated stories told by Teddy Roosevelt, who journeyed up the Amazon in 1913. Schultz was once so put out at Axelrod's grabbing a passing snake by the tail that he refused, on principle, to come to the doctor's aid even though his screams for help indicated that the snake was about to win out. Dr. Axelrod managed to escape unscathed, but Schultz did nothing more than lie in his hammock with a look of anguish. Considering Dr. Axelrod's foolhardiness, he has done reasonably well in the jungle. His only mishap occurred last November when, exhausted from netting rare fish, he settled down to sleep on top of several fire-ant hills that escaped his usually keen eye. He was bitten severely, and he had to spend a month in a hospital in Manaus getting mammoth injections of cortisone.

In Dr. Axelrod's absence, Schultz collects fishes on his own. Named after him is *Hyphessobrycon haraldschultzi*, commonly known as Harald Schultz's tetra, first cousin to *Hyphessobrycon herbertaxelrodi*, the black neon tetra. Not long ago Dr. Axelrod received a letter from Schultz announcing that he had at last found a fish beautiful enough to be named for Schultz's wife, Vilma, and the fish, which had a bright-red belly and two metallic blue spots, was subsequently called *Copella vilmae*. In addition to genus *Hyphessobrycon*, Schultz and Dr. Axelrod also have a double entry going for them in *Symphysodon aequifasciata haraldi*, the blue discus, and *Symphysodon aequifasciata axelrodi*, the brown discus. A species of goby, *Butis butis*, rediscovered by Lee Ching Eng, a renowned Jakarta fish exporter, is widely known as Axelrod's crazy fish. It so happens that when Dr. Axelrod entered Lee's establishment late one night in 1959, the proprietor shouted, "Dr. Axelrod! I've discovered a new fish!" The doctor looked at the fish, which likes to swim upside down, and remarked, "I doubt that it's new, but it sure is acting crazy." From then on, Lee called it Axelrod's crazy fish.

The honor of bestowing a scientific name on a new species of fish belongs to the taxonomist who describes it and not to the discoverer. Fish have been named after Dr. Axelrod largely in recognition of his forays into unknown areas, but the fact is that the doctor has the knack of finding new fish where others have looked long and hard. A prize example of this (and one that he likes to cite) occurred in Trinidad several years ago. The island of Trinidad has more fish collectors per capita than any other place in the world. It has been thoroughly combed, so much so that the government has imposed a closed season on collecting for fear that the island's fishes are in danger of extinction. One afternoon, net at the ready, Dr. Axelrod landed in Piarco airport and immediately seined a small pool at the edge of the runway. As onlookers gasped audibly—the doctor vividly remembers the chorus of sucked-in breaths—the net yielded hundreds of specimens of bright red fish that had never been seen before by any Trinidadian or any taxonomist in the world, for that matter. Flying on to Rio, Dr. Axelrod dropped off some specimens with Dr. Haraldo Travassos of the Museo Nacional, who classified them as belonging to the tetra family. He named the species *Aphyocharax axelrodi*. Ordinarily Dr. Axelrod does not boast about discovering a new species, but he is rather proud of this find, which is marketed widely as the red pristella. "It was like going to a high-school ball game and finding five Babe Ruths, four Lou Gehrigs, two Pee Wee Reeses and one Duke Snider," says the doctor.

Dr. Axelrod's knack for discovering the unusual is not confined to fish. While dining recently in the best restaurant in Bogota, he detected a bitter taste in his cup of Colombian coffee. Drinking it down, he discovered a cockroach, and instead of being dismayed he was elated. He took the cockroach back to his hotel room, popped it in a bottle of formalin and sent it to the Smithsonian in the hope that it might be a new species. If it is, the suggestion has been made that it be named after the restaurant.

The Axelrod knack also extends to people. While returning from the Brazilian jungle for a rest in Manaus, he met a fellow scientist in the elevator of the hotel. The scientist turned out to be Dr. Jean-Pierre Gosse, adviser to Leopold III, former King of the Belgians. Dr. Gosse refused to believe that Dr. Axelrod was *the* Dr. Axelrod—Gosse, too, had heard the rumor that the doctor was well into his seventies—but Dr. Axelrod was finally able to prove his identity by citing the name of a species of fish, *Neolebias axelrodi* (what else?), then under taxonomic dispute at the British Museum. Dr. Gosse introduced Dr. Axelrod to King Leopold, who was staying just down the hall, and Axelrod, in turn, had his doubts that King Leopold was really King Leopold. The King finally was able to confirm his identity to the doctor's satisfaction, and the two of them had a joyous week together on the Amazon spearing game fish, *Arapaima gigas* by day and *Osteoglossum bicirrhosum* by night. Dr. Axelrod, incidentally, was the first man to capture young *Osteoglossa*, which are carried in the mother's mouth. The fish always swallows her young when speared or netted, but the doctor showed Leopold how to obtain the young by severing the mother's head with a swift slice from a machete. Upon the King's departure for home, Dr. Axelrod presented him with a pet jaguar that had a nasty habit of biting the doctor's ankles, and Leopold, forewarned, gave the animal to the Brussels zoo. Since then the doctor and the King have exchanged visits in Belgium and Jersey City, and last year Leopold presented Dr. Axelrod with a brace of Belgian racing pigeons. They are now ensconced in the luxurious lofts atop TFH headquarters, but the doctor, a member in good standing of the Ideal Racing Pigeon Club, has not entered them against local competition on the grounds that it would be unfair, because Belgian pigeons are the fastest in the world.

In Brazil, Dr. Axelrod has also become very much involved with Willie Schwartz, an eccentric German-Jewish refugee who fled the perils of Nazism for the relative safety of Matto Grasso. Together they helped gather creatures for a couple of Walt Disney nature epics. One of Disney's more difficult orders was for a pair of rare black jaguars. Schwartz and Dr. Axelrod managed to capture one, but they were unable to come up with another. Finally, Dr. Axelrod suggested that they catch a run-of-the-mill jaguar and convert it. They did, Dr. Axelrod administered an anesthetic, and he and Schwartz trucked the beast to a hairdresser in Manaus, where it was bleached and dyed and shipped off to Hollywood.

Life in the wild still spells joy for Dr. Axelrod, but in recent months his thinking has turned more and more toward the booming business of TFH. "I'm really a deep thinker sailing far out into space," says the doctor. "I can sit in a chair for hours just thinking until I'm numb. I'm a great thinker. I go to sleep thinking, and I wake up thinking. I go to sleep with my hands folded behind my head. I have grandiose plans. I never think small!" A couple of years ago, after a bout of deep thinking, Dr. Axelrod seized upon the idea of the Fish-In-A-Flash kit. "It was the most successful flop I've ever been involved with!" he exults. He took the eggs of *Nothobranchius palmquisti*, an East African fish that lays eggs that can survive drought, to a toy trade show in New York and showed how they would hatch in a glass of water. Wholesalers and mail-order houses piled in with $8 million worth of orders. Dr. Axelrod started his own hatchery to produce eggs by the millions for kits, but he had to cease production because the initial customers were disappointed. The hatched fish were almost microscopic, and the customers had difficulty seeing them. "They expected—pop!—two-inch, beautifully colored fish," says the doctor. "It was a bust."

The doctor tried a new scheme last year with Quaker Oats, manufacturers of Cap'n Crunch breakfast food. TV commercials for the product feature a Cap'n Crunch, who skippers a ship called the *Guppy*, and the doctor thought that this looked like a natural. He made arrangements with Quaker Oats to supply a pair of guppies to any tot who wrote in, enclosing a Crunch box top and nineteen cents, but the deal fell through when the doctor refused to guarantee that the guppies would live. "Who knows what a kid is going to do to fish?" he asks.

The doctor's present grandiose plans fall into two categories. First of all, he aims to corner the entire tropical-fish market. "I have the total approach," he says. "The books, the livestock, the accessories." A couple of weeks ago he spent $1 million to acquire the second largest aquarium manufacturing company in the world, and he is rolling his eyes at the largest. He is also aiming to increase fish production on his Florida farms, because the size of the tropical-fish market is limited only by the number of fish available. Dr. Axelrod will go to any lengths to increase production. One day last winter he chanced to hear of a fisheries library for sale at $2,000, and, without inspecting a volume, he immediately offered to buy it. "Any one paper in it would be worth $2,000 to me if it gave a hint as to how I could get more fish production," he explains. "It may be that some little trick somebody found out a hundred years ago is just what I need." The doctor is always reading for clues and hints. Several years ago he was perusing an article on salt lakes and brine shrimp, *Artemia salina*, in a Russian fishery journal. The author noted that salt lakes having the right requirements for brine shrimp were found in Russia, Israel, California and Canada. At the mention of Canada, Dr. Axelrod leaped from his chair. He knew all about the lake in California; a fish-supply house in San Francisco had a monopoly on the brine-shrimp eggs, which are used as food for tropical fish. But Canada was something new. Discovery of brine-shrimp eggs there would be worth a fortune; the eggs bring more than caviar. The doctor ransacked reference literature, but he was unable to find the name of the salt lake. In fact, the best reference he could find mentioned one in Saskatchewan. He put in a call to a pet-shop owner in Winnipeg, who was an amateur pilot. The pet-shop owner agreed to fly up and down Saskatchewan looking for a lake with a white mark around the shore from salt. A month later he called the doctor. He had found not one lake but three, Manitou, Big Manitou and Little Manitou. Dr. Axelrod mushed north at once. The shores of the lakes were laden with brine-shrimp eggs. The doctor leased the lakes from the government, and then, in turn, he sold the lease to Wardley's, a tropical-fish supply house in New York, for a five-percent royalty.

For the past year Dr. Axelrod has been reading and rereading Alfred P. Sloan's autobiography, *My Years with General Motors*. The doctor feels that Sloan (assisted by John McDonald) has written one of the great books of the age, and he has underlined a number of sentences that have special meaning to him and the future of TFH. Among them are: "There is no resting place for an enterprise in a competitive economy," and "The urge for competitive survival is the strongest of economic incentives." The doctor has been applying these maxims to TFH, because the capture of the entire tropical-fish market is only part one of his grandiose plans. Part two calls for TFH to take over the entire *pet* market within ten years. In that time Dr. Axelrod foresees the gross of TFH swelling from $3 million this year to $20 million by 1970 and $100 million by 1975. "But it's not the money," says the doctor. "It's the power! The pet business is going through a fantastic boom that doesn't look like it's going to stop. The pet business is great."

As part of his grandiose plan for cornering the pet market, Dr. Axelrod plans to introduce a new pet to supplant the hamster in public affection. The doctor is down on hamsters. "We need a small, hardy animal!" he exclaims, and he has that small, hardy animal all picked out. It is the Mongolian gerbil. "The trouble with the hamster is that it is nocturnal, it sometimes bites, and it stinks," says the doctor. "The Mongolian gerbil has a longer tail, softer fur, is not nocturnal, doesn't bite and doesn't stink. The only difficulty is getting them to breed. I'm going to work on that. Right now I'm trying to tie up all the Mongolian gerbils in the United States."

After getting all the Mongolian gerbils to breed, Dr. Axelrod plans to set up retail pet and hobby shops in department stores, five & tens and discount houses all across the country. This will give him complete control of the pet market. "The shops will do everything from selling model airplanes and fish tanks to living fish and birds and chameleons and what-have-you," he says. "It will have a garden center. It will sell books, plants, seeds and microscopes. Everything and anything!"

But for all the fish, all the Mongolian gerbils, and for all the money rolling in, Dr. Herbert R. Axelrod occasionally sinks into gloom. "I'd be happy to be a pauper," he says, "if I could play the fiddle as well as Jascha Heifetz."

*   *   *

Dr. Herbert R. Axelrod, who now confines his business to publishing, has moved his base of operations, fittingly enough, to Neptune City, New Jersey, where he carries on in Axelrodian fashion. More than fifty fish have now been named for him. "I have genera named after me!" the doctor exults. "That means that everything in the genus has my name."